DUBLIN STREET LIFE AND LORE

An Oral History

By the same author

Georgian Dublin: Ireland's Imperilled Architectural Heritage
Dublin's Vanishing Craftsmen
Stoneybatter: Dublin's Inner Urban Village

DUBLIN STREET LIFE AND LORE
An Oral History

Kevin C. Kearns

GLENDALE

First published in Ireland by
Glendale Publishing Ltd.
4 Haddington Tce.
Dun Laoghaire
Co. Dublin

British Library Cataloguing in Publication Data
A catalogue record for this book is available from the British Library
ISBN 0–907606–970

Designed by Cathy Henderson and David Gregg, Kilmacanogue
Typeset by Wendy A. Commins, The Curragh
Printed by Colour Books, Baldoyle, Dublin

To my children, Sean and Megan, for their
love, understanding and support.

"Oral historians are haunted by the obituary page. Every death represents the loss of a potential narrator and thus an absolute diminution of society's collective historical memory".
(Cullom Davis, *Oral History: From Tape to Type*, 1977)

"Anecdotes and insights are the nuts and bolts of oral history".
(Ramon Harris, *The Practice of Oral History*, 1975)

Contents

Acknowledgements

From my first visit to Dublin some thirty years ago I was intrigued by the exuberant street life. In later years I occasionally gave thought to trying to portray something of the history and spirit of this unique feature of the city. But always I was dissuaded by the seeming impossibility of the task. How does a writer capture and do justice to something so variegated, spontaneous — chaotic — as Dublin's "living streets"? Eventually I realised that only through the words and experiences of the participants themselves could the story of Dublin's street life be creditably told. This, of course, meant seeking out surviving "old timers" such as jarveys, tram drivers, lamplighters, drovers and dockers. At the outset I was not even certain whether such earlier types still existed — much less where to find them.

Indeed, the search process proved highly challenging and often frustrating. It took three years of tracking to find the individuals whose oral narratives are featured in this book. To accomplish this I relied in part upon an extensive social network of friends and contacts which I have established over the past twenty consecutive summers of field research in Dublin, mostly within the older neighbourhoods. Many persons were thus found via this inner-city "bush telegraph". To the many city dwellers, publicans, shopkeepers and others who fuelled me with directions and tips I am most grateful. The following individuals played a particularly important role in the creation of this book by providing valuable information, ideas and insightful advice and to them I am especially indebted: Paula Howard, Head Librarian of the Gilbert Collection, Pearse Street Library, for generous archival assistance; Mairin Johnston, friend and fellow writer, for words of wisdom and moral support; Deirdre Kelly, Head of the Dublin Living City Group, for sharing contacts and insights on old Dublin; Bernie Byrne of the Marine Port and General Workers' Union; Pat Johnston of the Old Dublin Society; Joe Jennings of C.I.E.; and Uinseann MacEoin, Mary Dore, Mick Rafferty and Noel Hughes for their assistance in tracking down a number of notable street figures for oral recording sessions. Special acknowledgement is extended to the National Geographic Society for their partial funding of this research project.

Introduction

"Dublin has a strong history of street characters and street presences."
(Thom McGinty, 1988)

"Certain habitues of the streets are worth recording."
(Rev. Canon F.F. Carmichael, *Dublin — A Lecture*, 1907)

Dublin's streets have always been a grandiose stage for human events and expression — from noble, heroic, joyful to tawdry, bizarre and delightfully daffy. Dubliners have ever relished good street theatre be it a gala guild pageant, impassioned political rally, rebel uprising, clamorous parade, feisty "ruggy up" between two tipsy men, scathing exchange of street trader curses, or the amusing antics of balladeers and buffoons. Classical characters from Zozimus to Bang-Bang have graced the gritty streets of Dublin entertaining the common folk on their daily rounds. No less important has been the colourful galaxy of street figures such as lamplighters, buskers, jarveys, newspaper sellers, dockers, drovers, dealers and spielers who have contributed to the exuberance and drama of the streets. Yet, their distinctive role in creating Dublin's unique social streetscape has never been explored and chronicled.

Fascination with street activity has evolved as one of the most salient traits of Dubliners. In Medieval times they thronged the streets to witness spectacular guild processions and pageantry. And major political events, like the 1916 Rebellion and Civil War, have often been enacted in part out in the open streets. But apart from historic feats, Dublin's streets have always been a focus of daily action and excitement, teeming with hawkers, singers, newsboys, ragmen, tuggers, horsemen and coal block sellers, all issuing their energetic cries. Foreign visitors to the city, whether enthralled or appalled by the street mayhem, regularly commented on its raucous nature. Around the turn of the century the Reverend F.F. Carmichael declared that "Dublin is the noisiest city in the Empire".[1] In 1917 an anonymous Englishman in his book aptly entitled *Dublin Explorations and Reflections*, wrote that "the life of the Dublin streets must, I think, seem very odd and foreign and attractive to any Englishman".[2] He confessed to passing his time "very happily in a more or less aimless perambulation of the streets and in looking at people". Davies, writing about *Dublin Types* some seventy years ago, termed this the "free pageant of the streets", observing that the "life of the poor

11

people of Dublin is made bearable, even delightful, by the things they see in the street".[3] For the city's impoverished tenement dwellers the streets indisputably provided free shows and amusement, a welcome diversion from their struggle. But as Longford notes in her *Biography of Dublin* it appeared that all classes of Dubliner possessed this "passion for amusement" and were "devoted to walking about the streets."[4] It was conspicuously the most popular, egalitarian pastime.

The first half of this century was Dublin's heyday of animated street life with the bustle of open-top trams, "pirate" buses, newfangled crank-type motor cars, pioneering cabbies, rival jarvey brigades, hordes of bicyclists, dockland chaos and thriving cattle and horse markets. Add to this Dublin's rare abundance of local street figures and you have what John J. Dunne celebrates as the grand "cabaret of the streets of Dublin".[5] Modern social scientists confirm that such "street life" and "living streets" are a vital ingredient in a healthy urban environment. Indeed, city streets have been likened to a stage upon which there are actors, inter-acters and audience. The sheer spontaneity and pandemonium create a visual cornucopia and symphony of street sounds which are inticing and energising. Such street activity is part of what Jacobs calls the "drama of civilization" in cities.[6] Even *An Taisce* (The National Trust for Ireland) has declared "street character" to be one of the most important elements in Irish cities, lamenting that a "high proportion" of Dublin's streets have become discernibly "drab".[7]

Dublin's lively and colourful streetscapes have largely been moulded by the mosaic of motley "characters" and "figures" who have frequented the streets either by occupation or habit. Peddling postmen, cart-pushing chimney sweeps, torch-bearing lamplighters and whip-cracking jarveys plied their daily work rounds while street traders, spielers, newspaper vendors and drovers contributed their special banter and badinage to the scene. This was further embellished by performing buskers, clowns, mimes and pavement artists. All were part of the intriguing social collage of Dublin's streets which compelled Robert Gahan to vouch in the *Dublin Historical Record* a half century ago that the "most extraordinary characters" were to be seen upon the streets of Dublin:[8]

> *These old street characters of Dublin may not be of the calibre which entitles one to a prominent place in the history books, but they and their doings were an integral part of the everyday life of our city while they enlivened its streets.*

Paddy Crosbie nostalgically agrees: "these characters were ever-present during my boyhood ... they meant so much to life on the Dublin streets. Old Dublin would not have been the same without them".[9]

Collectively, Dublin's numerous street types make up a valuable repository of what has been termed "urban folklore". They possess their own heritage, customs, traditions and city lifeways comprising what local historian Eamonn MacThomais calls Dublin's unique "lore of the street".[10] Yet there is virtually *no written record* of Dublin's street figures and their lore in archival collections. It is paradoxical that they have been so highly visible, yet little known and documented. One can, of course, find charming vignettes about some of the legendary characters like Zozimus, Endymion and Soodlum. But what of those more mortal souls — jarveys, dockers, postmen — who daily lived out their lives working the streets quite unheralded? For example, sparse historical information exists about Dublin's renowned women street traders. Other than occasional journalistic snippets, what do we know of their origins, family life, struggle, traditions? Yet they and the others deserve to be recorded because they have contributed significantly to the life and character of the city.

Only recently have scholars devoted serious attention to the urban folklore of the "common" classes. Pioneering oral historians such as Professor Richard Dorson have strongly espoused the need to record oral histories of "ordinary and poor city folk", arguing that they "possess a culture and history well worth recording".[11] Similarly, Paul Thompson urges fellow scholars to write about the lives of common city people by detailing the "day-to-day life of the community and the street".[12] This can only be accomplished through the oral historical method or, as one academic put it, the "grass-roots" history approach.[13] In harmony with this goal, the 1980 Urban Folklore Project was launched in Dublin as a modest initial effort to gather the city's folklore "before an irretrievable part of our culture is lost forever".[14] Despite this admirable endeavour, attention was not given to the street life realm.

The purpose of this book is to chronicle and preserve a part of Dublin's rich street life as it has existed in this century through the vivid oral narratives of the participants themselves. To capture the life and lore of such individuals is a challenging task. Old-timers such as lamplighters, chimney sweeps, tram drivers, jarveys and dockers are a fast vanishing breed, few in number and diminishing. Conversely, surviving market traders, buskers, spielers, car parkers and the like tend to be highly independent spirits, often wary and evasive. Hence, taping sessions ordinarily had to be held on their turf and their terms. Respondents were allowed to tell their tales in the inimitable vernacular of the street. From ninety-year-old lamplighters and jarveys to fresh-faced pavement artists on College Green, all are part of the human tapestry of Dublin street life past and present.

It is important that their lives be duly recorded before they vanish from the scene as have so many of their ancestral street kin from bygone days. One such individual, Margaret O'Connell, whose grandmother sold cockles and mussels on Moore Street, was out in the old Daisy Market selling vegetables and skinning rabbits alongside her mother at twelve years of age. Now seventy-three and one of the venerable "old crowd" of Daisy traders herself, she confides with sadness:

> *The Daisy is nearly on its way out. There's just ten of us left now. Oh, we'll go on until God takes us. We had a good, happy life but eventually you're going to see no traders. All the Molly Malones will be gone and there will be none of us left ... and Dublin will not be the same.*

13

It is hoped that this book will convey a sense of the history and continuity of Dublin's street life and generate an appreciation for that which survives in locations such as Moore St., Henry St., Cumberland St., Thomas St., and Grafton St. This unique heritage deserves to be recorded and preserved for future generations of Dubliners.

Chapter 1

Dublin Street Life and Oral Urbanlore

Think of a city and what comes to mind? Its streets. If a city's streets look interesting, the city looks interesting; if they look dull, the city looks dull. Streets and their side-walks, the main public places of a city, are its most vital organs.
        (Jane Jacobs, *The Death and Life of Great American Cities,* 1961)

Listen to Dublin. Listen to its heart beating. Listen to the dealers in the streets, and the jingle sounds of silver and copper coins in their aprons … the most colourful thing about Dublin is its people.
        (Eamonn MacThomais, *Me Jewel and Darlin' Dublin,* 1974)

O'Connell Bridge: Before the era of automobiles and buses, the trams, jaunting cars, carriages and bicycles all competed for traffic space
COURTESY OF NATIONAL LIBRARY OF IRELAND

15

Sights, Sounds and Characters

"Dublin delighted to watch a free show" proclaimed Seamus de Burca in the *Dublin Historical Record*.[1] Indeed, by the fifteenth century the city had a reputation for gala street life. Webb, in his book *The Guilds of Dublin*, describes the renowned pageant put on by tradesmen on Corpus Christi Day dating back to the Medieval Age:[2]

> *A pageant that for sheer picturesqueness can scarcely have been excelled in any town in Europe. The pageant consisted, not of a series of tableaux vivants, but of a succession of mysteries or miracle plays performed in the open on movable stages which were transported from street to street. The actors had for an audience all Dublin, every man, woman and child.*

Coopers, blacksmiths, tailors and their brethren exhibited a dazzling extravaganza with floats, plays, processions, music and mimicry delighting the crowds lining their path. This annual spectacle, along with numerous other events held during the year, became part of Dublin's street tradition. As O'Neill confirms, by the 1700's the flamboyant processions and pageants had become so popular that even Englishmen were lured over to witness the sight.[3]

> *Trade processions took place in the city and were a great attraction. In the 18th century when travelling was not the simple thing it is today, crowds attended those pageants — even crossing from London for that purpose.*

Free street shows were always most important to the city's massive poor population which huddled in dreary dwellings and struggled to eke out an existence. They provided diversion from daily monotony and hardship. Even a small event or incident offered welcome entertainment for the downtrodden. Davies found that "one great characteristic" of the poor was their "sense of drama" drawn from the most mundane occurrences:[4]

> *They are loquacious, fiercely interested in their neighbours, in the things they see in the street. In the free pageant of the streets the poor take a delight which many of their jaded superiors can neither guess at nor imagine. A funeral, a scuffle with a policeman in Parnell Street, a crowd, a group of well-dressed important people, the look of the shop fronts in Grafton Street — all such things brighten the lives of the very poor.*

Years ago when people tended to act out more of their private lives in the "full public gaze" observers derived great pleasure from watching the drama played out in the street, whether it was happy or sad. Bill Kelly portrays a typical clash between two tenement women:[5]

> *Two of the oul wans, at odds with each other ... like two she-elephants*

*disputing a bull they collided in mid-fight, claws grabbing for hair,
eyes, or clothing, as the neighbours tried to separate them, and the
word spread along the street like wildfire — "Ruggy Up" — and the
crowds poured in from nowhere. It was cheap entertainment for the
masses.*

*College Green: Early in the century trams ruled the roads and their drivers were
the elite amongst transport men*
COURTESY OF NATIONAL LIBRARY OF IRELAND

Dublin's street life was as much a matter of sound as sight, especially early in the
century. One was literally bombarded by clamour – horse-cart wheels on
cobblestones, passing trams on steel tracks with bells clanging, honking motor
cars, barking jarveys, balladeers singing, organ grinders churning out hurdy-gurdy
tunes, sundried sellers vocally advertising "coal blocks", "five oranges for
tuppence", "violets", "sweet lavender", "Dublin Bay Herrin's", along with the
strident tones of "rags, bottles and bones" collectors and the piercing cries of
"Evenin' Heral' or Mail" from the barefooted newspaper boys. To this add the
stentorian shouting of drovers, spielers, dockers and one can understand Rev.
Carmichael's complaint that Dublin was the noisiest city in the Empire:[6]

> *The city is full of noises ... the cars and carts whose wheels the owners
> never dream of oiling, which go on for ever grunting, grinding,
> screeching and excruciating, without pity or remorse ... perpetual
> noise. Savages, bold children, drunken men and women, lunatics and
> vulgar people delight in it.*

Despite his distaste for the auditory onslaught, he had to concede that it was part
and parcel of the daily street life so relished by the natives.

No feature of street life has more charmed onlookers than the abounding characters. As Dunne boasts, "Dublin was ever a city that knew no scarcity of colourful characters".[7] Some of the more notable ones like Endymion, Soodlum, Jack the Tumbler, Johnny Forty Coats, Fat Mary, Hairy Lemon, Damn the Weather, and Bang-Bang have been identified in print. But apart from typically brief descriptions of their appearance and behavioural traits we know little about them. Most exist as mere caricatures in our mind. A few have gained legendary status and are better documented. Michael Moran, better known as the storied Zozimus, is probably best known.[8] Born in 1794 in the Liberties, he rose to become Dublin's premier ballad monger. Attired in long frieze-type coat and cape, soft brown beaver hat, baggy cordouroy trousers and blackthorn stick, he would traipse about spouting eclectic ballads to enraptured audiences. McCall importantly notes that Zozimus and the many street kin who came before and after him are actually all part of a great *tradition* of Dublin street characters.[9]

For some unknown reason, Dublin has always seemed to breed street characters in marvellous profusion and variety. Because of their entertaining, unorthodox or eccentric behaviour they became prominent figures widely recognised — sort of icons for the community. Indeed, locals have always taken pride in their amusing or deviant doings, boldly declaring, "Oh, he's one of our great characters". Exactly what constitutes a bonafide "character" is open to dispute. Local historians MacThomais and Crosbie contend that most regular street figures like dealers, ragmen, lamplighters, paper sellers, jarveys and chimney sweeps were legitimate characters in their own right, known for some pleasing idiosyncrasies. Of Dublin's street dealers one writer has declared that they are *all* "invariably characters".[10] Though most street characters never become famous enough to warrant documentation in written form they are well imprinted in local oral history and urbanlore. And the oral narratives of the more than fifty street figures in this book give unmistakable credence to MacThomais's proclamation that "Dublin still has many (street) characters … talk to them and get the feel of real Dublin".[11]

The Concept of Living Streets and Streetscapes

The grand assemblage of sights, sounds and characters creates what social scientists term the "living streets". And, as Jacobs attests, "watching street activity" has throughout history been one of the primary pleasures of city life.[12] But it is important to note that street life is not confined to the geographic centre of the thoroughfare itself — it is also found along the pavement and fringes of the street proper. This comprehensive street scene is what geographers term the *streetscape*. For example, while jarveys, tram drivers, cabbies and drovers charted their course down the middle of the street, the buskers, postmen, signwriters and pavement artists used the footpaths. Whatever their precise positioning, each is part of the holistic streetscape mosaic.

The social dynamics of city streets are unique because people of every imaginable type are brought together closely as in no other setting. In Dublin, where people have a natural proclivity toward strolling and watching, this has always been strikingly evident. For example, Henry Street spieler Liam Preston marvels at the variety of faces, dress and demeanour of those gathered around him — posh society matrons in their fur coats, raggedy-clad tinker children, dignified professionals in pin-striped suits, dowdy housewives and beggarmen. All stand shoulder to shoulder to get a good glimpse of his spiel. Nowhere else in Dublin would you find so curious a social mixture.

The motor car age dawns along Dame Street
COURTESY OF NATIONAL LIBRARY OF IRELAND

Some street activities which thrived earlier in the century, like droving, lamplighting and tram driving, have died out. Other once-vital elements of the old streetscape such as pawnshops have declined drastically. Only a few have survived into the modern age as relics of hard times past. In the 1930's they still numbered about fifty and were a central feature of inner-city streetscapes in the poorer districts, highly visible with their gleaming brass balls and queues of chattering women laden with parcels of every description. Though the actual financial transaction took place over the shop counter inside no one would deny that the pawn has long been one of the most conspicuous components of the Dublin street scene. Similarly, the old Iveagh and Daisy markets, though now sheltered overhead, remain tattered fragments of the city's earlier street life. All of the women still active in these markets are traditional street dealers, having inherited the trade from their mothers and grandmothers before them.

Since the 1960's many of the city's once-charming streetscapes have been adulterated or obliterated entirely by insensitive urban redevelopment. *An Taisce* recognises this loss and champions the cause of preserving those living streets which have survived. Dubliners, too, seem increasingly aware of the need to protect their street life heritage. In the early 1970's when the survival of Moore Street was in serious question the U.C.D. School of Architecture undertook a study to determine the importance of the street. Its final report declared that the street carried a "strong sense of tradition" and that most Dubliners wanted it saved because they regarded it as an "important part of life in Dublin".[13] But the only way to ensure the preservation of the street life heritage is to orally record and chronicle the rich lore of the remaining street figures before the last opportunity is lost.

Oral History and Street Lore

"Oral history provides a people's history ... it charts the history of the unknown people who have not before been considered important; people who do not figure in documents and records".

(John D. Brewer, *The Royal Irish Constabulary: An Oral History,* 1990)

An illustrated broadsheet printed in 1775 entitled *The Dublin Cries* depicts in sketches the women fruit traders, flower girls, oyster seller and rag woman. Constantia Maxwell, reflecting on this picture in her book *Dublin Under the Georges, 1714–1830*, speculates that "there must have been many pleasing characters among them".[14] Regrettably, we know precious little of these "pleasing" street types because they have been ignored by historians. Simply put, "ordinary" or "common" city people have traditionally been deemed unworthy of serious documentation by academics. The belief was that they didn't possess a history and experience which merited recording. This seems particularly true of the lower echelon street groups. In his study of Victorian Dublin, F.J. Little found that street dealers and their like were perceived in Dublin society as a sort of "sub-class", devoid of historical significance.[15]

With the advent of oral history, attention was finally given to common people excluded from the written record. Initially it was applied almost exclusively to the rural setting, gleaning information from the likes of Appalachian mountain families in America or Gaeltacht dwellers in Ireland. But by the 1960's pioneers like Thompson and Dorson began focusing their efforts on collecting oral histories from ordinary *city* people exploring their everyday neighbourhood and street life. As oral historians mined the urban milieu they extracted primary historical testimony from the forgotten working classes. This is what Morrisey terms "grass-roots" or "demotic" history, stating proudly that oral historians are a "vanguard of scholars" practicing their craft in the "real world".[16] Or, as Starr more adventurously puts it, those "modern muses armed with tape recorders in quest of firsthand knowledge that would otherwise decay".[17] Recording city lifeways and lore has given rise to a new genre of literature which historians and folklorists term "urban folklore".

Grafton Street: The appearance of noisy, newfangled motor cars on the Dublin street scene created havoc with the horse-drawn vehicles and gave rise to a new cadre of car parkers
COURTESY OF THE CHANDLER COLLECTION

In Ireland oral history and folklore are still strongly associated with rural life and customs. Indeed, to many in Ireland "urbanlore" might seem a contradiction in terms. People do not normally think of the city as a repository of old customs, traditions and folkways as they do the countryside and village. Nonetheless, in recent years three notable books have focused on the lore of ordinary workers in Irish cities — Messenger's *Picking Up the Linen Threads*, Kearns' *Dublin's Vanishing Craftsmen*, and Munck and Rolston's *Belfast in the Thirties: An Oral History*. These works have provided a fresh approach to the study of Irish urban social history.

Dublin is particularly conducive to the extraction of oral urbanlore because of its surviving antiquated neighbourhoods, inner-city traditions, large elderly population, and thriving street life. Yet little oral history has been gathered in the capital. To be sure, there are some fine works devoted to Dublin's old lifeways, such as Mairin Johnston's *Around the Banks of Pimlico*, Crosbie's *Your Dinner's Poured Out!* and MacThomais' *Me Jewel and Darlin' Dublin*. These, however, are largely personal and descriptive recollections rather than oral historical accounts. But in recent years the concept of collecting Dublin's folklore via the oral historical method has gained credibility and support. In part, this is due to *Comhairle Bhealoideas Eireann* (The Folklore of Ireland Council) which came to recognise the "similarity between the traditional customs and social attitudes of

21

Gaeltacht people and those of native Dubliners", thus promoting the "importance and urgency of recording the lore and idiom of Dubliners".[18] Coincidently, Professor Seamus O'Cathain of U.C.D., lamenting that "ordinary people have been largely written out of history" in the city, launched the Dublin Urban Folklore Project in which students were dispatched to collect oral recollections from elderly residents.[19] Similarly, authors Sheehan and Walsh in their 1988 book *The Heart of the City* drew heavily upon what they label "Dublin folklore" from the 1920's and 1930's. The publication a year later of my work, *Stoneybatter: Dublin's Inner-Urban Village*, an historical reconstruction of an old community through the oral narratives of the elderly residents, further illuminated the potential of applying oral historical methodology in the urban environment.

Despite the belated recognition of Dublin's oral urbanlore, virtually no attention has been given to street life and figures.* Yet, within the urban setting there is surely no more "grass roots" or "real world" history to be unearthed than that of the street itself. The prevailing notion that street people are unimportant and unworthy — even unapproachable — has doubtless dissuaded many scholars from exploring this source. Another deterrent is probably the perception that street types, unlike organised factory workers, tradesmen, and merchants who have historically had their own guilds and organisations, function freely on their own, quite independent of any cooperative contact; thus they couldn't possess any significant social history beyond their own personal experience. Simply stated, we tend to see street figures as lone operators. In truth, this is largely incorrect. Their oral testimony confirms that even those seen as the most humble street people — traders, newspaper sellers, car parkers — have long shared a sense of unity and cooperation, even possessing their own customs, traditions and codes of street conduct. This is expressed by eighty-two year old Moore Street trader Lizzy Byrne who was out playing on the street in 1916 when the Rebellion erupted:

> *My mother was a trader before me and me grandmother. All of us on this street were reared in a basket ... or a banana box. And we all followed the trade. It carries down. Oh, it's in the blood, definitely. But people had hard times. There was one trader here had twenty-one children. Me own mother had fifteen. We all helped one another, never let one another down. We're all like one big family here.*

Henry Street's horde of traders also had their own traditions, one of which was the annual laying-claim to coveted pitches for the prosperous month of Christmas. Ellen Preston, fourth generation street dealer, fondly recalls the scene:

> *Now for Christmas month there was a five shilling licence and we used to have to go and sleep outside in Henry Street the night before to get your place. It was a tradition, because if you didn't sit down in the street you wouldn't get your place. We'd go down the night before about 10:00. We'd all sit there with our boxes in place waiting for the next morning. We'd relieve each other for an hour and then go back again.*

*One notable exception is Eilis Brady's book *All in! All In!*, a marvellous collection of Dublin's old street names and songs.

But one family member would always be there. All sit there and send for a few chips and have tea and a bit of laugh, a bit of crack, and we didn't feel the cold. Once it was morning then you just had to put your board out and that was it. When you put your board down that place was yours for the whole month and nobody touched it.

Bustling street activity along Liffey Quays, circa 1890's
COURTESY OF THE CHANDLER COLLECTION

Like the women traders, Dublin's fraternity of newspaper sellers also inherited their trade from parents and competed for pitches. A half century ago this was legalised through a system of police licensing. However, even when one held authorised entitlement to a particular street corner if a rival attempted to steal the pitch the tough "law of the street" prevailed. Christy Murray, one of Dublin's famed barefoot newsboys who was selling papers outside the Bewley's on Westmoreland Street in 1918 at the age of eight, remembers well:

Oh, I sold in the snow in me bare feet when I was small. There was an awful lot of newsboys. You had competition all right. You had to have a half crown licence. You'd get it at the police station. It was like a piece of tin and a strap and had a number and you had to wear it on your wrist. If you had a place you'd make a pitch of it and no one else could stand there. Oh, there was often boxing matches over fellas claiming pitches.

Early in the century Dublin's pioneer bicycle and car parkers faced a similar situation. Apart from acquiring licensed status from the police they even formed their own protective union against interlopers. Henry "Ginger" Kelly started minding bikes and cars back in 1927 in front of Wynn's Hotel in Abbey Street.

Now eighty-three, he reflects with pride on his street role in the city's early motor car age:

> *I was made "official". The police gave you a badge and licence. I had me cap and badge and a badge on me arm. Hail, rain, snow in winter, it didn't matter. All I'd get was four or five shillings a day in copper. I* worked me heart out *and got very little thanks for it. We led the way, the early pioneers of the motor car (age). There's not many of us left.*

Jarveys, tram drivers, busmen and cabbies also felt strong camaraderie with their mates, abiding by established street codes. As traffic worsened in the first quarter of the century the often-rambunctious jarveys and free-wheeling cabbies were subject to licensing, regulations and strict inspections. George Doran, born in 1898, recounts his experience of driving a crank-type cab in the 1920's:

> *I broke in first in O'Connell Street. There was no driving exam but you had to get a badge from the police. You had to get two households to sign for you and a letter from your parish priest. And if you had been up in the court for breaking a window or mitching or anything when you were young you got no licence. The police ran it and inspected your car mechanically and everything else every year. Oh, yes, if you had a dirty car you'd get a summons. We wore a suit and you must have a collar and tie, that was compulsory. And the police, they'd check your shoes and if you weren't shaved they'd tell you to go and shave.*

These few oral extracts are evidence of the type of street history and lore missed by historians. Most Dubliners would not have imagined that "lowly" car parkers actually had a licence and union some fifty years ago. Yet every street group featured in this book had their own distinctive customs and codes. By recording their lifeways and lore we create a unique historical chronicle of Dublin's renowned street life to be preserved for future generations.

A Note on Taping Oral History

Many street individuals had to be tape recorded in the outdoor environment on their own turf. This familiar, non-intimidating setting was the most conducive to the flow of natural, spontaneous conversation. This sometimes meant turning on the tape recorder in lashing rain, wind, pedestrian traffic and motor noise — less than ideal conditions. Some preferred to chat over a pint in their local pub and a good number invited me into their homes. Because of their vulnerable position, street traders, spielers and buskers tended to be the most wary and evasive. Many are still subject to occasional harassment by shopkeepers, being "moved on" by police, or actually arrested under the archaic 1848 Vagrancy Act. Understandably, they were initially more reluctant to be taped "for the record". In such cases, several casual visitations were necessary to establish trust and rapport. Conversely, those holding more formal positions — bus drivers, postmen — were most inclined to cooperate.

Many individuals learned of their occupational heritage through the oral tradition — accounts and stories passed down by word of mouth through the generations by relatives or others in the trade. Chimney sweep Bernard McGuinness, whose detailed knowledge of the trade goes back to Victorian times, explains simply, "I've studied it up as much as I can from the old sweeps". In some cases there was a sense of responsibility and even urgency to relate oral history for the permanent written record. John Clarke, self-appointed custodian of oral lore in the old Liberties bird market, shares his concerns:

Crowds along Earl Street as tram approaches, circa 1910
COURTESY OF THE CHANDLER COLLECTION

The bird market originated with the Huguenots and that was in the middle of the seventeenth century. As far back as I can remember it's been part of my life. But the bird market is going to die out eventually. The old fellas are dying and there's nothing written about it. When it's gone, it's gone. It's the end of it. I want to let somebody know about it so that if I'm gone tomorrow at least somebody knows about it. Now with you I know that it's going to be recorded somewhere.

Most respondents possessed remarkable powers of recall and description. Having been on the streets most of their lives, stimulated by daily interaction with others, seems to have heightened their observational and recollective senses. In the simple vernacular of the street they spoke with great candour about poverty, struggle, family life, conflict, and personal traumas. But mostly they dwelled on the sheer joys of Dublin street life and their part in it. Taping sessions normally lasted from one to three hours. In some instances individuals were revisited and taped a second time. Their oral narratives have been condensed and organised to create a coherent flow but their words and expressions remain unchanged.

Military incident along Abbey Street excites crowd, circa 1920
COURTESY OF THE CHANDLER COLLECTION

Despite hardships, all loved their work and cherish their experiences. Even the most humble ragman, pig raiser, drover expressed unmistakable pride in the honest work they performed; each understood his special niche in the city streets. Collectively, they exhibited a sense of history about their role in the evolution of Dublin's street life. Some clearly saw themselves as a vanishing breed. Tom Flanagan, at eighty-five the last of Dublin's real lamplighters, typifies these sentiments:

> *The old lamplighters ... oh, they were a* hardy *breed of men they were. And they loved their work. Every one used to walk miles in the day and they'd take up a pace like a half trot as they'd go from one lamp to another. Had no bicycles. Oh, the children would follow you and you'd get a chorus of that little song "Billy the Lamplighter". The old lamplighters, everyone knew them. And when they'd make their rounds at Christmas they'd always get a free drink at the pubs — and didn't light half the lamps after that! It was the best job in the world — but it was a dying business. I was the last lamplighter to use the pole in Dublin.*

Chapter 2

Historical Perspectives on Dublin Street Types

I

STREET FIGURES OF YESTERYEAR

To many Dubliners the street characters of the past are nostalgic symbols of a simpler, happier age before the city was modernised and "progressivised". Only a few decades ago they were ubiquitous figures along the streets. Their images have been captured in old photographs. They variously bicycled, walked and pushed handcarts carrying sacks, boxes, poles, ladders and other paraphernalia. They knew almost every cobblestone and person in their path. Local people could nearly tell the time of day by their appearance. Back when the tempo of life was more leisurely and conversation savoured they regularly engaged in chat along the way. They were social fixtures along neighbourhood streets — part of the community itself. Street life would not have been the same without their presence.

Lamplighters

No street figure has been more romanticised or rhapsodised than the lamplighter, as the old song goes:

> *He made the night a little brighter*
> *Wherever he would go*
> *The old lamplighter of long, long ago*
> *He turns them on when night is here*
> *He turns them off when dawn is near*
> *The little man we all loved long ago*

His arrival in blue serge suit and uniformed cap adorned by a badge carrying Dublin's coat of arms was as regular as clockwork. He made his rounds either on bicycle or walking with his torch always borne aloft. When darkness fell people awaited the lamplighter with his magic wand to light the glass globe so that children could play relievio or other street games and men could congregate beneath the glow to chat, sing or play cards. As Redmond poetically put it, the lamplighter put the "sparkling sequins in Dublin's midnight black hair".[1] And his familiar image with friendly greeting was always reassuring to those wandering home late at night.

Two small girls going down the street carrying a jug – for milk or jill (porter) for Granny?

Children especially delighted in his arrival, usually scampering behind him chanting in unison some doggerel rhyme like "Billy with the lamp, Billy with the light, Billy with his sweetheart out all night". Or, in more taunting tone, "Billy with the lamplight, Billy the fool, Billy with the wooden leg, wouldn't go to school". Only when bold children would swing dangerously by rope around *his* lamp-post or mischievously climb up the ladder behind him would he have to exert his authority and chase them off — it was all part of the game.

Despite the romanticised image, the lamplighter's task was not an easy one. By 1909 there were some 4,400 gas lamps in Dublin that not only had to be lit and extinguished but also cleaned and repaired.[2] This meant trodding the streets seven days a week in the fiercest of weather and without relief. However, as lamplighter Frank Wearen, now ninety, tells it, the rules could be bent:

> *I'd do hundreds of lamps and I'd no bicycle. You'd carry your pole over your shoulder like a rifle, like a soldier. If it was raining you had to keep going. You'd be* saturated. *Now if you were hungry you could drop into a shop or have a pint ...* quick! *Oh, it was against the rules. But your tongue would get dry in your mouth running and trying to settle everything right with the lamps.*

Some lamplighters, as members of the I.R.A., played a clandestine role on the streets during the Troubles. When the feared Black and Tans stalked the streets after curfew in search of violators the lamplighters, as official Corporation night workers, had free reign to roam, carry messages and even conduct missions — so long as they were crafty enough to conceal it. As Wearen confides, they were very valuable men:

> *Lamplighters knew everything.* Everything! *They seen everything. But they kept their mouth shut. Oh, we had a few of them in the Movement ... oh, they were* very *useful. If it was curfew they'd be stopped by the Black and Tans but you carried a permit when you're a night worker for the Corporation and they'd let you go. They always carried a bunch of keys for opening the lamps and they could open a lamp and shove a gun into it and shut it if they were after doing a job. That took place.*

In 1912 the Dublin Corporation initiated a programme of change in the public lighting system from gas to electricity. However, it took some forty-five years to make the full conversion and the last gas lamp was quenched in 1957, though the Office of Public Works still maintains gas lighting in Phoenix Park. With the disappearance of the last lamplighters from the streets the night lost its special glow but, as Nolan observes, they linger in the mind as a "reminder of a bygone age."[3]

Postmen

Postmen, like lamplighters, were always a welcome sight in neighbourhoods, either peddling a basket bike or ambling along with pouch slung over shoulder. Their uniform was respected, worn with great pride and brass buttons burnished and gleaming in the morning sun. Years ago postmen stuck to assigned districts and got to know everyone personally. They were the street carriers of news, both good and bad. It could be welcome letters and money orders from distant relatives or bills, eviction orders and numbing telegrams notifying the family of a soldier's death during the war years. All had to be delivered. Yet postmen seemed forever cheery and gregarious, entering the dim hallways of old tenements and roaring out the names as people from the top levels would clamber down. And fifty years ago postmen like Jeremiah Crean delivered items unimaginable today:

> *I did the tricycle delivery with the basket on front. It was to deliver parcels. The basket was larger than the cycle ... the balance wasn't so good. A great thing in those days were the egg parcels from the country. And we had fowl and fish. The fowl still had the feathers on them and the fish were wrapped in rushes and reeds.*

Negotiating the streets on a shaky bicycle was hazardous duty, especially in slippery weather. But as Joe O'Neill found, back in the 1930's you simply learned how to cope with the conditions:

> *Most traffic then was trams and horse traffic. On your bike you were out in all weather. The bicycle had an oil lamp. The most difficult thing getting around was the cobblestones on the wet days and crossing the tram tracks. There was an art in crossing them. If you tried to cross them slant-wise the tyre of the cycle got caught and it'd throw you off.*

As Dublin experienced urban redevelopment old neighbourhoods were obliterated and residents moved out to the suburbs. Sometimes rougher social elements moved in and some postmen grew "afraid of the challenge of the streets", preferring office jobs.[4] The days of the inner-city neighbourhood postman are nearly gone now. In retrospect, Crean likes to boast that he has been in "every dump and dive in Dublin and I've never come to any harm". But that was before there were mean streets in the city.

Dockers

No part of the old Dublin street scene was more explosive than dockland. It was a world of masts, funnels, towering cranes, barges, carts, horses ... 'a hundred sounds becoming a symphony of dockland".[5] Thousands of men bustling about, shouting orders, heaving mightily and dashing frantically from one "read" to another in hopes of getting a day's work and wage. There was never a dull moment on the docks. Indeed, Dubliners were instinctively drawn to the quayside streets to watch the activity. One of the major attractions was always the dockers themselves, reputed to be the toughest men on Dublin streets. Skirmishes were common as rivalries developed and factions formed. Eighty-two year old docker Tommy Bassett saw his share of clashes:

Oh, Christ, tough men ... *toughest men in Ireland they were. It was no place for a clergyman's son, I can tell you that. There was certain docker crowds fighting one another, like Ringsend and the Northside crowd. Now rows in them days, there was no knives or bottles. Oh, I remember some trouble with bats ... but it was a fair fight.*

The dreaded Black and Tans imposed curfew on street life in Dublin
COURTESY OF THE CHANDLER COLLECTION

To old dock hands no memory is more vivid — or traumatic — than the morning reads along the streets at Liffeyside. The docks provided the main source of employment for the working classes of the North City and competition was Darwinian. The tension and emotion were palpable with sometimes hundreds of men desperately vying for a few dozen precious jobs and the stevedore perched above the crowd like a dictator. Willie Murphy, who began his life as a docker in 1927 at fourteen, still shows strain in his facial expression as he recounts the scene of which he was so often a part:

Stevedores had great power, terrific *power. A hundred, two hundred men might turn up for a reading and for maybe sixty-three jobs. So he'd get on the bridge of the ship and we stood on the wall. Stevedores would call you from their minds. No lists. They knew all the names. And if they didn't get a job that just put them down in the depths ... heartbreaking. And they'd run from one read to another. Some we'd call cross-country runners cause they could run that fast to get to another read.*

This wrenching experience was part of the street scene each and every morning. Dockers survived it but say they never got used to it. Once the most pulsating street section of all Dublin, dockland is now essentially dead as old dockers refer to it sadly as a "graveyard". They saw the end coming and knew it was inevitable, as Pete St. John's lamentful tribute tells:[6]

Sure the Dublin docks is dyin'
And a way of life is gone
And Molly it was part of you and me.

Chimney Sweeps

Their trade is one of the oldest and their presence on the streets goes back many centuries. Chimney sweeps were a solitary sort, highly visible but little known. Like some Dickensian character they traversed the streets blackened with soot, lugging long rods, brushes and sacks, shouting out their cries to women peering out of tenement windows. They could also be seen on rooftops along the streetscape clearing chimney stacks with long chain or rope and metal ball. Some were so blackened that their age was indeterminate and they could be frightening to small children. Most, in truth, were kindly but kept their social distance. In part, this was due to perceptions about them. Bernard McGuinness, who learned the trade from his father and has been at it for more than forty years, remembers when sweeps were plentiful and competition keen:

Sweeps were their own breed ... loners ... rivalry. We never liked to see other chimney sweeps in the area where we were sweeping. And the public looked on sweeps as a kind of lower class person. I didn't like telling people that I was a chimney sweep.

Though he was embarrassed to identify himself as a sweep when he was a lad starting out, he now takes obvious pride in his heritage. Recognising the honourable antiquity of his trade, he has patiently culled information and stories from the old sweeps via the oral tradition. One of the last sweeps in Dublin cleaning chimneys in the traditional manner, he is a valuable source of oral history and lore.

Signwriters

A half century ago most shops and pubs in Dublin had handwritten signs and signwriters were much in evidence ornamenting and embroidering the fringes of the streetscape. Through their wizardry with paint and brush they could spin magic upon the fascia board, leaving behind a wondrous display of colourful lettering and ornamentation. They gave dowdy little shops and stern pubs marvellous facelifts. They lovingly etched the character lines into the face of Dublin, bestowing upon the streetscape an artistic and personalised ambience for which it became renowned.

Signwriters were always popular street figures, says Kevin Freeney, one of the city's master craftsmen in the 1930's. By his own admission he has done "at least 700 pubs and shopfronts" in Dublin:

> *I often remember pushing a handcart with ladders on it eight miles to a job and back again along the street. I liked working to create relief. People on the street would stop and gather around.*

Indeed, the sight of a gifted signwriter perched atop his ladder doing a bit of three-dimensional lettering or fancy ornamentation invariably drew the rapt attention of an admiring audience. It was one of the best free shows on the street. Sometimes the crowd would grow so large that it would interfere with the flow of pedestrian traffic and a policeman would have to disband the people. Admirers and friendly critics might try to engage the signwriter in conversation which could be both an annoyance and distraction. Some would take mischievous delight in pretending to point out a misspelled word. But most signwriters were flattered by the attention and enjoyed a bit of chat. In the 1950's when plastic signs assaulted Dublin the signwriters began disappearing from the streets and only a few of the real old masters are still around today.

Fortune Tellers

Virtually all inner-city women who were around in the 1920's and 1930's remember the fortune tellers quite well. Back then it was Ireland's Romany gypsies who were reputed to have the "gift". Though most circulated the rural districts a few settled in Dublin, mostly around the Liberties and Stoneybatter. They assumed an important role in the street history of Dublin's poorer district. Some had their horse-drawn caravan on a vacant site along the street while others would tell fortunes in such secreted places as Thundercut Alley in Smithfield. Queues of women beside their caravan or alleyway were a common street sight. Despite condemnations by the clergy, women flocked to their fortune teller for "readings". Back in the more conservative times it was often the wise and non-judgemental fortune teller to whom women could turn in troubled times, revealing secrets not told to husbands, family or priest. a few gained an astonishing reputation and following, not only among the poor but also among middle-class and upper-crust patrons. Indisputably, the most legendary is eighty-four year old Gyspy Lee whose horse-drawn caravan was parked on vacant ground in the notorious Monto District in the 1930's:

> *There were these crowds coming to the caravan. I used to do forty and fifty people a day. Many times outside the caravan there'd be queues ... mostly women then. Some people came in* terrible *trouble. I'm glad I've had the gift and helped them.*

Pawnbrokers

As Hudson documents, Dublin pawnbrokers were a "central figure in working-class life for more than two centuries" and yet they have been "almost totally ignored" by social historians[7] The three brass balls affixed to pawnshops was one of the most identifiable symbols along Dublin's poorer streets. Dublin local lore has it that they symbolise "faith, hope and charity". Even his nickname "Uncle" signifies what a personal relationship the pawnbroker had with local folk. To poor families facing hunger, destitution, eviction he was indispensable. In 1870 there were sixty pawnbrokers in the city owning seventy-six pawnshops. By the 1930's there were still about fifty pawnshops, most strongly associated with such streets as Queen, Dominick, Summerhill, Gardiner, Marlborough, Bride, Francis and Dorset. On Mondays and Saturdays, the major pawning days, streets were visibly more alive with the commotion of women streaming towards the shop laden with bundles of every description. Some early morning trams were even christened "pawn trams" they were so packed with women. Patrick Carthy, whose shop on Marlborough Street is one of Dublin's last, recalls that some mornings the "queue outside our pawnshop went down the street and around the corner".[8]

Known as the "people's banker", the local pawn would take in almost anything and give out a few bob for survival's sake. Clothing, bedding, shoes, pots, wedding rings, religious pictures were all collateral. The interest charged was 2p on the pound per month. On a good day there could be 500 to 1,000 women beating the familiar path to the little local pawn. Thomas Lyng, counter manager at Carthy's, came into the business in 1938 at fourteen years of age in short pants:

> *The place was absolutely loaded with customers ... it was like going into hell, really ... the place was packed from morning to night with all women wearing their shawls and petticoats. We had queues going out into the street. Pawning all kinds of sheets and bedclothing and old suits, shoes. All that was taken in was old and smelled and the sheets and clothes would have fleas and everything in them.*

Pawnbrokers and their assistants were required to live above the shop to meet the needs of the masses. Almost all treated customers with genuine friendliness, dignity, even humour. Lyng explains that pawn day was a social occasion for women and their quips and banter enlivened the scene:

> *Pawn offices were very easy-going, had a jolly kind of air ... always a great sense of fun in the whole proceedings. The women, they'd be laughing and joking, a great feeling of solidarity among them because they'd all be in the one boat.*

Dublin delivery boy with basket bike – Circa 1920
COURTESY OF THE CHANDLER COLLECTION

This oral testimony clearly refutes the perception held by many that the pawn office was a grim, sad scene. Also, some popular mythology portrays pawnbrokers as greedy and mercenary, exploiting human misery. This may have been the case with some pawns in Dickensian England but in Dublin people unfailingly testify that the local pawnbroker was almost always a decent sort. Because of the prevalent misconceptions, Hudson contends that the oral historical method is most reliable for dispelling myths and discerning truths about pawnbrokers. For example, even in Dublin today the belief prevails among many that decades ago most pawnbrokers were of Jewish extraction. This may be due to the fact that so many Jewmen (as they were locally known) were involved in scrap collecting and moneylending. However, the oral evidence of Lyng debunks this myth ... "nearly all the pawnbrokers were Catholics. There were no Jews in it at all hardly".

Today there are only three remaining pawnshops in Dublin, a way of life almost gone. But when inner-city women reminisce about life in the old days they invariably laugh about trekking down to the local pawn with their neighbourhood pals — it was just a weekly street ritual.

II

DEALERS, SPIELERS, VENDORS AND COLLECTORS

Dealers

'Street traders are a part of Dublin heritage and tradition. Can any Dubliner imagine the city without 'the dealers'?"
("Street Traders", *Irish Times*, 1985)

Dublin's quintessential street figure is that of Molly Malone hawking cockles and mussels along "streets broad and narrow". This sentimentalised image is found in Irish song, literature and legend. Dublin's famed ruddy-cheeked women dealers, attired in apron and crying aloud their fruit, vegetables and fish for sale, are true survivors of the hard life on the streets. Centuries ago local shopkeepers complained — as some still do today — that they were a "constant annoyance" obstructing traffic and interfering with business.[9] As early as 1660 an attempt was made to abolish street traders except for those duly licensed, but to little avail.[10] Following the Great Famine and exodus to Dublin of impoverished rural families, the number of street dealers increased markedly. As social historian Daly states, men had little employment opportunity and dealing became "predominantly the refuge of women".[11] By the 1800's the proportion of females engaged in this activity in Dublin was "far in excess of most other cities".[12]

Many dealers were destitute widows with children to feed. Charitable agencies helped them get a basket and some produce to sell rather than having to rely on begging and handouts. Commonly they reared their children beside them and put them to work when they were of age. By 1900 juvenile street trading was widespread. As O'Brien explains, it was "as much evidence of straitened family circumstances as youthful enterprise".[13] Most of these "trading waifs" were between ten and fifteen years of age and from the poorest families. Bedraggled, barefooted urchins standing rain-drenched in the streets selling, was a pathetic sight. Often it was no more than a pretence to disguise begging. But despite the harshness of street life it was argued by some authorities that it was actually better for the children to be out and active on the streets than confined to the unhealthy, rat-infested and diseased tenement slums in which they lived.

Old Anglesea Street market showing parts of iron bedsteads, hanging clothing, bowls and pictures for sale

COURTESY OF RSAI

This century's women dealers are descendants of their nineteenth century kin; most can trace their trading roots back at least several generations. Reared as babies along the street in a box beside their mother and granny, theirs is a heritage of struggle and hardship — but also of pride. It was naturally expected that they would follow in their mother's footsteps. As they like to put it, it was "just tradition ... generation follows generation". Like their mothers, they wore shawls, pushed wicker barrows and balanced baskets on their heads. Now they and their daughters wear aprons, push prams or stand before stalls. Though no longer hawking cockles, mussels or rabbits, they still sell fruit, flowers, vegetables, fish, poultry, clothing and shoes in the old-fashioned way.

The "old crowd" of Dublin dealers — as they like to reverentially refer to themselves — are mostly between sixty and eighty-five years of age. They are found primarily along Moore, Henry, Thomas and Parnell Streets as well as the Daisy and Iveagh markets. As they tell it, street life in the 1920's and 1930's was every bit as tough as in their grandmothers' time. Like their mothers and grannies before them, most became street traders because of family tradition, limited education, jobless husbands and sheer desperation. Henry Street dealer Ellen Preston epitomises the plight of the Dublin street dealer in this century. Having had to raise twelve children off the street, she does not forget the hard days:

I'm part of the history of the street ... yes, I am. Trading goes well back in my family, over a hundred years. My mother and grandmother sold vegetables and fruit on Parnell Street. My mother had fourteen of us. Very, very hard times ... you had nothing at all. There was no work for the men. The women traders, they held the families together. They were the whole upkeep because they had to go out. It was very rough.

I was about twelve years of age when I started selling. Every day I pushed me pram on the road in the traffic. Every day. Over the cobblestones and it was really very hard it was. And there was horses and cars and we'd be walking through them ... keep walking. Some days was miserable. I often come home with the rain beating off me. You'd be drowned but you had to do it. I remember one day I went out to sell and it was snowing and the snow was getting into me shoes and I was expecting one of the babies at the time and I brought me little parcel with me and I went straight to the hospital and had me baby. And I was out on the street again then in a week.

Despite the rigours of trading, women relished the independence and social life of the street. Friendly banter, bargaining and haggling with customers was invigorating. Even better was the social interaction among dealers themselves which revolved around animated chat, crack, gossip, story telling and pranks. Singing and dancing commonly added to the mood of merriment, especially after a good funeral or around Christmas. At the Daisy and Iveagh markets where characters abounded women would regularly get their jill or half-jill from the nearby pub, dress up in absurdly comical old gowns and hats — even men's baggy suits — and burst into song and dance. For Nanny Farrell, at eighty-four still seated behind her little stall, it always made her day when two Daisy pals would put on a good performance:

You'd see them all be dancing and singing. Used to take a few pints and dancing and singing all day to their heart's content. They were a good laugh. They kept everyone alive. Two howls they were. Oh, I could listen to them all day ... two devils they were. It was grand.

Dealers and customers alike would gather around to watch. The more ridiculous the antics, the better the show. Some women dealers were notorious for their uninhibited prankish behaviour, parading their act around the streets and even invading the sacred male sanctuary of the local pub in full costume and song. The men howled even more loudly than the women.

Apart from their humorous nature, Dublin's street dealers have always been known for their kindness and generosity, to friends and strangers alike. It is more than just part of Moore Street lore that the weathered visage, sometimes gruff manner, and tart tongues of some of the veterans belie a "heart of gold". Stories of their helping the needy are countless. For those in trouble they always had an understanding ear, compassionate word or a few bob. As Daisy trader Annie Ryan relates, both the poor and the outcast could always turn to the dealers for help:

The dealers were always soft. It was just a tradition. They had time for everybody, especially if anybody was down-and-out or a knockabout or a "poor unfortunate" ... they were prostitutes. You always had time for them.

Busy street market in Cole's Lane (looking toward Henry St.) with a variety of hanging clothing, shoes, boots and furniture pieces for sale. Shawled women and barefoot children may be seen
COURTESY OF RSAI

Back when times were hard it was quite respectable for Dublin working-class families to buy the essentials of life in street markets. Like the pawnshop, it was a necessity of life and sign of the times. Street stalls and markets were crammed with customers. Crowds could be so thick that people had to queue up to get in on the action. Kathleen Maguire, who began as a child, recalls the boom years at the Daisy:

Oh, it used to be packed. There'd be everything. Everybody was looking for a bargain and everybody got a bargain. It was grand. The market would close around 3:00 and the man would have to come around with the bell to get the crowd out.

In addition to food items, the market dealers sold heaps of second-hand clothing, shoes, furniture, hardware, pots, pans, jewelry — even rosaries. Families were completely outfitted at the markets. Dealers acquired most of their merchandise from pawnbrokers' auctions and "jumble sales" where competition was stiff and hackles rose. Underbuying and underselling could lead to anger and words

39

exchanged. Friendly competition in selling was fair enough but if one dealer was caught trying to "steal" another's regular customer by unscrupulous means it could result in a scathing exchange of curses and even a most un-ladylike tussle on the ground, as Margaret O'Connell verifies:

> *Oh, and if they had a few drinks that would be it! Throw off the shawls and that was it. You'd see knickers and all. Have a row ... hair pulling and all. More than blows ... a real* fight! *Then they'd forget about it and talk.*

The halcyon days of street trading in Dublin are now a thing of the past. Famed Moore Street, however, is still thriving and seems sacrosanct. Street trading began in Moore Street about 1760. In 1968 there was an inquiry into abolishing street trading but proponents of preservation argued successfully that "street traders have a claim on Moore Street because they have been there for so long".[14] Similarly, Henry and Thomas Streets are still buoyant but trading along Parnell Street has largely withered away. Perhaps most dramatic and sad has been the decline of the Daisy and Iveagh markets, once hives of activity. There used to be eighty dealers or more at the markets and hordes of customers. Today the Daisy has about ten and the Iveagh a few more. "We're the last of the flock", intones Annie Ryan, "the market is going to disappear and we'll disappear with it". Out of lifetime habit they still congregate each day beside their rickety stalls sipping tea and chatting away as in days of old. But now it's clearly for the social company ... "there's no money left in it today", they all concur. They are openly depressed by the barren and dilapidated condition of their setting which was once so cheerful. Equally dispiriting are the health inspectors who probe about mumbling about sanitation and "E.E.C. regulations" while threatening closure. For Ida Lahiffe, who inherited her father's stall in the Iveagh, it is not only a personal tragedy but an historical loss:

> *It was great here in the old days. The market would be packed. Every stall was full. You could find almost anything you wanted if you came in here ... everything. It got people through the hard times. Ah, you'd hear a lot of people coming in here saying, "Oh, I reared me family out of here". The Iveagh, it has an awful lot of historical significance, but it's nearly finished.*

Spielers

Spielers are the most elusive street figures; also among the most intriguing. They appear suddenly in the midst of a crowd, squat down with their wares spread tantalisingly before them, make their spiel to draw an audience, collect the profits, and then vanish back into the crowd. In one form or another, spielers have long been part of Dublin's street scene. Compared to the more passive dealers, they are aggressive, canny, polished sellers. They are a special breed akin to the old-type carnival barker and smooth, fast-talking side-show pitchman. They have sometimes gained an unsavoury reputation as con-artists bilking the public out of money by offering fraudulent merchandise. But they have also been lauded as consummate salesmen and performers.

Mason's Street Market by Horseman's Row showing clothing on hooks, women's straw hats, metal washing basin and cabbage heap on table
COURTESY OF RSAI

Dublin's spielers may be found along any heavily pedestrianised thoroughfare but they are most commonly encountered on Henry Street, the mecca for Irish shoppers. They may wear swank London-type suits or casual shirt and slacks. Ordinarily they sell jewelry or perfume which are small, portable and bring a fair price. Rather than being dishonest dupers, they are hucksters out to charm and lure customers. The street is the stage upon which they perform their entertaining selling act, honed to precision. Liam Preston, born into a large family of street dealers, is Henry Street's premier spieler. He explains the art of spieling:

> *We "spiel" them. Spieling means to get out and actually give a speech, a good line. You've got to get them to stop first and then hold them. Make 'em think "it's too good to be true" — three gold chains for only three pounds! That's a stage there. Ah, I see myself as a performer. I have jokes and all. People themselves are like sheep, really, they want to be led.*

The usual scene is that of spieler squatting before a semi-circular crowd of twenty to fifty curious observers. The goal is to convince them that they are being offered a "once in a lifetime" bargain. There are subtle hints that the gleaming gold chains so enticingly arranged on velvet might have been illicitly obtained and thus literally a "steal" at the asking price. Timing and theatrics are vital to success. An element of trust and rapport must be established. Country Irish are especially good prospects because they find spielers an exotic attraction. Crowds intuitively detect the shifty spielers and they do not survive long on the street. As Liam knows, "a lot of them have tried it and failed".

For the most part, Dublin's spielers offer an honest product at a fair price, but under the guise that it is a great bargain. Though not defrauding customers, they do often violate street trading codes. For this reason, they employ a "watcher" to keep a vigilant eye out for blue-uniformed police who, fortunately, tend to stand out about a half foot higher than crowd level. When alerted, spielers slam shut their case, scrape up the pound notes, then vaporise into the crowd — only to resurface about ten minutes later at the same pitch. It's street theatrics at its best.

Newspaper Vendors

Fifty years ago, before radio and television were standard home possessions, newspapers selling for one penny were the principal source of daily news and information and Dublin streets were filled with sellers. They were posted on virtually every corner and scattered in between. One historian has proffered that the newspaper vendors were as ubiquitous as street traders and their cries even more audible.[15] When the evening papers hit the streets in late afternoon their din was sometimes deafening. Early in the century the Rev. Carmichael wrote of the "ear-piercing shrieks of our newsboys. Newsboys yell like Apaches on the war-path, like Zulus in a charge".[16]

In his work *Rakes and Ruffians*, Walsh notes that historically in Dublin the poor, crippled, deformed and blind often ended up on the streets as newspaper sellers.[17] Hence, they were sometimes objects of pity. Though not disabled, the city's shivering, barefooted newsboys were often pathetically poor and ill-clad, eliciting compassion and generosity. Christy Murray tells of his caring customers back in the 1920's:

> *It was a poor life. You had to struggle to exist. Sure, I don't think I wore boots till I was fourteen. And your fingers would be freezing. When I'd go around with the papers I'd get fed. People in them days was great.*

Most paper sellers began as young lads and grew into stationary figures holding the same pitch for decades. Known by hundreds of regular customers, many were regarded as great characters. They prided themselves on having witnessed first-hand every imaginable sort of human behaviour from their stool perch along the street. Wise to the ways and sights of city life, they were regarded as something of street philosophers. But the few who have been recorded in writing were more notable for their comical traits. As Gahan writes in the *Dublin Historical Record*, one was "this character" known locally around Stoneybatter as "Blind Joe" Sadler.[18] Despite his disability, he was able to distinguish papers by feel and unerringly delivered them to the proper hands. He delighted in advertising by shouting out the news of the day after being so informed by a friend. However, some waggish mates occasionally took mischievous fun in fuelling him with bogus news stories which he excitedly disseminated through the neighbourhood — until he sheepishly learned the truth. Another chap was

An old Dublin newspaper and magazine vendor
COURTESY OF THE NATIONAL LIBRARY OF IRELAND

labelled "Paddy the Liar" because of his habit of spreading "fantastic lies to sell his paper".[19] Unblushingly, he would concoct sensational stories of murder and mayhem but when buyers searched the pages the story was not to be found.

It was the mad scrambling of the boy sellers that most enlivened the newspaper trade, as they darted wildly about the streets and through dangerous traffic to make sales. Some, like Murray, were innovative and daring:

> *I used to jump up onto the trams to sell the papers. Just hop on and dash upstairs to see who wanted a paper and hop off and then onto another tram. I was young like a hare and I'd dodge the horses and traffic. I done the* Mail *and* Herald, *a penny apiece, and on a good day you'd earn a couple of bob.*

Back when the inner-city was densely populated there was a large workforce trekking home each evening and plenty of business in the paper trade. But with the onset of decentralisation and suburban housing development in the 1950's the urban population dwindled and business declined. Bill Cregan, doyen of the O'Connell Street newspaper vendors, remembers better days:

> *Donkey's years ago this (O'Connell) was a great street. Forty years ago on a good day I could sell 500 papers, just evening papers. Oh, you'd get loads of people. Everybody lived in the city. These days I can't sell 200 evening papers. It's not the city anymore ... the heart of the city has gone to the suburbs.*

Scrap Collectors

Plying Dublin's streets were also the scrap collectors, better known in the old days as "rag and bones" men. They combed the streets with sack, push-barrow or horse and cart in search of salvageable items to cash in at the scrap merchant's yard, normally owned by a local Jewish man. Their typical cry was "any rags, bottles, jam jars?'. Sometimes they would hand out delft, balloons, windmills or picture cards in return. Besides the "rag and bones" men there were also small armies of "tuggers" and "pickers"who worked for the scrap merchants. Tuggers were mostly women who plodded the suburbs with wicker boxcars collecting second-hand clothing in exchange for delft. Pickers were usually men and boys who dug through city dump sites for bottles, brass, scrap metal or anything else of value.

Ragmen with horse and cart were especially preyed upon by children who loved to scut the back, climb aboard, or snatch a few bottles for cinema money — everyone, it seemed, had their ploy for making a few bob from the street. Scrap collectors worked the streets well into the 1950's but have hardly been viewed as historically important. In actuality, they performed a useful scavenging and recycling role in the inner-city. One such individual, "known by all as Dan the Ragman" around Parnell and Gardiner Streets in the 1930's, was immortalised in print.[20] In his sixties and walking with a limp resulting from a World War I leg wound, he clambered through the streets with horse and cart calling out for rags and bottles as women poked their heads out of tenement windows to yell back at him.

Rough cobblestoned streets, laneways and alleys were the playgrounds for tenement children

COURTESY OF RSAI

Scrap collection in Dublin was dominated by a small coterie of Jews, some of whom were also moneylenders. In local vernacular they were known, without pejorative intent, as "Jewmen". Much misconception and mythology surround them. In such antiquated neighbourhoods as the Liberties and Stoneybatter they are very much a part of local folklore. One stereotypical image is that of a shrewd scavenger-businessman who made a "fortune" from collecting cast-offs from the poor and engaging in mercenary moneylending. To others, they were kind, benevolent men who could be generous to the needy. Many elderly city dwellers remember them without malice as merely "necessary evils" of the age. In truth, little is known about the old Jewmen because they usually remained behind the scenes relying upon their collectors to bring in the scrap. In many ways they were perceived much the same as the tenement landlords who were often invisible, having their agents collect the rents from the poor. For this reason, Kelly writes that still "dark suspicions and rumours anent the Jewman and landlord".[21] But by using oral historical inquiry we can demistify the Jewman and decipher fact from myth.

Some Jewmen became legends in their time around the neighbourhood and their "doings" became a part of local lore. As Crosbie confirms, one was the "famous" Harry Lipman who had his scrap yard off Brunswick Street and was "known far and wide".[22] Through the verbal testimony of Jimmy Byrne, who at twenty became his top assistant, we can historically reconstruct his role:

> *He was the Godfather of all the Jews in Dublin. Always known as "Harry Lipman the Ragman". Ah, he was a* legend. *It was only an old scrap store with bottles and rags and jars and that but, oh, he was a millionaire! People used to go around collecting with these basket cars they'd get from him, big basket prams made out of cane with a wooden handle and two wheels and a wheel in front. Now some of the people wouldn't collect the stuff, they'd go and pawn his cart on him.*

Byrne became so closely trusted by his employer that when Lipman died he left the business to him, in blatant violation of his synagogue rules that it must rightfully pass into the hands of another Jew. Byrne's "inside" account of the role of Jewmen and scrap collecting in Dublin is a prime example of the value of pure oral history.

III

TRANSPORT AND VEHICLE MEN

> *"The trams always seemed to belong to a more civilized age"*
> (J. Nolan, *Changing Faces*, 1982)

At no period in Dublin's history were the streets more madly chaotic — and exciting — than between about 1910 and 1945. It was a maelstrom of horse vehicles, trams, bicycles, buses and motor cars all competing aggressively for traffic space and parking places. And there were few regulations to impose order on the streets. In the words of ninety-four year old George Doran, pioneer bus driver and cabbie, it was an unmitigated "free-for-all". Rivalry ran rampant with newfangled motor cars challenging the horse, cabbies quarrelling with jarveys at hazards (ranks), renegade "pirate" buses out-speeding trams to steal away passengers and cyclists swarming like locusts through the vehicular traffic. It was a turbulent and reckless period but the streets were undeniably "tinged with excitement".[23] By 1930 when the new age of "automobilism" had conspicuously arrived, with an estimated 11,000 motor vehicles in the city and county of Dublin, the street scene was so frenzied that the *Irish Times* began warning citizens of the dangers of venturing forth.[24]

It was also the great age of public transport when people still travelled by rail and ship. Dublin's railway stations and docks were packed with passengers as jarveys and cabbies formed long queues awaiting business. The grand hotels and cinemas were concentrated in the very heart of the city and O'Connell Street was as congested as any in Europe ... "Oh, the streets were alive night and day", recalls eighty-five year old Johnny Rearden, an old jarvey and cabbie. It was also an age of elegance with the stately and "civilized" trams gliding along with bells clanging and trolley sparks flying, while bowler-hatted jarveys, fancy whip in hand, trotted courting couples out to the Phoenix Park and Strawberry Beds on a fine Sunday afternoon. In the evenings horse-drawn carriages pulled up in front of the Shelbourne and Gresham hotels and theatre crowds, dressed for the occasion, streamed along O'Connell Street in congenial mood. And, as former tram driver Paddy Lynch declares, Nelson's Pillar was the centre of the whole universe for Dubliners:

Nelson's Pillar was the meeting point for everybody, young and old, lover and the whole lot ... "I'll meet you at the Pillar". That was the focal point of every blooming thing.

Stately trams and simple horse vehicles had to share street space well into the 1940's
COURTESY OF THE CHANDLER COLLECTION

Jarveys

Jarveys were a colourful and rambunctious lot — real horsemen in the city centre. Back in the 1930's and 1940's "the horse was king ... the horsemen, each a character in his own right".[25] Proud and competitive, they drove the streets perched atop their jaunting cars or four-wheeled carriages drawn by often magnificently groomed horses with brass and leather gleaming. They did grand horse funerals, took spectators out to the races, and frequented the bonafides for midnight pints. They boasted quirky nicknames, clannishly hung out at their favourite pubs and were known for their gregarious nature and witticisms. Adding a sort of roguish element to the streetscape, they "made a decided offering towards the city's individualistic character".[26] They also contributed a romantic flavour to travel, as the "Song of the Dublin Jarvey" reveals:[27]

If you want to drive round Dublin
Sure you'll find me on the stand;
I'll take you to Raheny
For cockles on the strand,
To Phoenix Park, to Nancy Hands,
To Monument and then
I'll take you to the Strawberry Beds
And back to town again.

Jarveys were a particularly inbred bunch as sons inherited the trade from their fathers and, as old jarvey Mickey Sheridan discloses, "in me father's time a jarvey's son married a jarvey's daughter. The girl's father would give him a wedding present of a horse, hackney car and harness". Licensing and regulation were conducted by the Police Department and were strict. To obtain a licence a jarvey had to have two householders "go security" for him and a publican or priest submit a letter attesting to his good character. Though they were indeed men of fine character, Rearden confesses that when he started as a jarvey in 1923 they were also reputed for their ability to drink and tell tall tales:

Jarveys done their share of drinking. Some characters was known for their capacity to drink, others for to tell stories. The police could interfere with the jarvey if he'd been drinking and take him and the horse to the police station. It didn't happen often because the policeman didn't like handling the horse. And if he'd had too much to drink the horse would bring him home.

By the late 1930's jarveys were being displaced by buses, cabs and private cars. But with the outbreak of the second world war the situation changed drastically. With petrol rationed, private car use declined while taxis were limited in fuel and prohibited from driving passengers to horse races and sporting events. As a consequence, there occurred a great revival of horses and jarveys on the city's streets. Though veteran jarveys welcomed the reprieve, they had to cope with unsavoury competition, as Sheridan explains:

> *When the war broke out it was a free-for-all! Cars were off the road and taximen was under petrol rationing. All types of horse-drawn vehicles started to come back onto the hazards. There'd be 500 to 600 jarveys. In the war years I seen maybe seventy yokes on the hazard. But in the war years you'd meet the bowsies, the blaggards, the men only coming into the job. They were a rougher crowd. They hadn't the same class. They gave decent jarveys a bad name.*

Jarveys provided a valuable transport service during the war years but once petrol again flowed freely they were forgotten heroes. With people returning to motorised vehicles the jarveys found themselves sitting idly in their jaunting cars at queues with no business. In 1945 Sheridan went to Amiens Street station for "three days at twelve hours a day and never got a fare off it ... that'll tell you how bad it went". A few jarveys hung on part-time into the 1950's but the horse, once king of the streets, had become obsolete and a nuisance to modern motorists.

Tram Drivers

Horse-tram service began in the city in 1872 and by 1881 three different companies had amalgamated into the Dublin United Tramway Company (DUTC) which ran 186 trams and used over 1,000 horses.[28] In 1896 electric trams were put into service and the horse-trams disappeared five years later. The electrified tram system was a great success, heralded as "one of Dublin's minor glories".[29] In retrospect, these "galleons of the street" did indeed seem to belong to a more civilised time.[30] In old photographs they are an especially nostalgic sight for Dubliners.

If there was an elite corps of Dublin transport men it was surely the tram drivers who were legendary for their professionalism and personal courtesies. True gentlemen, they were regarded as aristocrats among the city's transport men. To them, the stately trams were ships and they the captains. They knew well that their behemoths ruled the roads. Most were four-wheelers but some larger luxury trams had eight wheels; some were open-top and others covered. Because tram drivers operated the largest vehicles, carried the most passengers, and controlled the street centre, they had great responsibility. They also confronted many obstacles from frosty tracks to belligerent horsemen to reckless motorists. Paddy Lynch coped with the strain and risks of the job:

> *You stood all day long, you never sat down. Oh, you couldn't take your eyes off the road. In frosty weather the tracks would be kind of frozen*

and you wouldn't have the stopping power and you'd slide. In a motor car you can brake real hard or swerve but in a tram you can't. Horses was one of the biggest problems. You'd know a horse was flighty, you could see his ears wagging. We were trained to knock off the current so we can go by them. And there'd be plenty of arguments between the tram drivers and the men with horses, especially the coal men ... the type of people they were, you know ... tough.

Open–top tram and proud driver in front of Trinity College
COURTESY OF THE CHANDLER COLLECTION

Tram drivers lived with the risk of reckless motorists who would speed up to pass them while trying to beat an oncoming tram from the other direction. As Lynch witnessed in horror, when a miscalculation was made "the motor car used to be sliced in two".

Despite their popularity and civility, trams gradually fell victim to what one observer called the "soulless busses".[31] The new fleet of buses with routes scattered more strategically throughout the city served the public closer to their homes and work places. In an increasingly hurried lifestyle, trams became viewed as slower and less convenient. The last city centre tram ceased service in 1949 and the famous Hill of Howth tram a decade later.[32] It was a cruel blow to the proud tram drivers, especially those who were transferred by C.I.E. to bus conductor duty. Tom Redmond, the last tram driver in Ireland, shares his emotions:

> *The 31st of May, 1959, was my last run. I was demoted from a tram driver to bus conductor. It was really dreadful. I mean, you go from being a tram driver where you were on the front, your own boss, just the same as the captain of a ship ...* people respected you *... and then you have to go to the back of the buses looking for fares. There were tears for the last old tram. It's history gone, a way of life. I was the last tram driver in Ireland ... I'm the last link.*

Busmen

In 1828 when the first omnibus service began in London, Dublin businessmen determined that such "buses" might serve their city as well. However, efforts to launch a similar bus operation in 1834 were thwarted by the jarveys — or hackney men as they were then known — who engaged legal counsel to show that buses would be illegal under the Dublin Carriage Laws.[33] Finally, in 1848, a new Police Act permitted buses on the streets. During the Victorian era most of Dublin's buses were of the double-decker type drawn typically by two horses and sometimes four. Eventually the jarveys ceased opposing them when they realised that there was plenty of business for everyone since buses were confined to set routes while they could provide transport to any destinations. With the advent of trams the horse-drawn buses became outmoded.

After the first world war independently-owned motorised buses appeared on Dublin streets. Described as "an extremely motley collection" of vehicles seating generally twenty or fewer passengers, they had the advantage of being able to speed around city streets, outrunning trams, stopping anywhere, and stealing passengers.[34] These "independents" or "pirates", as they came to be known, wreaked havoc on the street scene, detested by the respectable tram men, cabbies and jarveys for their outlaw habits and cut-throat activity. They carried such names as the Contemptible Omnibus Company, Silver Queen, Blueline and Excelsior Bus Company. Some owners, however, did not even bother to "dignify their vehicles" with a trademark or name.[35] During the 1920's they virtually ran wild and unregulated as rival buses engaged in "breathtaking races" through the streets to first reach a cluster of waiting passengers.[36] Doran, who drove a proper char-a-banc bus in the early twenties, abhorred their vulturous tactics:

> *The pirate buses used to go around to all different routes. Oh, they could go anywhere they liked. They weren't confined to one route — a free-for-all! There was no bus stops, anybody could just put up their hand and stop you anywhere. Oh, they'd cut one another's throat.*

Many of the pirate buses were not only driven recklessly but were poorly maintained and thus condemned by authorities for posing a danger to the public. After losing enough of their tram passengers, the DUTC in 1925 inaugurated their own bus service in competition. Their vehicles were operated more safely and efficiently and the pirates began to falter. But not until 1932 when the Road Transport Act was passed requiring all buses to operate under licence and on defined routes were the independents put off the roads. Throughout the thirties and forties the new respectably-run buses co-existed peaceably with the trams and jarveys. After the second world war the DUTC was changed to the National Transport Company of Coras Iompair Eireann (C.I.E.) and by the end of the decade buses had replaced the city's trams.

For the past fifty years buses have served as the major provider of public transport in Dublin, earning a very respected reputation during the early decades. C.I.E.'s bus drivers and conductors worked as a team and enjoyed a mutually respectful relationship with their daily passengers who they commonly knew by name and personally assisted. Busmen prided themselves on personal appearance, courtesy, and running on schedule. Hugh Maguire, who began in 1942, found working on the older variety of buses with open rear compartment both gratifying and adventuresome:

> *Now I enjoyed the job of conductor. They had a double-decker bus in service at that time known as the "R" Series. It was a fifty-five seater and was much more compact than the present double-decker that holds seventy-four. This was smaller, had steeper stairs to go up, and they were faster. They weren't heated and the platform on the rear was open. Conductors had to stand at the back and in the wintertime the rain would be belting in on top of you ... and the snow. And the kids would be throwing snowballs at you. And there was a great relationship between conductors and passengers, a great respect built up.*

Old busmen, without exception, lament that "things have changed". Nowadays, they claim, busmen often seem to "take no pride" in their work and appearance, lacking the professionalism and politeness of men in their time. For this they blame lax management as well as the new breed of busmen themselves. It's a sad commentary on the times, they say.

Bicycle and Car Parkers

Parkers are probably the most unacclaimed of Dublin's street figures; there is no historical record of their existence. Yet they have played a distinctly important part in "civilizing" Dublin's streets. Their role was borne of genuine need and after more than seventy years the solitary parkers are still to be seen on the streets assisting harried motorists. With their caps for identification, they stand out like beacons in the centre of the road scanning for approaching customers and making convoluted gestures to guide drivers toward safe harbour. They are most in evidence around Parnell and Mountjoy Squares and St. Stephen's Green. To appreciate their role on the streets, one must look at the early history of bicycling and automobilism in the city.

Newfangled sleek motor cars were a great novelty on Dublin streets
COURTESY OF THE CHANDLER COLLECTION

The appearance of motor cars was the "most startling transportation innovation" on Dublin's street scene.[37] It began modestly enough in 1896 and by 1904 there were only fifty-eight motor cars registered in Dublin (compared with nearly 3,000 in London). At first, motor cars were quite expensive, costing between £250 and £400 and thus exclusively the property of the rich. But mass production of such vehicles as Ford's Model-T made the £100 car a reality for buyers and by 1915 there were nearly 1,500 in the city. But it was during the 1920's that their popularity soared and by the end of the decade there were some 11,000 in the city and county of Dublin. From the very outset, motor cars disrupted the established street system. Aggrieved horse-vehicle drivers cursed the "infernal machines" which intimidated them and frightened their animals. For tram drivers they posed new obstacles and risks. But there was no holding back the tide.

Dublin was ill-prepared to handle the motorised mayhem. There was an absence of driving tests, traffic lights, enforceable roadway regulations and adequate parking space. As a consequence, the early years were deleriously unregulated and free-wheeling. Dubliners became notorious for their "negligent and furious" driving habits as the *Irish Times* took to warning citizens of the dangers.[38] For their part, motorists complained of the dire parking problem. The congestion of trams, buses, jaunting cars, delivery vans and bicycles could completely clog a streetway. In frustration, motorists sometimes simply abandoned their vehicles in the street and went about their daily business. In 1934 an article in the *Irish Times* noted that the law allowed only for persons to halt their vehicles for a "sufficient time" for the purpose of taking up or letting down passengers, but that this was summarily ignored. It was suggested that there be a strict limit for street parking, arguing that:[39]

> *The practice of making use of a busy street as a garage to keep a vehicle outside a place of business all day in order to have it immediately available on a few occasions during the day cannot be fitted into any effective parking scheme.*

Coinciding with the automobile boom was a colossal increase in the number of bicycles. Bicycles had become popular during the Victorian age but in the 1890's a good one was still prohibitively expensive for most. However, by the 1920's mass production had dropped their price to about £5 with easy payment terms for their purchase. City streets were soon besieged with cyclists of all sorts who zig-zagged through traffic with complete abandon. Charlie Dillon, a parker in the early 1930's, describes the scene:

> *It was nearly all bicycles at that time. Ah, thousands of bikes. I done the middle of O'Connell Street and there was no traffic lights at all — it was "go" all the time. Oh, you couldn't cross the road with the bicycles ... it was a disaster.*

The combination of worsening automobile and bicycle traffic during the twenties gave rise to the parkers as a unique Dublin street type. Most pioneer parkers began by minding both bikes and cars. Some eventually specialised in one or the other. In the early years it was often more profitable handling bikes because of the sheer volume, especially at sporting matches at Lansdowne or Croke Park where parkers like Dillon who had a prime pitch might get fifty or more bikes:

A person would come in and I'd mark the bike with chalk, the number on the saddle. And you had a double ticket and you'd stick one into the handlebars and give one to the person. It was threepence a bike. That was great money at that time ... it was only seven pence a pint.

Besides marking and minding the bicycle, the parker was responsible for taking it into the police station at day's end if the owner did not reclaim it. On big match days when men over-imbibed a weary parker might have to haul several bicycles down to the station.

Car parking was a more demanding job. Men commonly worked ten hour days in all weather. They not only directed motorists to a safe parking place and guarded their vehicles but when owners returned they were expected to open doors, choke and crank-start the car with big whip-lash handles and even give it a push if necessary to get it going. And since there was no set fee for their service they had to accept whatever was offered them. Normally it was a few coppers but sometimes only an apple, orange or few cigarettes. Back in the twenties "Ginger" Kelly simply endured the hardships:

When I started all the motor cars had a handle. You'd have to swing it and there's a back-kick with the big brass handle. Sometimes you'd get a rough looking bloke and he'd swing it himself. But nine times out of ten you'd have to swing it. The men were generally very sedate and delicate and if you cranked it for them you'd be lucky if you got tuppence. Women drove cars very little back then ... and they was all "ladies". All I'd get was four or five shillings a day in copper. It got us stew for the seven kids.

Parkers also took it upon themselves to "sort out" entanglements by directing street traffic around their pitch. They commonly released brakes on the cars they were minding so that they could push them around to clear jams and facilitate the traffic flow.

Toughness was an asset in the parking business and fistfights common as men had to defend their pitch against intruders. In the 1930's Dublin's hard-core of regular parkers received licences from the police, complete with cap badge and armband to make them "official". For solidarity against the many unofficial parkers, known as "bluffers", they formed a parkers' union consisting variously of between thirty and fifty men. Union men stuck together, handed down pitches to sons as a sort of inheritance, and monopolised areas like Croke Park. As Frankie Farrelly knew, bluffers had to be cautious:

I was a bluffer but I'd have me cap and put a green ribbon on it, to let people see that you're a car parker. I never worked Croke Park because there's a gang there and it was mostly inherited in the family going back to the bike days. See, a son, he'd be taking over his father's pitch.

There was many a scrap over pitches but if a man was tough they wouldn't touch him at all, wouldn't get near him for their life!

Car parkers have survived into the modern age because traffic is denser than ever and vandalism and car theft an ever-present risk in the inner-city. Today, protecting the owner's vehicle against violation is more important than providing a parking place. On a good day a man can earn up to £50, enough to keep a few of the old-timers like Dillon and Farrelly still working the street. But they complain that the new breed of parkers lack the sense of duty to vigilantly mind customers' cars and instead often take the money and head off to the nearest pub. For them, dutifully minding cars remains a matter of simple honour.

Cabbies

The already frenetic state of Dublin's streets was further "compounded by the proliferation of the motor-driven taxicab".[40] The decision to permit taxicabs in the city rested not with the Corporation but the police who were under the control of the British Government. When some English companies began applying for permission in 1908 Dublin's jarveys fiercely resisted by setting up an Anti-Taxicab Association to prohibit motor taxis on *their* streets.[41] Jarveys feared that the interlopers threatened their very financial existence. But late in 1911 approval was granted and the first cabbies made their appearance. At first, however, they could be hired only from garages or at fixed stands, not hailed at will by passengers on the streets. Thus, the jarveys held a comforting advantage.

Dublin's early cabbies were not required to take a driving exam but to be licensed they needed letters of reference from two householders and their parish priest attesting to honesty and character. If they had any court violation, even childish mitching or window breaking, they got no licence. Police not only inspected their vehicle for safety but checked the men for proper dress and cleanliness. Dirty shoes or an unshaven face could result in issuance of a summons. They drove vehicles with such names as Unic, Daimler, Humber, Chadron, Buick. Most were about forty horsepower, got twelve miles a gallon, carried spare tins of petrol and water on the running board and had roof rails for trunks. Rearden, who switched from jarvey to motor cabbie in 1927, recalls that his old Unic, for which he paid "ninety quid", was quite primitive:

It had a crank and you had to get it going yourself. Carried four passengers sitting face to face. It had a half windscreen and no wipers. The elements, they came in. Ah, and no electric lights. There was two oil lamps and a tail light and acetylene headlamps you filled with a mixture of carbide and water. In them days you could set the trunk beside the driver. See, there was no door on the lefthand side ... you got the weather.

By the 1920's cabbies were encroaching on the sacred terrain of the jarveys, pulling their motor taxis onto the same hazards beside the horses. Tempers flared and disputes erupted as verbal threats were issued and whips raised in anger. In some cases physical rows broke out. It was a clash between two ages and cultures and emotions ran high. Older jarveys were particularly distressed by the invasion while younger men saw its inevitability and tried to change with the times. George Doran switched from his char-a-banc to motor taxi in 1925 and witnessed the emotions of the conflict:

> *When the motor cabs come out the horse men felt very sick about it, especially the old horse cab men. They didn't like us pulling onto the hazard. Tried to keep us out. They'd put the amount of horses (allowed) on the hazard. Sometimes there was rows. Then they started to learn how to drive and they started to buy taxis. They'd switch over. Like on O'Connell Street we were mixing with the jarveys and by degrees you could see them fading away. But some of the jarveys couldn't take up taxis. Their heart wasn't in it ... no, it was with the horse.*

Ironically, in the late 1930's when motor taxis were replacing horse vehicles the war broke out and petrol was severely rationed. With cabbies limited in fuel and prohibited from attending sporting events the jarveys prospered. But it was a temporary triumph. By the late forties taxis had clearly established their supremacy on Dublin's streets. Rearden, who started as a jarvey in 1923 and didn't retire as a cabbie until 1981, reminisces: "Oh, Dublin was a grand old spot at that time ... more colourful with the horses. I saw the end of one period and the start of another".

IV

ANIMAL DEALERS, DROVERS AND FANCIERS

> *"Horses and cattle and pigs flying about the streets was a familiar sight when the cattle market was open up there. It was just part of the street life of Dublin".*
>
> *(Antoinette Cooper Healy, 1989)*

In the first half of the century Dublin streets could be so clogged with animals that it looked like fair day. Animal life was a normal part of city life, especially around Smithfield, Stoneybatter, the Liberties and the docks. By 1920 the cattle market at the top of Prussia Street had become the largest in the British Isles, selling weekly about 5,000 cattle, 7,000 sheep and 1,000 pigs.[42] British, German,

Dutch and other European buyers came every Wednesday and Thursday, employing local drovers to herd their animals to the docks for shipping. Streets were jammed with beasts, drovers and their dogs as pedestrians and motorists tried to dodge the onslaught. The shooing, waving, cursing and animal bellowing created an air of excitement. At that time it seemed that "every kid in Dublin wanted to be a cattle drover".[43] Indeed, as animals were driven past, many onlookers, children and adults alike, would pick up a stick or folded newspaper and give them a prod along their way. People on the street loved to get in on the act. In the wintertime the drama was heightened as streets became frosted and animals slipped and fell. Passers-by commonly joined in to get the animal back on its feet. But the best show was when cattle burst into tenement doorways or shops and had to be extricated by impatient drovers.

Horses, too, filled the streets. It must be remembered that well into the late 1940's most deliveries of coal, bread, milk, turf and other basics were made by horse-drawn vehicles. And during the war years when petrol was rationed the city literally ran on horse power. The sound of hoofs on cobblestones and the smell of dung in the streets were evocative of city life in those days. And the clamour and confusion created by the horses, cattle, sheep and pigs made for good street theatre.

Drovers

Dublin's drovers were authentic street types — weathered, tough, durable. They normally worked only two days a week for mere pittance, drank heavily, and fought fiercely. But mostly they just stood around the street together talking, smoking, chewing and spitting tobacco. They tended to be clannish and were conspicuous for their ritual of congregating at certain spots. One famous gathering place was Hanlon's Corner on the North Circular Road, just across from the sprawling cattle market. They also clustered in small cliques in front of pubs around Smithfield.

Long ago the drovers were known as "penny boys". As Maxwell writes, they carried bludgeons and "cruelties were practiced" as they beat the heads and legs of the animals.[44] They have always had the reputation for being a rowdy bunch, rough not only on their animals but on each other. Disagreements were often settled in the open street, lashing each other's flesh open with their ashplants. But, as drover Christy "Diller" Delaney tells it, most were poor but decent men:

> *Some were rough. They'd fight when they got drunk. Fight with sticks they would. Serious injuries. There was cow men which didn't like the bullock men. Sticks would be getting used on the head and across the shoulders. But a lot of them of very respectable type. You'd see them on Friday morning — as hard as they worked all day and night Thursday,*

exhausted and up to their waist in muck and cow dung — and they'd be dressed up with a white collar and tie at Hanlon's Corner. And they always wore what we called the dust-coat, some with a velvet collar. Work two days a week and they'd just stand around the rest, that was their routine.

On market days drovers ruled the streets, driving large herds of often unruly beasts down the centre, scattering people and interrupting traffic. It was like a scene from a western cowboy film. As motorists fumed in frustration pedestrians burst into laughter. But for the drovers, with great responsibility, it was serious business. Runaway animals posed great risk to people and property. Sometimes shops were demolished and individuals actually killed. Christy Donoghue, now seventy-three, began mitching from school and driving cattle down to the docks at twelve. To him market days were memorable and maddening:

Ah, the wild west wasn't up with us! You could have about 500 cattle being let out together going down at one time. Ah, it was murder going down that North Circular Road and you had people coming up the paths. Oh, they were afraid for their life! We always had a man on each side knocking them off the cars and trams was always in the middle of the road, always ringing their bells. And some fellas in their motor cars used to be stampeding them. They'd do it out of devilment. They could easily get out of control ... ah, they'd run their heart out.

When the Dublin Cattle Market closed in the late seventies the days of the drover ended. Many were unsettled by the sudden loss of their world. A scattering of old-timers can still be found around the local pubs reminiscing about the good old days when the streets were aswirl with beasts and scented with fresh dung.

Horse Dealers

In the first half of the twentieth century no other European capital city was more dependent on horse power for its daily functioning than Dublin. Firms such as Guinness's, C.I.E., Dublin Gas Company, coal merchants, bakeries, dairies, turf suppliers and countless others all used work horses by the thousands. Farriers and harness makers practiced their ancient crafts profitably in the city centre. It was the savvy horse dealers who made the whole system work. They attended horse fairs around the country, bought animals in large numbers and transported them to Dublin via roadway or train. It was big business involving great rivalry and profits. Like slick gamblers, they were shrewd and had their secrets of the trade. By all accounts it was a cut-throat business in which only the best survived the competition. Top horse dealers enjoyed an exalted status among animal men in the city. They made big money, drank the finest whiskey and were often too generous with mates. But the high style of life many lived during the horse revival of the war years was too good to last

Smithfield was the centre of horse trading in Dublin and here the horsemen congregated — haggling on the cobblestones, slapping hands when the price was set, and sealing deals with a pint in the nearby pub. The sight of a canny horse dealer displaying his strategies was a street event guaranteed to draw a close crowd around. It was almost with a sense of reverence that other horsemen watched him work as the act was played out. John Mannion was, by popular consensus around Smithfield, the best horse trader in the business — bar none. His reputation was hard earned over half a century:

> *I come to Dublin when I was about sixteen years old. Dublin was all horses then. You couldn't cross the road. Five hundred horses lining up on O'Connell Street in the morning. That's unbelievable … oh, yes, the jarveys, C.I.E., bakeries, very big work on the docks with horses. Small dairies running around delivering milk and people with pony and traps. In the* heart *of Dublin! I got in with the famous Cooper's of Queen Street in the strong horse business. Started buying horses at fairs for them. Horse dealers always carried only cash. I could carry £10,000 in cash, no trouble. We had* queues *for horses. Oh, during the war there would have been* no Dublin, *only for the horses and horse men. That is* true.

Mass motorisation in the 1950's spelled doom for the horse traders. Theirs was a trade no longer in demand. Like the drovers, they were perplexed and disturbed that their way of life so abruptly ended. But with the modest revival of the Smithfield horse fair a decade ago, after nearly twenty years of dormancy, a few of the real old traders like Mannion are back in fine form again, albeit on a miniscule scale compared with the past halcyon days. Nonetheless, on the first Sunday of each month Smithfield comes to life again for a few hours. The exciting mix of horses and horsemen harkens back to the "good old days" and visibly stirs the blood of admiring old-timers.

Pig Raisers

Pig raisers may have been the "poor cousins" to the horse and cattle men but their presence in city life was highly detectable, by sound and smell as well as sight. Only a few decades ago raising pigs in the rear yard was a commonplace family activity in parts of Dublin. Small back lane piggeries dotted the cityscape. When sufficiently fattened, father and sons would just take a stick and poke the squealing pigs along the street toward the market or abattoir, wending their merry way through the traffic and adding to the confusion. There were also a number of families who raised large herds of pigs as their sole business. Some kept several hundred pigs in their yard in the centre of the city. Behind closed gates they were often detected only by their hungry squeals or an odoriferous breeze. But years ago it seemed natural to the senses and neighbours seldom complained. Jimmy Riley, whose family goes back at least four generations in pig raising, still keeps about a hundred pigs in his yard off North King Street:

> *In me father's time there was a lot more piggeries. See, back in them times a family had a batch of pigs and they sold them a couple of times a year. A batch consisted of anything from six to ten or twelve. They'd just fatten them up and it was an extra few pounds a year.*

Once commonplace, pig raising in the 1990's is seen by some as a novelty, by others a nuisance. Owing to new sanitation regulations in the city, the Dublin Corporation seems determined to eradicate the last of the piggeries within a few years. Says Riley stoically, "I'm just seeing out an old thing".

Bird Market Men

Attending the bird market on Sunday mornings is one of the most enduring street customs of the Liberties. As one long-time devotee put it, it's just "part of the ritual associated with being a Dubliner."[45] Dating back to the Huguenot period it shifted sites several times. For the past 150 years it has been most strongly associated with Bride Street. It has traditionally been held in a small open yard along the street entered through a wooden gate. Birds were displayed in cages hung on the walls with nails. In its heyday bird men congregated by the hundreds every Sunday morning after Masses. Cronies debated, exchanged stories and extolled the virtues of their tiny feathered friends. Real bird men *never* missed a meeting.

Bird men were a conspicuous feature of the street scene. Apart from their Sunday streetside gathering they were constantly seen peddling their bikes carrying nets, poles and boxes heading toward the countryside to catch birds. Another highly visible element of the bird market along the streetscape were the many bird cages hung outside the windows of the grim bricked tenement rows. The poor occupants would buy a bird at the market for a shilling or two to add a bit of colour, song and cheer to their dreary environment. Many tenement rows were festooned with bird cages on both sides. This not only brightened the streetscape but also contributed to street socialisation because bird owners often sat beside their windows and passers-by often stopped to admire their bird and engage in chat. Sometimes a small crowd would even gather along the street beside a window to hear an especially beautiful birdsong.

Despite its longevity, there is no written historical account of the bird market. John Clarke, who has been part of the market scene since childhood, attributes this in large part to the notoriously competitive and secretive nature of the bird

ien themselves. Yet there is a wealth of local oral lore. Recognising this, he
egan patiently gathering verbal historical information decades ago from the fast-
iding older bird men. He is motivated by the realisation that the bird market will
kely not survive much longer and its history would die with the old men:

> *The old lads were very secretive. They've always been secretive. Even to*
> *the present day they're like that. That's why they never gave*
> *information to anyone, or interviews. I realised that the bird market is*
> *going to die out eventually ... that I'd have to get whatever little bits of*
> *information I could. So I talked to the old fellas. I want to let someone*
> know about it.

espite efforts by authorities to close it down in 1969 the bird market has

Man proudly strutting down Thomas Street in the Liberties with
a pet goose at his side

survived. It is still held on Sunday mornings about 11 a.m. in a small yard off Bride Street. As in centuries past, men enter through a small gate door, drop a few coins into a small cardboard box on the ground, then stray about admiring birds and chatting away in cliques. On a good morning there might be sixty men and a hundred bright, chirping birds. It is truly the last remnant of an ancient street tradition.

Pigeon Fanciers

Pigeon raising and racing, which originated in Belgium, filtered into Ireland via England and Belfast around the turn of the century. It especially caught on around the northside and dock area among the labouring classes and "boomed as a poor man's sport".[46] British soldiers stationed in Dublin who were pigeon fanciers helped to bring in birds and popularise the activity. But during the 1916 Troubles the British declared pigeon keeping illegal and tried to confiscate the birds, fearing they might be used as message carriers. Dublin fanciers had to hide their birds and smuggle them around.

Pigeon raising is a more important part of inner-city street life than many Dubliners (especially suburbanites) might realise. Tony Kiely, who started raising pigeons in 1936, reflects on the tradition:

> *Ah, pigeon racing has been a great part of the history of Dublin. You'd hear them talking about their pigeons in tenement houses and in pubs. See, pigeon racing was actually known as a poor man's race horse. In the poor tenement areas the pigeon fancier, that was his sole hobby ... that was his religion! This area of North Dublin around Ballybough and the North Strand was a hotbed of pigeon men. There were patches of open field around the back then and you could have four or five lofts in the one field, a vacant site. It was just a tradition here.*

Much of the activity took place on back streets, mews, laneways and vacant land where lofts were constructed. Pigeon men on their bikes with wicker baskets were a common sight on the streets. Harry Dixon, at the age of seventy-four one of the oldest members of the Dublin Homing Club dating back to 1924, as a youth used to regularly carry a basket of pigeons on his bike thirty miles out to the Curragh to release them for training. On race days the "sky became filled with a cloud of pigeons and there was great excitement in the street".[47] One ludicrous scene in the early days was that of men literally dashing down the streets carrying their pigeon in hand or in a basket heading toward the G.P.O. to have its race time registered by the postmistress. But, as Dixon recalls, the effort was worth the reward:

> *If you won a race there was a hooley in the house. Ah, banjo players*

63

and fiddle players. Oh, there used to be plenty of medals in our house.

Pigeon racing still flourishes today on the northside but in a financial and mercenary form which many elder men detest. High betting stakes and flying the "widowhood system" have taken the pure sport out of it while adding an element of cruelty. They insist on flying by the old rules — win or lose.

V

ENTERTAINERS AND PERFORMERS

The city's exuberant street busking performers have been hailed by one *Irish Press* journalist as "troubadours of modern Dublin".[*][48] Indeed, the tradition of street entertaining may be traced back to the troubadours of twelfth century Europe and well beyond. Since time immemorial Europe's city streets have been a stage for ballad singers, musicians, story tellers, pavement artists, dancers, clowns, mimes and magicians. Sjoberg, writing in *The Preindustrial City*, affirms that such entertainers were a natural part of street life in old feudal cities.[49] They are part of Europe's street *culture*.

Historically, Dublin has been blessed with an abundance of street performers of every imaginable sort. Balladeers were especially prevalent. MacLysaght, writing in *Irish Life in the Seventeenth Century*, notes that three centuries ago "street singers ... added their contribution to the general hub-bub of Dublin".[50] Later, in the post-famine period, many down-trodden Dubliners were forced to seek subsistence from the streets. As Phadraig contends in the *Dublin Historical Record*, by the 1860's itinerant musicians with their tin whistles and fiddles were almost as plentiful along the city's streets as hawkers.[51] Busking often amounted to little more than begging. Similarly, after the 1914–18 War many returned soldiers, too seriously wounded for normal work, turned to the streets to earn a few shillings with a song or instrument. Another "typical Dublin street singer" around this period was the woman standing beside the queue outside the Gaiety Theatre with an infant in one arm and leading another small child by hand while warbling a song for a few coppers.[52] As Davies sympathises, "if her songs are sad no doubt she does but reflect life as she finds it ... it would be a stony-hearted person who could refuse her appeal".[53] During the 1930's and 1940's street singers and musicians were familiar sights around the Liberties. Perhaps best known was John Wilson, an itinerant ballad singer. As he would stroll melodiously through the streets tenement windows would be thrown up and he was showered with coins. His contemporary counterparts along Dublin's streets

*The term "busker" traditionally applies to musicians and singers who perform outdoors for public donations. However, in Dublin today all street entertainers are known as buskers.

are part of a long historical lineage.

No Dublin street performer has been so famed as Michael Moran, alias "Zozimus", born in 1794 in Faddle Alley in the heart of the Liberties. Even the poet W.B. Yeats acknowledged that he achieved the stature of rector of Dublin's street ballad singers.[54] Actually, he was more of a reciter than singer and depended upon his eccentricity and bizarre attire as well as his musical talent to gain such a reputation. He spawned many imitators and followers and set some precedents for street entertainers. Interestingly, his old haunts were much the same as today's buskers — most notably Grafton, Henry and Dame Streets — and he regularly changed his pitch to cultivate a fresh audience.

In his paper entitled *In the Shadow of St. Patrick's*, read before the Irish National Library Society in 1893, P.J. McCall pointed out that Zozimus, like his modern-day brethren, was regularly harassed by authorities for obstructing traffic, blocking shops and encouraging pick-pocketing by drawing crowds.[55] For performing in the streets he was sometimes taken into court and officially charged with being an "obstruction and annoyance". Fortuitously, some of the dialogue between Magistrate and defendant was recorded for posterity. In one case, after admonishing him for blocking pathways and generally being a nuisance, the Magistrate queried, "What have you to say to this charge?" Replied the indomitable Zozimus, who often saved his best performance for the court:[56]

> *Your Worship ... what I sing is the praises of me native land. I love me counthry. She's dear to me heart, an' am I to be prevented from writin' songs in her honour? It is true that I can't see; but I can warble that which can rise the heart ov me counthrymen; an' if crowds gather round me how can I help it? ... Homer sung the praises ov his counthry on the public highways.*

Upon completion of his defence statement, he burst into one of his flowery recitations. So impressed were the Magistrate and court observers that he was merely issued a warning and the case dismissed. Today's buskers, when summoned to court for identical violations, often successfully cite similar historical precedents to convince the judge of their traditional right to perform on the street for the people.

Like their ancestors, today's buskers are the blithest spirits on Dublin's streets. They are the epitome of free enterprise in a democratic society, exhibiting refreshing creativity, artistic expression, individualism and self-initiative. Among themselves, clear distinction is made between the *real* buskers who live by their street trade year after year and the summer sunshine "chancers" out for a lark and a few quick pounds. True buskers are hardened and wisened by life on the streets, have perfected their skills, and remain undaunted by harsh weather, police interference, and discouraging days. Most have nomadic instincts and during the summer occasionally travel to other Irish towns and festivals to perform. Some busking veterans have been on the roads and in the streets for nearly sixty years, having travelled the thirty-two counties on foot, bicycle and horse-drawn caravan in their day.

Though the Irish climate does not favour buskers like the more sunny climes elsewhere in Europe, Dublin is regarded as a good busking city with appreciative audiences. As in generations past, buskers are most in evidence along O'Connell, Grafton and Henry Streets and College Green. Competition along the street is keen but they have established their own rules governing the establishment of

Old ragged–clad fiddler and street busker
COURTESY OF THE CHANDLER COLLECTION

pitches, setting discreet distances, and respecting one another's rights. Increased motor traffic, noise, pollution and human congestion have made their trade more stressful. However, their major problem remains the conflict with shopkeepers and police over charges of obstruction. Police routinely demand that they "move on" and sometimes arrest them under the archaic Vagrancy Act of 1848. Seeing themselves as a small fraternity of beleaguered struggling artists and performers, the city's diverse buskers formed the Dublin Buskers' Union in 1986 to defend themselves and champion their rights. Negotiations with local shopkeepers have resulted in a more tolerant attitude on both sides.[57]

Singers and Musicians

A talented busker can draw a crowd that spans the width of Grafton Street — much to the dismay of authorities. The entire streetscape comes alive with their music. People respond variously by watching in silent appreciation, tapping their feet, singing along, and sometimes dancing out of joy. Buskers may perform solo or in a group of five or six. On fine summer days with dense shopping crowds, buskers may be stretched along the entire length of Grafton or Henry Streets distanced discreetly about fifty feet apart. Bad weather is their arch enemy and they try to chart its course before setting up a pitch for the day. Summer is the prime season but generosity is greatest around Christmas and Easter. Financially, a bad day is less than about ten pounds and a decent day twenty or more. If everything is in his favour a busker can make fifty pounds or upwards.

Some old-timers like John Maher began busking as children, taking it up naturally from their fathers. Born in the caravan of a travelling family sixty-three years ago, he started out singing barefoot in the streets:

> *In those days me father often went singing in the streets. So I'd start singing the song. And then I'd start playing it with a whistle. I'd have been seven or eight at that time. It just came natural. And I often did a jig. I had a crowd around me and I'd play up to them. And I was raggedy completely. I had no shoes, me hair would be unkempt and trousers was always too big or too small for me ... something like out of Dickens in a way. People'd throw you money in the streets, ha'pennies and even farthings. I've often had me two trouser pockets full of coppers. When I appear here in Dublin now I get great crowds. One time I had a crowd of 400 to 500 people.*

First-rate buskers have the talent to perform in pubs and clubs. But owing to their nomadic instincts and independent spirit most eschew the regimentation of a set schedule and locale. They do, however, often "do a gig" for a night at local pubs around Dublin like the Wolfe Tone, the Chinaman, and the historic Brazen Head. This supplements their street income and provides refuge from harsh weather.

But most genuine buskers could never completely abandon the street for the comfortable pub setting. All assert that the intimate rapport and energising interaction with street crowds is their very life blood. Sixty-year old Frank Quinlan, one of Dublin's best buskers who prefers Henry Street working-class Irish crowds to the more cosmopolitan Grafton Street set, explains:

> *Busking is the same as getting up on a stage. As a busker you do more on the street than you would do in a pub. On the street when you're giving out, doing a pitch, when your crowd comes around they're all facing you and you're looking at them and the closer the contact you have with them the better. You're not only singing and playing but you talk to the audience, crack a joke or two. So you'll have more of a rapport on the streets than you will in a pub. I always stick with a certain number of Irish songs. You can see the smiles and the memories in people ... and tears.*

The busking life is no easy one. It's fraught with fickle weather, unpredictable crowds and police harassment. Straggling home in rain-drenched weather with only a few pounds in your pocket for six hours of a standing street performance can be discouraging. And there are no sickness benefits or pensions to count on for security. Essentially, it's a life of ups and downs and some buskers drink more than is good for them to ease the burden. Nonetheless, it is a life that most wouldn't relinquish. No one better epitomises the hardship and love of the busking life than the grandaddy of Dublin buskers, Paddy "Bones" Sweeney. At seventy he is now in poor health but can still be seen outside Croke Park or along Grafton Street with his harmonica and bohdran drum. Since boyhood he wanted to be a wandering busker and over the past half century he has paid his dues:

> *Years ago there were hundreds of buskers all around the country. When I become sixteen I decided to hit the road myself. So I packed up me gear one day and I was off. I went travelling around Ireland on a bicycle. I had a wattle tent. You cut the hazel sticks and make ribs and pull your canvas over it. You'd cycle about eight, ten miles and you'd come to a village. I'd sleep mostly on the side of the road. Sometimes I slept in grave yards. Then I had a horse and caravan and I travelled the thirty-two counties. During the bad weather you couldn't travel much ... keep out of the mountainy country. A lot of old buskers, they'd base themselves in Dublin for the winter.*

> *They all know me name in Dublin. Some say "You're the best in Dublin that we've ever heard" ... God, it's been a hard life. There's only a few of us old-timers left. But I'd do it all again. Going along the road, from place to place, whistling to yourself. It's been a beautiful way of life. No money can buy me lifestyle ... I've been free!*

Pavement Artists

Pavement art has been an element of European street culture for many centuries. During the Renaissance Period struggling artists would apply their talents to the pavement in order to draw attention and hopefully gain employment. It was a way to show off their work to the world while the contributions of passers-by put bread on their table. The pavement artform especially flourished in Italy and France where aspiring young artists competed for recognition. It is believed that a good many famous artists started out in this modest manner.

The origins of pavement art in Dublin are unknown. However, by the Victorian Age it seems to have been recognised as a legitimate, if somewhat unorthodox, form of art carried out by a free-spirited artistic breed. Early in this century Jack B. Yeats created an empathetic painting entitled *A Dublin Pavement Artist* in honour of the unacclaimed street artist. It depicts the artist, down on knees, over his works which included a Madonna and a landscape. The artistic recognition given this informal artform by the likes of Yeats conferred a degree of validity upon the pavement artist. Similarly, in 1917 poet Susan L. Mitchell celebrated the talent and struggle of Dublin's pavement artists in her poem "Out of the Dust". The poem appeared in the Christmas issue of *The Lady of the House* magazine accompanied by a picture of Yeats's painting. In part, it reads:[58]

> *Out of the dust I see him raise*
> *A timid look, beseeching praise,*
> *And his uplifted, anxious eye*
> *Scans every hurried passer by*
> *Less for gains that he may make*
> *Than for his inner vision sake.*
> *He feels the artist's joy and pain,*
> *Doubts and exults and doubts again*
> *O Passer by, do not despise*
> *Those gropings after Paradise*
> *Here in the pavement painter know*
> *The humble kin of Angelo*

Whether or not Dublin's contemporary pavement artists see themselves as the "humble kin of Angelo", they do have an historic sense of the European artistic street tradition. Brian Hudson, one of the most dedicated, sees even more distant roots:

> *I reckon that pavement art goes back millions of years, like what the cavemen used to do on the walls with burnt wood or whatever they used. Even Leonardo DeVinci used chalk in his painting.*

There are no more than about a dozen serious pavement artists currently working in the city. Living the stereotypical life of the "starving artist", they refer to themselves as "chalkies". Their favourite pitches are College Green and the corner of Westmoreland Street and Aston Quay. But they may be found wherever there is a good pavement surface for chalking. Most have travelled throughout France, Germany, Austria and Italy where pavement art is highly respected to practice their skills and learn from fellow artists. Some are evidently more gifted than others. Their work ranges from original creations to copies of Michelangelo, Ruebens and the French Impressionists. Religious paintings, landscapes, Celtic mythological scenes and sketches of such literary luminaries as Joyce and Yeats are especially well received by Dubliners.

No street figures are confronted with more problems than the pavement artists — angry weather, police harassment, interfering drunkards, indiscreet dogs, traffic fumes, self-appointed critics and thieving Tinker children. Unlike other street types who enjoy the mobility to shift sites if they wish, the artist is bound to his work site. They are typically down on their knees or haunches on the hard surface for five to eight hours, able to take a tea or toilet break only when a friend consents to guard their pitch for them. And hours of artistic labour can be obliterated in seconds by a cruel thunderstorm. Owing to the physical strain, pavement artists tend to be younger than other street types — their work is better suited to the young and pliable than to arthritic older people. About half are females. Most begin around seventeen or eighteen years of age and by the time they reach their late twenties they are true veterans. Despite the obvious rigours, pavement artists relish the independence and freedom of expression they are allowed on the pavement as well as the instant gratification of public reaction. Ursula Meehan discloses:

> *You have to be a free spirit. I've always felt that it was worth people giving money for street drawing because you've made something beautiful. I love seeing the colour that you're doing on the street. That attracts people and for the moment people enjoy it ... the colour that you add to the street and the way that people react to it.*

Mimes and Clowns

Some might argue that Dublin streets are sufficiently filled with clowning and buffoonery from the ranks of its ordinary citizens. But in the more classical sense, street clowns, mimes, jesters, jugglers and magicians were very much a part of city life during the Medieval Age. They played a significant role not only by entertaining but sometimes through re-enacting historic feats, mimicking public figures, or mocking unpopular laws. Mostly, they performed amusing stunts to cheer people, usually attired in colourful or bizarre garb. They have always been a great novelty along the street.

Dublin has had its fair share of street jesters like Bang-Bang and his many predecessors. There are still a few bonafide clowns and mimes who earn their living off the streets. Most famous is Thom McGinty, better known to Dubliners as "The Diceman".[59] He likes to refer to himself as the city's most notorious "street walker" — and, indeed, he is. In outrageously weird costume, he seems to glide without motion down Grafton Street, face frozen except for the occasional winks at transfixed observers. A highly gifted mime and clown, he exults in spreading happiness along his pathway:

> *You give people a visual delight. You're giving them a moment of making them laugh, amusing them. I very much have to have the personal contact. Oh, Dubliners are appreciative. I'm a street character, a street presence. People do see me as part of the history of street life in Dublin.*

Bardic Street Poet

It is said that the age of great Irish bards, who trace their decent back to the "dim ages of Ireland", ended with Turlough Carolan. But a few bardic descendants of lesser stature made it into the modern age. Such wandering poets and story tellers habitually trekked rural circuits in western Ireland visiting farms and villages. One well-known bardic figure named Peter Cunningham-Grattan actually roamed County Wicklow into the 1940's.[60] To local people he was known simply as the "Roving Bard". A sort of peregrinating tramp, he wandered the hills and valleys of Wicklow playing his tin whistle and reciting poems. Sadly, he died from exposure in a snowstorm and was found in a ditch along the roadside.

One does not normally think of "modern" bards since the term bard itself has an ancient ring about it. And cosmopolitan Grafton Street would be the last imaginable locale where one would expect to encounter the revivalist embodiment of the Irish bardic tradition. Yet here is found bardic-style poet Patrick Tierney, a charming cultural anachronism and surely one of the most unique sights on Dublin's streets. Utterly out of time and place, he devoutly recites poetry to small clusters of listeners.

He did not come to his lofty calling easily. Orphaned as an infant, he was raised by the Sisters of Mercy and the Christian Brothers and suffered cruelties. As a schoolboy he was inspired by the works of blind poet and bard Anthony Raftery who travelled around Counties Mayo and Galway some 200 years ago. He, too, felt within himself a need for poetic expression and had a vision of travelling a like path. In school he wrote poems which impressed his teachers. Thus, after leaving school at fifteen he began "wandering about" in England, America and Newfoundland, Canada. Patterning his life on the old bardic tradition, he travelled throughout Newfoundland from village to village gathering experiences and bits of history and stories. Along the way he would read and write poetry and make up songs. In return for offers of food and shelter he would recite poetry, sing songs, tell stories and perform chores. An article in *The Newfoundland Herald* proclaimed him a "modern day minstrel", an apt description.[61] Like the Celtic bards before him, his life on the road was an arduous one as he experienced hunger, cold, sickness and loneliness. But there was no better way to learn his art and discover himself. After nearly a decade in North America he returned to Ireland determined to bring poetry to people on the streets of Dublin.

Positioned along Grafton Street amid the noonday crowd, he flawlessly recites poetry by W.B. Yeats, Patrick Kavanagh and other Irish masters as well as his own work. At first, many onlookers show surprise at the sight of someone so earnestly spouting poetry in public. But those who question his sincerity or gift need only linger a few minutes — all doubts are quickly dispelled. His sense of mission is manifest as entranced listeners stay a spell to savour the small feast of words, then drop a few coins into his "poet's pot". To sceptics, his vision of reviving the bardic poet way of life may be quixotic. But as he tells of his dream one can hardly doubt the sincerity of the quest:

> *It was very romantic, very free spirited … rambling the roads in the sunshine and being your own man and singing to yourself as you walk the roads. I'd carry a backpack and a sleeping bag and a change of clothes and a few books of poetry and I'd find a sheltered spot. I had to write poetry as an expression. But I decided that I wanted to bring poetry to the streets of Dublin. To see if it was possible to revive the bardic tradition, this idea of the travelling poet. I think that poetry can be brought back to the people and it's as important to do it in the city as it is in the country areas. That's my contribution … bringing poetry to the people, doing it on the street. I can feel the words and the words become part of me. I can actually see people on the street trying to choke back a tear.*

Chapter 3

Street Figures of Yesteryear

FRANK WEAREN — Lamplighter, Age 90

At age ninety, his life has spanned the momentus events of this century. As an idealistic young man he joined the I.R.A., encountered the dreaded Black and Tans, participated in dangerous missions and survived an excruciating 27-day hunger strike. In the 1930's when things were more politically settled he was employed by the Dublin Corporation and became a lamplighter. The pay was good but the hours gruelling. As he puts it, lamplighters "knew everything ... seen everything". Many a curious and shocking encounter he had in the midnight hours. He was out tending his lamps only a few streets away when the German bomb fell in 1942 and all "hell" broke loose in the city. A man of great dignity and patriotism, he is proudly one of the last real lamplighters in old Dublin.

'At that time there was about forty of us lamplighters left. I was all around the Monto there, had to do Railway Street, Foley Street, part of Sean McDermott and Gardiner Street, Summerhill. I'd do hundreds of lamps and I'd no bicycle. Had to walk lamp to lamp, street to street. The quicker you were done, the quicker you were home. You could run. Some of the men'd run along like terriers and others would walk nice and casual. We were still doing it with the torch and pole. The pole was about five foot and the torch was eighteen inches. You had to be very accurate when you'd be going to light it or you'd break your mantel and that gave you more work the next day hanging a new mantel. You got the knack. You'd carry your pole over your shoulder like a rifle, like a soldier. You'd hold it standing up, not sticking out, so's no one would run into it. The pole was Malacca cane. The torch worked with acetylene and that was in a brass container you stuck down on your stick. You brought that in and put it in a socket and it would be re-charged for you.

'There was a pilot flame on the torch and you could rise it if you wanted a light in a dark lane to show you your way on. It would rise up nine or ten inches. And if a dog run at me I'd switch the long light on and give him a dart with it. And that dog would never come near a lamplighter again! Now I'll tell you a story. There was two dogs having a fight and a crowd around 'em trying to drag them asunder. Says I, "stand back, I'll separate them". They all got away and I switched on the long flame and stuck it between them. Well, you never seen dogs so gone like that. Oh, it done the trick, all right. Them dogs did go flying. There was a cheer and I was tapped on the back and everything.

'Children would all run after you and shout "Billy with the lamp, Billy with the light, Billy with the lamplight out all night". In a rough district where children would be throwing stones at one another they might accidentally hit a lamp and then they'd all run ... scatter. And children used to climb up and switch off the light. They *did*. They got away with that. Now if I seen children swinging on the lamps it was my duty to cut the rope. If you cut a rope on them they'd jeer you ... "he cut me rope, that old fella". So when I seen the young ones with a rope I'd cut it and say, "you tie it up when I'm gone".

'The old lamplight was like something you'd see on a crib, a Holy crib, like the light over the manger. It wasn't bright. It was soft. In the fog you could see it about ten or twelve feet all around. And in the snow the heat of the lamp would melt the snow and it would slowly slide off. And you had to maintain your lamps and keep your lanterns clean. You were supplied with a duster and a sponge and a tube of solution. You cleaned it with the solution and the sponge and then you polished it off with your chamois. You might do eight or ten lamps in a morning. Your ladder was a light ladder, a sort of cane, made especially for the lamplighting. You'd carry it from lamp to lamp on your shoulder. And you got a chain and lock and you could lock it on any railing. Often, when the jet wasn't lighting I'd no ladder and I had to monkey up the pole and strike a match and light it. But I was told *never* to climb up. And we used to monkey up if we had broken lamps. If the glass was broken the wind would blow the mantels out and the gas was leaking, blowing like hell, and you'd put your back to the wind so the gas would blow from your face.

'Wages worked out to between three and four pounds. You had an extra four shillings for working Saturday and Sunday. In the summer time you started off at half nine and you were working till after midnight. Go home then and come back at half past three in the morning to start putting them out. In the winter evenings you started at a quarter past four and in the mornings started to put them out at a quarter past seven. Very few young men would stick it in my time cause the hours were erratic. Oh, Jesus, the wife had no husband. No home life. So they were mostly older men who wasn't able to do manual work in the Corporation and they'd take on the lamplighting because there was no strenuous work attached to it. But the bloody hours used to annoy them. Oh, very cranky they used to get. I didn't like the hours. You were going out to light the lamps seven days a week. And you had to go out Christmas morning and Christmas evening ... oh, it was terrible.

'And if it was raining you had to keep going. The rain would run off your shoulders down into the legs of your trousers. You'd be *saturated*. Now if you were hungry you could drop into a shop, or drop in to have a pint ... *quick!* Oh, it was against the rules. But your tongue would get dry in your mouth running and trying to settle everything right with the lamps. Oh, there was many lamplighters sacked over drink, over being drunk on their routes. See, they had inspectors and he'd be either in a motor car or on a bike and he'd follow you around. The old lamplighters, they were *all* fond of their pint. You couldn't be a sober man and be a lamplighter!

'Lamplighters knew everything. *Everything*. They *seen* everything. But they kept their mouth shut. And there were a few of them in the Movement, too, you know. Oh, yes. We had a few of them in the Movement. Indeed, we had. Oh, they were very useful. If it was curfew they'd be stopped by the Black and Tans. But you carried a permit when you're a night worker in the Corporation and they'd let you go. They always carried a bunch of keys for opening the lamps and they could open a lamp and shove a gun into it and shut it if they were after doing a job. That took place.

'Now I had this route at the back of the Abbey (Theatre) and I used to light these two lamps regular. This inspector came down one night and the two lamps was out. This was after I was lighting them that evening. Says he, "this is the second time I've found them out. There must be somebody operating in that lane". I says, "what do you mean 'operating'?". "Do you ever see any lady in the lane?". "Jesus", says I, "there's two of 'em". "They're two prostitutes", says he, "and they must have some way of putting out them two lamps". They were doing their *business* up there in the *lane!* And if they seen a policeman coming up from the light on Abbey Street they'd run and he wouldn't capture them. So the inspector says, "I'm going to send you a helper to watch and see who's putting out the lamps". And along came one of the women. She went over to a gateway, she knelt down and put her hands under and pulled out a big long six foot length of wire. It was *thick wire*, as thick as that poker, and she had a little hook on it and she'd put it up and pull the lever and out went the lamp. So a special policeman was put on that lane the next night and she was captured. They collared her. She was charged with interference with the public lighting and she got three months. And six months for soliciting. So there was no more of that.

'Another night I was lighting a lamp and I seen a clergyman, a *drunken priest*. And he was sitting on the step outside the back of a Protestant Church in Abbey Street. I went over to him and says, "Beg your pardon, but this is no nice place for a clergyman to be sitting". "And why is it any business of yours?", says he, "I'm waiting ... I have an appointment, so go off and mind your business". He was drunk, a big strong hefty man. A Bobbie comes along and so I explained to him. "I'll look after him", says he. Months went by and this policeman spotted me again in Abbey Street. "Well, I looked after him. He (priest) said 'nature is nature" (awaiting a prostitute) and I said 'I understand'. "And don't you be talking about it to anyone either … you'll be letting down the prestige of our clergy if you do". "Ah, you must tell the truth", says I. But I never bothered about it.

'In 1942 when the bomb dropped on the North Strand I was starting to put out me lamps in Gardiner Lane. I got the blast and I nearly collapsed. It was a German plane and he thought he was in British territory. All my lamps was gone, blown out into the middle of the road. There was no gas. See, the gas main was blown up on the North Strand. Everything was in dark. Oh, it was dreadful. Jesus, I come up to the end of Summer Street and there was a crater twice the size of this (house). Oh, it knocked the houses down like a pile of snow. Down to the very root they blew it. Ah, there was a good few killed on the North Strand, twelve or fourteen of them. Jesus, every ambulance was flying and the hospitals was full. People that wasn't caught in the bomb collapsed and fainted with the fright. Had I been a bit earlier I'd have gone with the lamps! But I got through it and didn't get home until nine that morning and my wife was out on her bike and two of me sons searching for me. They didn't know where I was. And I says to me little one, "where's your mommy?" "They're out looking for you, Da, they thought you were blew up!". They thought I was blew up … but I wasn't. So she was delighted when she come home, I'll tell you.'

TOM FLANAGAN — Lamplighter, Age 85

His father and uncles were lamplighters before him. In 1924, at age seventeen, he began his career caring for gas lamps in Phoenix Park. For the next fifty-one years he was a familiar figure, riding a bright red bike with ladder balanced across the handle bar while his little dog followed faithfully along. To untold thousands of regular park visitors, Tom was truly the "Old Dublin Lamplighter", the last man to use the pole and torch. In 1988 over a hundred gas lamps were restored in Phoenix Park to rekindle something of the old atmosphere and it was only appropriate that Tom's two sons got the job of lighting and maintaining them — it's the family tradition.

'Me father was a lamplighter before me in 1894 with the Board of Works and they run Phoenix Park at that time. On each gate the gatekeeper used to light the lamps himself but me father and his two brothers were responsible for the lamps on what we call the "backroads" of Phoenix Park. They done the hand lighting at night all around the park … and the three of them walking! No bicycles at the time.

'Now I was taken on as a helper for me father. I was seventeen. Oh, there's no doubt about it, I was the proudest man in the world when I started. I got one pound, fifteen a week and I was doing immense! And I got a bicycle, a blaze red bicycle. I was on the bicycle fifty-one years. Oh, not the *same* bicycle. I had three or four bicycles. They were ordinary standard Rally bikes. And I went through a good many tyres as well, I'd say. I had no uniform but I always wore a coat and tie. I always felt you were never dressed without a tie. But they did supply me with a short waterproof jacket and a pair of pull-ups.

'I was responsible for 195 lamps in the Park. I done the lamps with the pole and it had a carbide torch. You'd put the pole up with the flame on it and meet the gas head and the lamp was lit. Next morning you'd come around with the pole and turned it off. I'd carry a ladder around on the bicycle and you had a little tin box on the back of your bike for mantels and spare brass fittings and a few tools like pliers and screw drivers. The old lamps were great. With a gas light it's a warm glow. It sends its rays down like in a fog. Oh, a warm little glow. In the summer it was *excellent.* And you just got used to the cold and snow. If there was bad snow or frost, like in the 1940's when there was ice here on the ponds and they were ice skating, I wouldn't cover the whole park. Icicles would be hanging off the lamps and you'd have to knock them off to open the lamp.

'I had a little dog that would come around with me and sit at the foot of the lamp there when I'd go up. Oh, she was great company. She'd know which way I was going and she'd turn that way. And children always loved to see a lamplighter or a postman. Oh, children would race from one lamp-post to another and follow you and you'd get a chorus of a little song ... "Oh, Billy the lamplighter at the garden gate, how I used to remember where you used to wait". It was a real song at the time. Children would monkey up the pole and put a rope around it and have a swing on it. They'd do no harm. And when you went up the ladder if you didn't keep your eyes on it a lad would come half way up after you. But it was only a ten foot ladder.

'At that time it was the back streets and back lanes in Dublin that was the last lit with gas lamps. And I done Killester out on the Howth Road after the first world war. There were thirty lamps there and I used to clean them. I used to meet other old lamplighters in the Corporation and get to know them. Oh, they were a *hardy breed* of men they were. And loved their work. And every one used to walk miles in the day and they'd take up a pace like a half trot as they'd go from one lamp to another. Had no bicycles. The old lamplighter, everyone knew them. And when they'd make their rounds at Christmas they'd always get a free drink at the pubs wherever they went — and they didn't light half the lamps after that! But there was no pubs in the Park for me. Occasionally at the American Embassy I'd get a bottle of whiskey for Christmas or cigarettes. And if you went up to the President's house maybe you'd get a drink or a pound note.

'This was the last stronghold of gas here in Phoenix Park. I done me work and there was never one complaint against me in the fifty-one years I was in it. I worked till 1975. *Never bored once.* You met every sort in the park ... old age pensioners, the high-ups, the tramps. On every road you went you met characters. It was a pleasure and I was me own boss. And if it was a good summer's morning and you're going down the main road there'd be a couple of buses laden with tourists coming along and the driver'd pull up and the next thing out come the cameras. Right and left taking pictures of me. And the bus driver would be saying, "now this is the last lamplighter in the country". Oh, I was more flattered than anything else. I enjoyed every hour of it. It was the best job in the world! But it was a dying business. I was the last lamplighter to use the pole in Dublin.'

TOMMY BASSETT — Docker, Age 82

As he tells it — with a conviction no listener is apt to question — dockers were the "toughest men in Ireland" engaged in "cruel, hard work" to feed their families. There is still a discernible tightening in his facial expression when he speaks of the despised scabs who took the docker's jobs in the 1920's strike. After toiling manually on the docks for nearly fifty years he retired in 1979 when mechanisation replaced manpower. Though he now resides in the Sheriff Street flats beside the docks he seldom goes down to dockside, explaining that it makes him too melancholy.

'I was born in 1910. Me father was a fitter and turner on the Great Western Railway. We lived on Newfoundland Street and ninety percent of the families there was dockers. When I went down to the docks the first time I was nineteen and the docks was open to anyone. There was no unions then and anyone could come down. You stood in a read and if you got a job you got a job. The men would start gathering in a circle. There would be hundreds of men. Businessmen, teachers, professors, if they lost their old jobs, if they were in disgrace after having spoiled themselves, they could come down. There was a place for everyone. They'd give them a day's work. I worked with professors meself out on the boats. If you didn't get a job the only thing you could do was walk home with your tail between your legs.

'So the men would be in a circle and the stevedore got up on a platform — and I seen them getting into empty wagons — and there'd be a reading. He'd first call "Mick, John, and Joe" that belonged to his own family. Then he'd call other fellas. Reputations was very important. There was fellas knew how to work and fellas didn't know how to work. My first day three or four of us was left in the read but there was a good bit of work up and so he called us. She was a big boat from Australia and all timber and canned fruit. The fruit come up on trays and you had to stack it in sheds and the timber went into piles on the quay wall. It was hard work. And when we were finished old Patsy Kelly (stevedore), he called me back and says, "anytime I have a read, you stand in it". Whether he was watching me or not I don't know.

'Ah, there was some good stevedores ... and one or two bad fellas in it. They'd eventually call you. They were fair in that sense. If you let something fall or done damage they may leave you a week idle just to chastise you. And stevedores kept to themselves. Oh, stevedores had their special place in the snugs in the pubs. They didn't mix with dockers. Because it would be bloody hard if they went out and drank with dockers ... they'd have this fella and that fella asking for a job. People would even go to their wives to get their husband to give their sons a job and all. There was plenty of poverty at that time and you couldn't very well blame them. Their doors would be nearly tore down, men looking for jobs. Men currying favour with them, they'd leave a "hanger" at the public house for the stevedores. A hanger was a baby Power's Whiskey and there was a little corkscrew on the top of it and they used to hang it at a counter for the stevedores. But a stevedore might get on to him and kick him ... "I never took that off a man in me life, you *gurrier*".

'Northside stevedores always gave northside men the first preference for jobs. And the Ringsend men then, naturally, give their men the jobs. Human nature ... and politics. And there'd be jealousy. Now Ringsend, they were a little village on their own at that time. They were always suspicious of strangers. Had their own law and all. Very clannish. It was like the islands in the west of Ireland ... always suspicious of strangers. And if a girl married a fella from the city you wouldn't get a house in Ringsend! She'd have to get out. It was a tradition. And there was certain docker gangs fighting one another, like Ringsend and the northside crowd, or parish-minded people. Like it could be three or four brothers from each side, a family. You know, that sort of thing. And if anybody interfered, well, some other fella'd take him on! Now rows in them days, there was no knives or bottles. Oh, I remember some trouble with bats but it was a fair fight. But then they'd have a pint together.

'In 1925 there was a docker's strike. They brought fellas up from the country to dig the coal boats. Scabs! No one would let them in. And wouldn't be served in the pubs. Had to go somewhere foreign to drink. They couldn't get a lodging house. They slept in Liberty Hall. There was murder there. There was one fella sentenced to death. He killed a fella with a hurling stick. They never forgave a scab, you know? Didn't forget him or forgive him. And that was generations passed down to sons. It never left. Even if you met them in the street you wouldn't recognise them or give them the time of day. Oh, once a scab, *always* a scab.

'Outside work was a sort of easy job. It was harder for the men inside the lower holes. It was cruel hard work. It was no place for a clergyman's son, I can tell you that! Oh, Christ, *tough men* ... very tough. Toughest men in Ireland they were. We imported a lot of brown raw sugar and there was twenty-one stone in a bag and two men would lift that. Tough men. The hardest job in the lot was a pitch boat. This pitch stuff, it was real hot, like slacky coal, like tar, and they'd get all the by-products out of it. You used to have to go down and shovel it into tubs. The air off it would burn the eyes out of you and your nose burned. You used to have to wear a girl's stocking mask over your head. And the grain boats was hard because there was pollen off the grain, the dust. Used to bushel it into bags and that created a lot of dust, powder. You inhaled it. It'd all gather in your chest. Dockers used to say, "take a half of whiskey" and that seemed to ease it off. But you'd go home after four or five pints of porter and get a feed and the next morning you couldn't breathe. You'd get up and across there (chest) you'd think someone was after beating you with a hammer. The old grain porters, they died worse than the miners with lung trouble. Ah, sure, they all died around their forties.

'Dockers, they worked and drank, worked and drank. They were paid every job, every day. They'd enjoy themselves that one night. Oh, Christ, dockers only lived for the one day. They were *millionaires* when they were working ... that night. But they may be paupers for the rest of the week. Now tradesmen had their own corner in the pub and the dockers would be on the other side. Oh, they'd talk to one another but they'd never have a drink. Tradesmen had their place in the pub, same as stevedores. They didn't drink with dockers. See, dockers had a very bad name ... some of them. Terrible rough characters. It was probably that. Ah, but dockers was some of the finest men in the world.

'Now I was single at the time and maybe got fifteen shillings a day. That would be all right if you were getting it *every* night, but you might only get it two or three days of the week. Your drink could be put on credit — put it on the "tick" or the "slate". They were very honest and the first job they got, they paid. And if a docker died and the family wasn't insured the publican would bury you. Great sense of community. He'd say, "go up and get the undertaker ... I'll pay for it". And you'd pay him maybe a pound a week after that. And they'd carry him, the coffin, on your shoulders three times around the chapel and stop in front of his house for a couple of minutes.

'The second world war was a fiasco. Hitler's submarines was all around. Ah, Christ, there was nothing here at all in the war years. The grass grew on the docks. The only thing we used to do was a bit of turf on our own boats from the bogs. Turf boats used to come in but no coal. *Nothing* was coming in. So a lot of dockers joined the British army and we near all went to England to work. I went over and started building airfields around the midlands. After the war in 1945 I come home, right back to the docks cause it was improving all the time. There was work. I was on the Red Cross and cattle boats, trying to save Europe. They fitted out them Liberty ships for cattle. There'd be Red Cross stuff down in the lower hole and between decks would be all cattle pens. A boat would hold 750 head of cattle. I seen more cattle in one day than a farmer would see in his lifetime. Oh, and plenty of horses being sent away to the Continent. Drovers would bring the cattle and horses down. Drovers and dockers got on very well. We were married to one another's sisters and brothers and we were all intermixed. Drovers and dockers, they'd drink together and everything. But drovers was lower than dockers ... and that was low enough! Anyway, I worked on the cattle boats as what you called a bullock man, to look after the cattle and milk the cows. See, it was a three-day trip to Amsterdam and the cattle had to be milked and watered and fed. There was one man had to look after thirty cattle. Then there were passengers coming back and maybe she'd load stuff for Ireland, bring back tomatoes and peaches.

'After the war, in 1946, there was 2,000 dockers here in the Dublin port. Then the buttons come out, the union thing. There was 650 button men and he (stevedore or foreman) had to employ them first. The others were in the union but they was "casuals", hadn't got the button. The first 650 buttons were given on their years of service on the docks. From that onwards you had to be a son. When a man died he gave it to him. It was left with the mother to choose the son. Me own son went down there and didn't get a button because there was no buttons available. That was the poorest form of seniority in the world.

'Dockers was always proud and independent. I worked nearly fifty years in it. I wouldn't have any other life. I was always happy at it and I reared a good family. I got layoffs but I was always handy and could mend a pair of boots or paint a ceiling. I've no regrets to tell you the truth. I was happy as Larry because it was like a beehive down there and you'd listen to them all night telling yarns in the pubs. But I retired in 1979 and I don't believe I was twice down there since. It's sad ... very sad.'

WILLIE MURPHY — Docker, Age 79

He went to work on the docks in the 1920's at age fourteen amid rough times and tough men. His thick, knobbly hands tell of a life of hard, honest labour. In his day dockland exploded with daily activity and drew a colourful array of read runners, bookies, hoggers and prostitutes. Powerful stevedores reigned like dictators and dockers and scabs brawled in the streets during the strike. Never a dull moment. Then in the 1970's the docks died and became a "graveyard". Each day he still walks the quays, full of memories but sullen in spirit.

'The docks in my young days ... it was magic. My father was a docker and my grandfather was a shipwright and me great grandfather was as sea-going captain. I was born on Fitzwilliam Street (Ringsend) and I loved being around the docks. In them days there'd be horses and cars going in every direction. *Fantastic* activity! Hundreds of horses going in all directions. And cobblestones, the square setts. That's what the whole docks was. And heavy trucks with steel frames and wooden handles pulled by men. Big thick heavy steel wheels. Two men pushing and a man doing the "horse" as we called it. Everything was manual. Really hard, tough work.

'My first memories was carrying my father's dinner over there. I was eight years old. All the sons done that. That was the ritual in them days. It was a 1:00 bell and you *had* to be there, dead on. There was a rowboat bringing the dockers from Ringsend over to the North Wall, so I was rowed across with his dinner for a penny each way. It might have been a coddle put in a bowl and there'd be a saucer to fit over the top so it was enclosed. And wrap it up with a woman's woollen sock around it that kept it warm. And then a red handkerchief for me to carry it with. Always a red handkerchief with white spots. In those days the men tied them around their neck to keep the sweat from coming down, then use it for to wipe the sweat off the brow. That was always washed and cleaned, a priority that it was a fresh handkerchief going over his dinner. He'd be eating that on the deck of the ship. And an old galvanised tea can that'd hold about a pint, with a lid on it. I'd put it on the galley fire and heat it for him. And if they were working a grain ship maybe I'd get to fill a can and bowl full of grain and corn coming back. All the people around this area had hens and they'd give me tuppence for a bowl of grain and tuppence for a can of corn. So that's the way we'd get our ferry money and we'd make a few coppers from that.

'Dockers liked betting and every day I had to bring the midday racing paper. He wouldn't eat his dinner if he hadn't got that. Every day my Da had what they called a rapple, a few bob — like you were betting tuppence and sixpence. Oh, I used to be a runner for me father. Bookies were illegal but they'd come down the dock steps out of sight of the police and take the bets. All the dockers would bet with them. So he'd look through the racing paper and pick out the horse and write it out and I'd bring it across to the bookie. And maybe next day he'd say, "there's so much coming back". We had an altar in the corner of the room at home, a small altar like the Blessed Sacred Heart, and a red light burning and an altar cloth underneath. Well, he'd say, "put it under the altar cloth" ... and he'd know where it'd be when he come home.

'And there were some prostitutes on the docks. Most of them were country girls and a couple of Dublin girls as well. They used to pick up the sailor and go off drinking and then go aboard the ship with him. Now we had two — I always used to call them "two ladies" ... they were unfortunates — and they used to have a stand at the back of the Gas Company. There was a long, dark walk and a wall there. These two ladies were well known and pretty good looking, too, although they were around forty or forty-five years old. And anybody who felt like going down there they just paid a shilling, that's all they charged. They earned their living for years at *one shilling*.

'My father died when I was fourteen. And I had one brother and ten sisters. My father's brother was a stevedore on the docks, a rough, tough type of guy. I was just gone fourteen years of age and he said, "you'd better get yourself over there!". And I was still in short trousers. I made me Confirmation at twelve and I was still wearing my Confirmation suit. That had to last you a long time. So I got a pair of dungareens — what you call jeans today — and the heavy boots. Most of my uncle's work was these small hand trucks like they use in the warehouse. He discharged all the fruit coming from Spain — apples, oranges, onions, melons — all in cases. You put one on your little truck and away you went running with it. They called us the "greyhounds" … always running. That was my first job.

'Stevedores had great power, *terrific* power. A hundred, two hundred men might turn up for a reading. And for maybe sixty-three jobs. He'd get on the bridge of the ship and we stood on the wall. The family of the stevedore would be the first called — nepotism from the very word "go". Now after that he'd call whoever he liked. Or the best workers. They all had favourites. They knew all the names. Stevedores would call you from their mind. No lists. And stevedores were very strong, very independent in their ways. Physically and mentally very strong. And they walked very tall as well … in their attitude. Like "I'm the stevedore", you know? They always looked different to the ordinary dockers the way they dressed. They'd wear beautiful suits and ties and a big gold watch and chain and a soft hat, a trilby. They were done up to the nines! But he'd call whoever he liked and bribing went on. If a stevedore come into the pub they used to do it undercover sort of. They'd leave a small whiskey for him, or a "ball of malt" they used to call it in them days. Well, that was for to get a job! Stevedores would take that.

'At readings men had it in their minds that there was something at home wanting on that table. And if they didn't get a job that just put them down in the depths. Heartbreaking. It's true … you could see the tears in their eyes. And they'd run from one read to another cause there'd be readings for other ships. Like some of them we'd call cross-country runners cause they could run that fast to get to another read. As soon as one reading was over you could see them run … flash! They were gone. And there were some men that had an old bike and they'd jump on that and had an advantage. Many a time my name didn't get called at readings. I felt down in the dumps, really down in the dumps. Many a time. A life of ups and downs. You never got a smooth run on the docks. *Never.* Good times and bad times. It was a way of life. And that was it.

'When I went on the docks we were after having a big strike in 1925. The union imported labour from all over Ireland — scabs for to take our jobs. When the scabs come in there was killing. Terrible! Real violence during that time. Police charged with their batons and hit the pickets. Knock them to the ground and kick them. I mean, it was *so tense*. Scabs was afraid to come out after finishing a coal boat so they used to sleep in the stables overnight and come out in the early morning to avoid a confrontation with the pickets. See, in 1927 when I was starting these men who scabbed it, they were on a list and had priority over us. Ah, yes. They got this privilege cause they scabbed it. Of course, this created *anger.* You'd say, "look at the scabby bastards going in". Even when the strike was over the stigma was still there. You'd get it brought up in a pub, especially when they'd get a few drinks on them. You know, calling them a "scabby" and the man would have to get out of that pub. You wouldn't drink with him. Ah,

83

and there were digging matches all over the place. Even in the holes of ships. They'd come to punching one another. In them days it was fists. There was no iron bars or knives or anything used. It'd be bare hands. Just make a ring and let them have it. No one would interfere. Let the best man win. It'd be settled. But the stigma *never* died. And it's still going on. People have memories and they still bring it up to their sons.

'Back then you had grain ships and coal ships and phosphorite for fertiliser, and iron, timber, flour, fruit. Working in the hole you'd put a little pebble or a button or a little piece of coal in your mouth and that'd keep your mouth moist all the time. Now in my opinion the hardest job was the copper ore, what you call iron ore. It was so hard to get through it with a shovel ... it was so heavy. You used a number five shovel, a smaller shovel, for it. That was physically the hardest job. And on top of that you got *acid* from it. You could get the acid into you and your teeth would go black and your tongue. You'd come home and give the teeth the old brush. I used to use salt and soot (from the fireplace).

'Then I worked guano ships, bird droppings from them islands (off the coast of Peru). You had a five grain fork and you'd dig down and loosen her up with that and shovel it into bags. And when we went deep down in the thing (deposits) it'd stand up the height of the wall there and then you'd dig under it with the fork and you'd get a fall. Everybody'd run for the ladder cause you had to get out from under it with the fumes. See, there was ammonia sprayed right through it as it was going aboard the ship, to save infection. The powder and the ammonia would burn your eyes and made you bleed from the nose. You used to put a handkerchief around your face to keep from breathing it. It was very hard to get men to go to them ships. Very, very hard. And it was hard times then. And still, men would only last one day. They'd get paid for that one day and they'd be gone. Couldn't stick it any longer. That was *some job!*

'I enjoyed working the bag boats, say, cacao beans. And the smaller bags of sugar, the eight-stone and ten-stone bags. But I worked *twenty-four* stone bags of sugar. Me and my mate would lift them into a rope. And it was always a pleasure to work in your skin working timber. Because the job was so clean. Nothing to get on you, no dust or anything. And back then the two-masted schooners, they'd be bringing in the red bricks from Chester River in England. We used to take them by hand and pitch them out of the boat. Two bricks at a time. I'd be in the hole and I'd pitch you two bricks and you'd catch them and throw them up to the next man on his platform. We were expert at throwing them and catching. And the bricks never separated going up. I done that with bricks and slates as well.

'If you were called to do *anything* you were able to do it — pulling a truck, tiering in sheds, slinging in the holes, driving a winch. And you took *pride* in doing it. But there was always danger working on the docks. I saw a man being killed with a tub of coal. He was a workmate. We were working the ship's gear and the wire broke on the winch and it just *buried* him in the coal. And I always felt that the long steel rails, thirty or forty foot long, was a very dangerous job. Always afraid of wires bursting in overweight when you were hoisting it. And it *did* happen. And I carried eight-stone bags of cement on me back, it'd burn the back off you. You know, cement has its own heat. Well, we used to get a pad, like a woman's silk blouse, and put that inside our shirt across here (upper back) and that'd prevent us from getting this soreness. Just get an old silk blouse ... you know how silk is so nice.

'Dockers were big drinkers. The work was so hard that drink, it was a beverage to build up for the sweat you were losing during the day. Plain porter, that was the docker's drink. The plain pint. It was eight "P". I seen men drinking — *honestly* — fifteen to twenty pints in the one day in maybe two sessions. And I'm telling you, they *wouldn't be drunk!* He'd know what he'd be talking about and be singing old songs. Now whiskey was always three "P's" dearer. In them days whiskey was a gentleman's drink. Or a tradesman. And you'd *never* see a tradesman drinking with a docker. We were always looked down on by tradesmen as the poor relations ... always downgraded.

'Now when Guinness's discharged their barrels after being emptied in, say, London or Manchester, Liverpool, they'd bring them back and load up empties there at City Quay. Big casks and small casks. Now the "hoggers" — hoggers was men looking for free drink — they'd shake the barrels. They were knockabouts. And dockers often done it. Yeah, a docker often went and had a sup ... "fond to drink it out of an old boot", we'd say. They'd shake the barrel and hear it and say, "we have one!". So they'd put it up on top of another barrel and tip the porter into the rim of the barrel and then they'd go down and suck it up. Now they always had red raddle that goes around the rim of the barrel. Well, this red raddle used to go into the porter and when they'd finished up their mouths would be red, like if they were painted. And you'd say, "there's a hogger", cause the red raddle would be on his lips.

'I saw the end coming a long time before it came. And I even told others. It started first about 1961 with palletising the cargo, putting it on pallets and just lift it up, a ton or two on a pallet. And then the forklift trucks for just going under the pallet and run it into the shed. Then small thirty foot containers coming in. Then they wanted gangs reduced ... "too many men on the docks". They started realising what was happening here then. The crisis came about 1971 when we lost at least 250 men in one go. And now it's gone. It's terrible. Sad. The atmosphere is not there anymore ... the old crack we used to have when we'd put in the day. It was part of history and now it's not there. I go over there and now, to me, it's a graveyard.'

JEREMIAH CREAN — Postman, Age 63

*As a postman he boasts of having been in "every dump and dive" in
Dublin without meeting harm. During the war years he had the sad
task of delivering death notice telegrams to relatives. On his tricycle
with basket he delivered fish, fowl and eggs from the country to city
people. And he dutifully served the most squalid tenements where he
would enter the dark hallway and bellow out names of those on the top
floors. After nearly a half century he's still at it.*

'I did the exam for boy telegram messenger around Easter of 1944 and I've
worked ever since. There were thirteen of us in my family and it was a *job*. The
earliest a messenger started was seven and on your late nights you worked till
nine. Normally you were going out with five or six telegrams and you'd have a
reasonable line. You wouldn't get one on the North side and one on the South
side. They issued a slip for every dispatch and they had a good idea how long it
should take you on your bike and it was very strict. They would watch your time.
You could go out the best part of five miles. A run now on a bicycle in those
days from the G.P.O. to Dollymount, well, a lot of it is coast road and the wind
would play a hell of a part in it. And you had to go out in all weather. You got
rain gear, a cape and pull-ups, and the rain just rolled off the cape when it hit
you.

'When the war was on quite a lot of those telegrams was about a son who had
been killed. They would stick up in the corner of the envelope a little red sticker
and that was very urgent. In fact, they used to do that, too, for the Sweep
winners, they always got a telegram. Many people got telegrams that their sons
had been killed in the war. You feel a terrible sadness. During the war the saying
was, "no news is good news". In one case a girl about my age opened the
telegram right in front of me with the news that her father had been killed. She
knew it had to be bad news. Oh, it was a very jolting telegram. As a matter of
fact, that girl had only a sheet around her and it fell off … when she got the
shock. I'll never forget that morning.

'At eighteen you went to a postman and only got a week's training in all aspects
of the postman's work. You'd just go into Pearse Street for training in sorting.
Then you were committed to carrying a bag that weighed about thirty-five
pounds. It's a terrible drag on you. My big grievance in this life is against the
architects who, knowing that a postman can have a bag of letters, stick a letter
box six inches from the ground. Now there were three deliveries in those times.
Seven a.m. was the Irish, ten was the English, and three was the midday post. I
started on Parnell Street and up North Great George's Street, Hardwicke Street
and Dorset Street. In the forties there wasn't nearly the volume of mail and it was
only a penny for a letter and an open letter was only a ha'penny. There's a big

difference today!

'If you were on walking duty you could have up to 500 houses. For instance, I done duty in Fairview and I'd know them all. Years ago people would ask you in for tea and breakfast. It was strictly against the regulations. But if it were a cold day you'd just go in and get a quick cup of tea in your hand. Oh, but it's not an easy job. When I was a young postman what we called the "pressure period" started on the 18th of December. We often went from six in the morning till twelve at night.

'That English delivery I had on Parnell Street, now that was all tenement houses. People in the tenements, they got it rough. You didn't have the same social welfare you got today. Tenements were in a fierce state of repair and the people were very, very poor. Oh, God, they were desperately poor. They got quite a lot of English delivery up there because practically every family had got one or two in England. In the tenements you called out in the halls. Oh, you needed a lamp because in the tenements in the mornings you'd get pitch darkness. You'd go in and call out so they'd hear you on the top flight. I had to shout out "postman!" and then I'd call out the surnames. And they'd come down. I've been in every dump and dive in Dublin and I've never come to any harm. I must say that for the people of Dublin. You wouldn't do it today.

'In those days you did the tricycle delivery with the basket on front. It was to deliver parcels. The balance wasn't so good. Overloading. It was a basket about three and a half or four feet long and three feet high. Oh, the basket was larger than the cycle. And, of course, a great thing in those days were the egg parcels. An awful lot of eggs came in from the country to be delivered to ordinary individuals. Their relatives in the country sent eggs up to them in Dublin. They were properly packed in a hard cardboard box and very seldom would they break. And we had fowl at Christmas. And fish. The fowl still had the feathers on them and a label around the neck and a duplicate one around one leg in case the label was lost. And a lot of fish were sent parcel post. They were wrapped in rushes and reeds, salmon would be. They were fresh enough unless they were undeliverable. If they couldn't be delivered for some reason or another they used to hold a weekly sale of perishables in the return letter branch. It would be advertised for the staff to go to the sale at three in the afternoon for the perishables. You couldn't do that today.'

JOE O'NEILL — Postman, Age 74

He started off at fourteen as a boy messenger in the depths of the Depression. Back then, when you worked for the Post Office and flaunted a uniform you were "somebody". He covered the entire city on his bicycle and motorcycle, dodging tram tracks and horse vehicles.

Working in the sorting office during the war years was tiring but amusing as people tried to smuggle everything from silk stockings to rashers through the post to relatives.

'I'm a Dublin man, born in 1918 on Ballybough Road. My father worked as a bread driver in Kennedy's Bakery. There was eight children in my family. Now how I happened to go into the Post Office, it was during the Depression and my father was unemployed and two brothers and one sister unemployed. Unemployment was rife in Dublin. I was only fourteen at the time. So I made an application for the exam for boy messenger. There were fifteen vacancies advertised and there were 350 sat for it. See, it was a *permanent* job. And I came in thirteenth. I was elated, to say the least. But I wasn't as elated as my mother was! My pay starting out was ten shillings and seven pence old money per week. Oh, it seemed like a lot back then. Back then a postman was better paid than a policeman and you were well clothed, well shod. A uniform and boots twice a year. And you were somebody when you worked in the Post Office. You were *somebody.*

'I went in on the 9th of October, 1932, and the G.P.O. was only after being reopened after the Troubles. The inspectors brought you in and gave you a bicycle and you mounted and rode up the street and back, to test to see if you could ride — and that was it. And when you were given a telegram to deliver you had no map with you. You'd say to one of the supervisors, "I don't know where that is" and you'd be told, "well, you'll know when you come back!" So you asked one of your senior messengers where it was. And in no time you got used to the city. See, the city at that time was like a small town compared to what it is today. The canal bridges were the perimeter of the city and I'd say Raheny would be the farthest you'd go on a bicycle.

'On your bike you were out in all weather but you had a water-proof cape and pull-ups and boots but you had no gloves. And on the bicycle you had an oil lamp. You'd have to light that up with a match and it fulfilled the requirements of the law. Of course, the lamps were always going out. You'd just go off without a light but the guard might stop you and you'd say, "oh, it's gone out again". He wouldn't mind. When you came in at night the lamps were taken off you and left on a table in the bicycle shed. There were two messenger boys and their duty was to take each lamp and clean it, the glass, the wick, refill it with oil, polish it up and leave it ready for use that evening.

'Most traffic then was trams and horse traffic. Some motor cars. Oh, you could get around faster than today. The most difficult thing was the cobblestones on the wet days, and the tram tracks — there was an art in crossing them. If you tried to cross them slant-wise the tyre of the bicycle got caught in the track and you couldn't get it out and it'd throw you off. Now when you reached the age of sixteen you went onto the motorcycle for delivering telegrams and they provided you with gloves and leggings. The old motorcycles we had then, they were

British, and you could throw them around the place and run into a wall and you wouldn't do any damage. The motorcycle had a carbide lamp. Just under the saddle was a carbide flask and a container of water. You just turned on the water for a few moments and once you created the carbide gas into the burner for the headlight you put a match to it and lit it. Now Thursday was the cattle market day and telegrams coming in in the morning were delivered to buyers and cattle dealers around there. At that time there was a Depression on and the biggest demand for cattle was from Germany. That market couldn't start until the German buyer got a telegram telling him how many beefs were required. Every Thursday I'd wait at the City Arms Hotel up there on Prussia Street until the German buyer came out and deliver his telegram and he'd give me a half crown. *Every* Thursday. I got the telegram by chance the first time ... then I made it my business to get that telegram every Thursday.

'You became a postman at eighteen. First you did a fortnight's training in what was known as sorting out the letters to the different districts. All the furniture and boxes were designed for right-handed sorting and left-handed men weren't allowed in the sorting rooms. Then you were designated a walk, that's a delivery. You learned from another postman. My first delivery was the Fitzwilliam Square walk and the Harcourt Street section. I'd be in Pearse Street (office) at half past five. You'd set in your walk, tie it up, and be out on delivery by seven. Oh, you were proud of your uniform and always had to have your brass buttons cleaned up. You had to wear a white collar and black tie, black socks and your boots shining. Back then there was respect for postmen ... and for clergy and nuns and for schoolteachers. There's no respect now!

'You were given a postbag with your number on it, a canvas bag with steel rings. You could always adjust the size you made your bag. You turned it inside out and got a piece of string and tied it to the bottom and then turned it back inside. That made the bag smaller and more convenient for your shoulder, depending on the weight you would have and the walk you were on. Thirty-eight pounds, I think, was the maximum weight. If you were doing a delivery in a commercial section, like on Dame Street, it would be very heavy. If you complained that it was too heavy you could ask to have it weighed. Then you left behind the overage, but it didn't pay you to do it. It paid you to take the extra weight. Because you'd have to wait on your delivery until a van came around and gave you the remainder. It would be delivered to you on your walk. So you might as well take it out because you could be waiting for ten or fifteen minutes for the second bag after having finished the first one.

'What I remember most about the war years was the American mail. This was before air mail was introduced. It would come in maybe once a week or fortnight up from Cork or over from Southampton. Mostly, American post came in the form of money orders, especially to the west of Ireland. They were all flimsy little things, difficult to handle, that would annoy you. And the addresses on them were vague at times. The most boring thing you could ever be put down to sort was these American money orders. Everybody had to do a few. And when the American mail would come in there'd be a lot of work to be done in the parcel traffic. There was an awful lot of old clothes parcelled to relatives. Bags and bags and bags coming over from America of old clothes to go out to the country, like to Mayo. It would have a declaration on it "old clothes" and customs never opened them. And chocolate candy would be enclosed in among the old clothes, just as a present.

'Now in the sorting office if there was anything you were suspicious of, like prohibitive literature, you sent it to the customs. Like the *News of the World* was banned in this country. People used to try to get that through by putting it in another newspaper. Of course, it worked the other way, too, because during the war years there was a scarcity of silk stockings in England and a scarcity of rashers, meat of all description. Well, an awful lot of people here used to get the newspaper and a bit of tin foil for a half a pound of rashers and wrap it up in the tin foil and roll it up in the newspaper and address it over to their sons and daughters in England. You'd have a suspicion with the weight of it but you'd never stop it. Oh, it made it most of the time.

'Some of the best years of me life in the Post Office were those I spent on the travelling post office from Dublin to Cork. See, when I started they were *steam engines*. Big engines. Oh, I liked the steam, it was very romantic. The whistle going off and this big "puff, puff, puff". But I retired at sixty years of age in 1978. I could have stayed on till sixty-five. But the *reason* that I retired was that *discipline* collapsed. I think there should be respect for one's work and one's supervisor and that had become foreign to how I started my life in the Post Office. There's no satisfaction in their work today. I was forty when I was promoted to Inspector, and I was very young. Today they'd be in their twenties! So I retired on a Friday ... and the first woman postman came in the following Monday!'

BERNARD McGUINNESS — Chimney Sweep, age 54

At age sixteen he began learning the old trade from his father who was also a sweep. Over the past forty years he has gathered a wealth of lore from other old sweeps he has encountered. Proud of his traditional role, he still cleans chimneys by hand with cane rods and muscle power. He has cleaned clogged chimneys from the meanest tenements to the most elegant chambers of the rich and powerful — and learned much about human nature in the process.

'Me father's uncle used to do chimneys and then me father became a chimney sweep. He was at it till his seventies. I started when I was sixteen. My father didn't order me to do it but there wasn't a lot of work at that time and there was a few bob to be made in chimney sweeping. It's one of the oldest trades and there was a natural handed-down ascendency if you like. But when I was that age I didn't like telling people that I was a sweep. I felt embarrassed. The Dublin public looked on chimney sweeps as a kind of lower-class person ... a lower trade, a lower mentality. The image was a type of roughness about you, doing something that maybe was undignified. It looks gruesome dealing with this amount of black soot which looks *uncontrollable.* Your hands are all black and every part of you is black and people maybe picture a kind of hideous man in black that lives in caves like a stoneman aloof from the rest of the world. Even a lot of poorer people wouldn't let their child become a chimney sweep. They would think that they were lowering the class of the family. And, yet, the chimney sweeps themselves could see a dignity in it because it's one of the oldest trades.

'In the Dickens days chimney sweeps was actually more dignified, a man of standing in the society, and he could be classed as a master sweep. I've studied it up as much as I can from the old sweeps. In the old days a man would bring his son and maybe have two or three young boys with him. They were generally orphans. It was actually a form of slave labour on unfortunates. Child sweeps was generally runts. They had rickets and were very badly fed and were actually older than their size. A lot of them were in their teens and they only had the bodies of six and seven year old children. They would climb up the paving steps in the chimney at maybe two or three o'clock in the morning in Dublin, in London. See, the gentry of the day wouldn't want sweeps knocking around during the middle of the day and the servants could clean up after them and everything would be grand and fresh the next morning. But at two or three o'clock in the morning maybe the fire hadn't *gone out* the night before. And a lot of those boys, of course, were lost. It was a scandal of the period. It was commonplace in Victorian times and that applied to Dublin and Cork and Belfast. It was known that in the early part of this century in Cork it was still carried out, children still climbing chimneys.

'Chimney sweeps were their own breed. They were loners, kept close to the family and didn't come out of their circle much. They were secretive. Rivalry. Like we never liked to see other sweeps in the area where we were sweeping. You kind of feel that that's your territory. The strange thing about them is that families that were related were very "anti" one another. The main families on the southside of the river were the Curry's. Very prominent in chimney sweeping, one of the oldest families. A strange thing about people in them days, if you weren't a Curry they wouldn't accept you as a chimney sweep. You wouldn't be trusted. Wouldn't get inside the door! The Curry's were in Mespil Road and two Curry's in Donnybrook — families of chimney sweeps and they never spoke to one another. They *hated* one another. The Curry's on Mespil Road used to have a big sweep's brush up on the wall outside their door and a Curry in Donnybrook had his sign up saying "Established 1832". Another famous chimney sweep family on the southside was the Moran's. On the northside I'd say the Rooney's was the best known. They were on the North Strand. Even up to twenty years ago I can remember old Rooney cycling out to Howth on a bicycle at ninety-four to sweep chimneys.

'They used bicycles and some of them had push carts or horse and carts. Up to the fifties they had bicycles and used to put the rods on the side. The bicycles were very well made in them days, big strong steel bicycles. You wouldn't see one of them now. Some sweeps used to walk with them (rods), just carry them on their back. Walk down the street and shout out "sweep!" and people would say, "would you come over to me?". A lot of them would wear old clothes handed down from the gentry they were doing chimneys for, a waistcoat or something like that. And they had a peak cap and might wear a scarf.

'We used to get the rods from England. They were six-foot rods made of Malacca cane which came from Burma, which you can't get today. It was strong but had give in it, about an inch in diameter. Rods had a brass top with a screw so you could join one to another and it could go up. A man would take out about fifteen or twenty rods. And you could get a very big chimney brush about fourteen inches in diameter right down to four inches. I still use the Malacca rods. I still sweep in the same way it was done for hundreds of years. You always have to do a good job because as a chimney sweep your *name* is the main thing. I work twelve months a year but the busiest time is from early autumn to about Christmas. About forty years ago it cost four shillings. Today it's about ten pounds. It's unbelievable isn't it?

'Chimney sweeping is very masculine and has that roughness about it. You know, you grab the brushes and rods and you heave and you push and sweat. You're always down on your knees. I've got welts on both knees like callouses. Now on a street like this here they're four storey (18th century Georgian) and you could use maybe twelve or thirteen of those rods joined. It's very tough. Tremendous for your shoulders. It takes great strength, no doubt about it. A lot of sweeps got cancer of the scrotum from bringing the rods through their legs and the soot rubbing off of them here. And we can never see up the chimney, it's all on feel. You join each rod and you might meet a bend. In the old days individual builders had their own way of doing a chimney. You like the challenge. Some would put a corkscrew bend in it and there'd be no way of getting out of the top. So you'd take a ladder and go from the top down. And when it's warm, it's rough doing chimneys. There's a certain amount of thirst. Sweeps were known to drink because of the dust. They drank plain porter and some were also great whiskey drinkers. They would always have money in their hands because they would get money as they worked each day, while the rest of the tradesmen would have to wait till the end of the week.

'Now we never put glasses or goggles on. And strange enough, it's very rare that cinders come down in my eyes. It's more *dust* than heavy stuff. Now the idea that soot would infest your lungs and clogs your lungs up ... these men *ate* soot and they were still happy at it. Soot is very pure and you'll never get any germs. I often cut meself and put me hand in soot to purify it. There's nothing as good for curing a burn than soot. And I remember this old woman when I was doing her chimney and she told me when she was young the midwife used to deliver babies and go over to the chimney and rub her hands in the soot and rub it around the baby's mouth, into the mouth, to stop any impurities. And people would use soot for cleaning their teeth, with salt. There's no doubt about it. There's *my* teeth now!

'In some of the tenement houses we cleaned in the old days they *really* depended on the fire ... where there was nothing else, no gas or electricity. They'd call out their window and ask you to clean their chimney. There was a terrible lot of chimney fires in Dublin during the early forties because we couldn't import coal. They used to bring in coarse turf. Chimneys would be hard with wood or turf that couldn't come off with an ordinary brush. What a lot of sweeps devised in them days was to put the crank of a bicycle — where the chain goes — on top of a rod and go up and scrape off the rough turf, the tar, with the teeth of the crank. And we used to "ball" chimneys from the top. We used to get an iron ball, like a canon ball. The last one I got was one of the balls that was used outside the Bank of Ireland, on these ornate metal chains. I got one and put a ring on it and put a rope through it and it'd roll right down the chimney and clear it right down to the bottom of the fireplace. Every sweep would have this steel ball. It was called "balling it".

'Chimney sweeps were thought of as lucky as weddings. The Protestant gentry used to like to invite a sweep to the wedding with the soot on his face. It was classed as lucky. The custom was that he'd kiss the bride and he'd be *black*. And that wouldn't be the end of it. The gentry would shower him with silver. They'd throw it on the ground, *gush* it on the ground, and he'd go around picking it up. That was part of the ritual. They wouldn't hand it into his hand, see, because he was *below* them. I know this from the Curry's. And me own father has even been asked to weddings. The Curry's and all the older sweeps did that, especially in good areas. There's also a superstition that it was lucky for a chimney sweep to go into your house on the New Year's Day, especially if he was black haired. Even today, people still come over to me in their house and say, "you're lucky" and rub me hand to get a bit of the soot on their hand. That still happens a couple of times a month.

'It's amazing that I've been to so many eminent people. I go into their personal chamber. I've been to Garrett Fitzgerald's house, been to De Valera's, Lynch's. I've met distinguished writers and painters. And they've always treated me very equal. I've been in de Valera's house when he was *there*. I swept the chimney beside his bed. He lived a very frugal life. He'd no fancy trimmings in the bedroom, just an ordinary bed on ordinary boards. But I've seen some sad sights in the tenements. Oh, there was some *terrible* poverty. Their chimneys were smoking and they were living in dire poverty. It was absolutely like something you'd see about three hundred years ago. One day — and I often think about it — I was in Henrietta Street and I was in the top bedroom of this tenement doing this chimney for this lady and her mother was in the bed beside the chimney. Now I'm *sure* the woman was dead. And her daughter looking after her ... immune to her being dead. The woman never moved and she looked dead, looked like death. Yellow and pale. I don't know whether it was because the daughter wasn't right upstairs ... or couldn't accept it. I never forgot it.'

KEVIN FREENEY — Signwriter, Age 67

Signwriting goes back at least three generations in his family. Back in the 1930's he rambled through Dublin's streets on bike or with pushcart carrying his paints and brushes. In that period the city's streetscapes were elegantly embroidered with handwritten shop and pub fascias. Having done "at least 700 pubs and shopfronts" in Dublin, the most famed streets — O'Connell, Henry, Grafton, and Capel — carried his personalised three-dimensional relief lettering and ornamentation. His fellow craftsmen hailed him as a "master".

'My father was a signwriter and my grandfather was also. My father unfortunately died when I was eleven. My brother was a signwriter and I learned most of the trade from him. I went through an apprenticeship at age fourteen. Wages were very low at that time, eight shillings and three pence per week. We all went around by bicycle and had a little carrier on the back of the bike with all our tins and pans and brushes. I can remember cycling twenty-eight miles to a job and writing a fascia board and riding twenty-eight miles back. And I often remember in the 1930's pushing a handcart with ladders on it eight miles to a job and pushing it back again along the street.

'In the 1930's most pubs and shopfronts had handwritten signs. Signwriting was a specialty in the painting and decorating trade. Standards were very high. You learned lettering, shading, highlighting and gold guilding on shopwindows. Having my brother was a great advantage, picking his brain so to speak. He was very good. We'd often work together on a fascia board and we knew each other so well that I could work on the back and he could start at the front and we'd end up correctly! I just have that gift. Just make a few marks and I know where each letter is going. You just acquire it. I wouldn't know where to start to each it to anyone. I see the younger signwriters sketching it all out with a pencil and rule and a compass. But I always find that if you do that the lettering looks very stiff. There's no *freeness* to it.

'Now I worked with Brendan Behan when we were serving out time in the painting trade. At that time, of course, he wasn't famous. He was always a renegade, you know, Brendan. A very obstinate man, contrary to work with. He'd come in in the morning and throw on his overalls and read the paper first on the boss's time. Wouldn't start work until ten whereas we were in from eight. I remember working with Brendan on the same plank which was about fourteen feet long. You worked as a team. You'd put the bucket in the middle of the plank and you done your half and your partner done his half. But when I was working with Brendan I done two-thirds of it. Oh, he was a desperate character, that man. You'd be doing most of his work as well as your own. Oh, and he'd never stop talking!

'Signwriters competed for business and one lived by his reputation. We didn't encroach on other people's territory. A good job spread by word of mouth. I'm freelance and I never had to advertise in my life. I'm so well known that I get away with it. Now a bad habit I have, I start at the back rather than the front when I'm signwriting. Just get up on the ladder and start at the back. It does create a good deal of curiosity. And I like trying to create relief. There was a pub at the corner of Stephen's Green and King Street many years ago and the fascia board lettering was done (carved) in timber with the letters brought out to a "V". They had a fire and they couldn't get anyone to reproduce the side fascia which had been burned. So it was up to me to create (in paint) the impression of the side fascia … to create relief. It's a nice compliment when someone says to you, "is that in relief or is it in paint?"

'When you'd be working on a pub you were entitled — it was an unwritten type of thing — to a drink, usually when you were knocking off. The owner would come out to check the work. Actually, signwriters never liked working on pubs because the people who frequent the pubs always had the criticism and the barman or man who owned the pub was more inclined to listen to the customers because it was they who they were pleasing. People on the street would stop and gather around to witness the work being done. It never bothered me. I've often had to work on the inside of a shop window doing some glass guilding and they'd be less than a foot away from your head (outside) watching you. It's flattering to know that they would be interested enough to watch.

'We never had to give up work because of heat — just cold. And you can't work in the rain because the board has to be dry. On cold days I would wear mittens with fingers out. It was very, very difficult in winter when your hands would get cold. Some days you just couldn't work. I remember working on a fascia board one time down on the quays by the side of the Liffey and there was as much snow in the pot as there was paint. But times (1930's) were so hard that you didn't get much money for it and you just had to keep working whether you liked it or not. And on a wild day the ladder could shift. It was usually held on top (roof) by a fifty-six pound weight tied with a wire rope. But it didn't always hold the ladder in position. We used to put our leg through the rung to hold onto the ladder and then you'd have both hands free. But you'd get the fright of your life when the ladder would move. I remember Johnny Doyle, a very small man with a bowler hat and black box and he had this little gait where he jogged along. Old Johnny worked on high ladders into his eighties.

'For a long time handwritten signwriting on pubs and shops went out of fashion and plastic signs came in very popular. The authorities should never have allowed plastic to creep in the way it did in the fifties and later on. Oh, you've only to look around St. Stephen's Green now, that's destroyed with plastic. I've often seen an old building maybe being demolished and they take down the plastic sign and "lo and behold" there's a lovely job underneath ... maybe your own work. And you think back to when you were doing it, what you were thinking about at the time. Handwritten signwriting is on its way back now and I'm in great demand for it. I love signwriting ... *love* it. I cannot imagine life without it ... the self-satisfaction. There's very few streets in Dublin on which I didn't have at least one fascia board painted. There aren't many old signwriters like myself left.'

THOMAS LYNG — Pawnbroker, Age 68

At age fourteen, still in short pants, he began his seven-year apprenticeship as a pawnbroker. Back in the "Hungry Thirties" women were queued down the street and around the corner waiting to deal with "uncle", as the local pawn was known. Entering the jam-packed shop, he remembers, was like "going into hell". From morning till night he took in countless bundles of stenchful clothing, rotted shoes and God knows what else. But after more than a half century behind the counter of the "people's bank" he likes to reflect on the dignity and kindness of the people. He is now the manager of Carthy's Pawnbroker Shop on Marlborough Street, one of only three pawns left in Dublin.

'My father was an orphan and at age fourteen he had to leave the orphanage and go out on his own to work. He wanted a job where he could live-in on the premises because he had no home. This was 1906. So this job appeared in the paper for an apprentice for a pawnbroker on Talbot Street and he applied and got it. The wage was one pound a year and he could live-in which meant he had all his meals. You had to sign an indenture form to stay and serve out your apprenticeship for seven years. The pawnbroker was more or less your master and could do what he liked with you really. This was just ending when I came in. See, the manager and all the assistants lived-in. Employers didn't want you to get married. Wanted everybody to live above the shop and be at the beck-and-call of the pawnbroker. There was a great deal of animosity for many years between the pawnbroker and the assistants.

'Pawnbrokers around the city at that time — and when I came into it — wanted to build up this reputation for fair dealing with the people. Because there had been this exploitation in earlier times. Pawnbrokers got a bad name from about

1700 when there was a lot of exploitation here in Dublin. They used to charge exorbitant interest and had huge stocks of goods they used to sell off at a great profit. That's why they brought into Parliament so many acts in the pawnbroking business, to make sure they'd charge a proper rate of interest. The Government had pawnbrokers get recommended by people around the district where they had their shop. Five or six businessmen had to sign forms to say that this man who was running this pawnbroking shop was a reputable man and wasn't up to any hanky-panky. And, funny thing, nearly all the pawnbrokers were Catholics. There were no Jews in it at all hardly. And nearly all pawn offices were handed down from their fathers. Very rarely did you see a pawnbroking establishment up for sale — very rarely.

'In 1938 when I came into the business (Amiens Street shop where his father was manager) there were around fifty pawnshops in Dublin. And there were still people living-in above the different pawnshops. I was just fourteen and in short pants. Most pawn offices had to have at least five people. I had to serve my seven-year apprenticeship. Here in Dublin it was always called the "people's bank" because the ordinary person could come in and get a few shillings just by taking off their coat or anything. You could pawn almost anything then. There was great competitiveness between certain pawnbrokers in Dublin. They'd have their own customers and if one of them brought in a ticket from another office (by mistake) they'd really give him a great telling off for going to another pawn.

'In the old days it was really a weekly business — *in* on Monday and *out* on Saturday. The places were absolutely loaded with customers. It was like going into hell ... really, the place was packed from morning to night with all women wearing their shawls and petticoats. Very rare to see a man in the place. We had queues going out into the street. It would be pretty rough, you know, but you were young and glad to be working. And a pawnbroker would take in *anything*. Things then were at a very low level social-wise with regard to living accommodations. Most people were living in tenement houses and they were pawning all kinds of sheets and bedclothing and old suits, shoes. Every pawnbroker was filled to the top of the house with clothing of all descriptions. There was nothing new. All that was taken in was old and smelled and the sheets and clothes would have fleas and everything in them. There were articles being pawned that weren't worth a quarter of what they were being pawned for ... old shoes, suits full of holes and threadbare. But they'd still give the money on them because they knew the customers and they knew it would have to be taken out at the end of the week. A pawnbroker was dependent on the interest more than anything else. I remember taking in shoes and they would be so worn that the best part of them would be the *laces*. People didn't have money to buy new shoes then. I remember a man pawning his shoes and walking out into the street in bare feet.

'Nearly all the people went to one particular office that was near them and they were used to being with the man behind the counter. They'd all be looking for money and you'd know them all by their names. They were hardship cases at that time. For a lot of them it was mishandling of the little money they had because their husbands used to drink a lot and they had to try and fend for the family. It meant that the women had to do all the running to the pawn office and accumulating any few bob they could get. But there was always a great sense of fun in the whole proceedings in a pawn office. The women, they'd be laughing and joking, very lighthearted about the whole proceedings. There'd be a great feeling of solidarity among them because they'd be all in the one boat. The managers of pawn offices were very easy-going, had a jolly kind of air and a great rapport with the customers. And the man behind the counter, most of them had a great sense of humour and they'd always be having a chat. Always there was this constant joking. That's what, I suppose, made it so easy to work in.

'The fifties were difficult years here. We had queues going out into the street. The pawnbroker would just have to take in whatever he could and everything was in chaos. We just started taking in musical instruments, crutches, false teeth, spectacles, walking sticks, knives. All kinds of ladies underwear — unmentionables — were pawned. Tailors used to pawn their scissors and barbers pawned their open razors and shavers. Skeletons brought in by medical students. A woman used to bring in a bird in a cage on a weekend and leave it for a shilling. And a ventriloquist used to pawn his dolls here. He'd bring them in in his suitcase … used to call them his "family". And women now would come in from the better parts of the city, who had seen better days. They'd put in maybe little pieces of silver, little clocks, bits of things from home. You'd know by their accent that they were a different type … and by the way they dressed. But still, they'd have their respectability and their way of speaking. The sixties were boom years in Ireland. People weren't buying old, used clothes anymore. We were the first here to stop taking in second-hand clothes. We just started taking in jewelry, radios, electrical equipment and stuff.

'There's great social history in pawnbroking. I think they should be remembered as playing a very important part in the social life of the city. All the business was done on a very good relationship with the customer and never overcharging or anything like that. Pawnbrokers played a very active part in promoting good relationships with people in need … with dignity.'

THE GYPSY LEE — Fortune Teller, Age 83

If there is such a thing in Dublin as a "living legend" surely it is the famed Gypsy Lee. She began telling fortunes nearly sixty years ago in her brightly coloured gypsy caravan parked on a vacant open yard in the notorious Monto district. In the 1930's women queued up outside the exotic caravan was a daily street scene. Her reputation spread by word of mouth among the meek and the mighty — from tenement dwellers to upper-crust matrons, stuffy professionals and even T.D.'s. To the working classes of the inner-city she is a major figure in the urbanlore of Dublin. She is devoutly religious, compassionate and possesses power and wisdom which are, quite simply, incomprehensible to mere mortals. Among Dublin's poor she is as much loved as respected. At eighty-three and in ill health she still opens the door of her Hardwicke Street flat to a select few in dire need.

'I was born in 1909 in Aberystwyth in Wales. I was born in a castle. My great grandmother was a relation to the Prince Flewelyn of Wales. My full name is Elizabeth Flewelyn Meredith. My mother's family were all in business. It was quite a happy childhood ... very kind, quite strict. But every opportunity I got I went to where the Romanies were and they weren't very far from the castle. And I *loved them*. There was a fascination there, a great fascination. They were a very kind people, very understanding, interesting.

The Gypsy Lee, legendary Dublin Fortune teller

'I was just nearly on eighteen when I met my husband there. I put it down to fate. I do believe that everybody's born into fate ... perhaps a little we can dominate our own destiny. I met him where he lived in the camp with beautiful caravans and they travelled all over Wales. I had good schooling but they were not educated ... well, they were very much educated in a *different way*, and a very good way. Hand-knitted linen on their tables and hand-knitted lace and silver forks and spoons and knives, Crown Derby dishes ... very elegant. My husband was twenty-three years older than I. But it didn't make any difference

99

because he was so very kind, so very good. A lovely looking man. I was married in Wales and there was an objection about the marriage in my family. They sort of split up over this. My husband's family, they welcomed me all right. But there was jealousy when strangers (other Romanies) came along the roadside and would pull in while travelling, or if we would pull into their camp on the roadside. The people would turn and say, "that lady doesn't belong to this tribe! ... she's so *different*". It used to annoy my husband. We travelled all over Wales and it was a horse-drawn caravan in those days. I kept in contact with my own family periodically.

'My mother-in-law, she was *brilliant*. A lovely looking woman and a very kind woman. She couldn't write her own name but she was brilliant in languages. She could speak her own Romany language fluently and Welsh also. And she had this "gift" ... *really had* this gift. She could tell you what you were thinking about! Before you'd come through the door she'd get this feeling of what's wrong with you. And she often dreamt things that'd come true.

'My mother-in-law and father-in-law came into this country travelling and they had a little boy named Edgar at the time and he used to sit upon the front of the horse-drawn caravan with his father. But before this child was born they were camping and she was laying on the bed of the caravan and she was looking into a glass cupboard and she saw this beautiful blue bed and this lovely blue room. She often talked to me about it. Well, when this little baby was born it was a boy and at the age of seven going along the road on the caravan he said to his father, "stop, Daddy, look at that cross over there! It was one of those funeral undertakers. "Oh", he (father) said, "that's lovely, but that's for the people that's dead". "Oh, but I'd love it", he said. Well, by the time they got to this little town this little boy took a desperate temperature and they fetched a doctor out to him. "Oh, My God", they said, "this little boy has diptheria". Now diptheria in those days in this country was a killer. It was a *killer*. They demanded that they take him into the isolation hospital because he was contagious and very dangerous for the other children. But she (mother) said, "unless you let me go in with him and *stay with him* until he's better or he dies, I won't let him go out of my arms". Well, they decided to let her go in and stay with him. And when she went into this room ... "Oh, My God!", she said, "my child will never come out of this room". *That was the room she saw* before the child was born! The blue bed, the blue room. As she had seen it. And he died.

'It was through my mother-in-law that I got the gift of palmistry and different things. She'd teach me ... and I got that. She'd show me the lines of the hand and the signs of the Zodiac. And I've often dreamt things that'd come true. She gave me the gift. I took to it naturally. I started reading palms at about nineteen. When people came to me and I told them things they'd say, "that girl is very, very *clever*". And they used to send people back to me all the time ... so many people. Palmistry, the crystal, and cards, that's what I've used. I let people make their own decisions about palmistry or cards or the crystal. You're born with free will. With palmistry everybody has different lines in their hands. No two people the same. But I think the crystal is the best. The crystal is a gift that you can get *into* people. When people come to me I can practically tell what's wrong with them before they sit down. I don't know what it is.

'We came to Dublin in 1937, just travelling. We came into the Monto part of Dublin, one of the worst places. It was the slums. But the *nicest* people we lived among. You could leave all your doors open, they would never steal. Terribly nice people. We was in a yard in the back of the cinema just off Talbot Street. That's when I really began to get into readings. See, when we were in the promenade in Bray (before travelling to Dublin) I met Justice O'Byrne's wife when she came into me (for a reading). It started from that. She gave me her address and told me to come there to do a feat at her garden parties. From the very moment I done that fortune telling there was people *following me to this yard*. I seen so many people and they thought I was very good. There were these *crowds* coming because they had been recommended to come and see me. They'd come to the caravan. I used to do forty and fifty people a day! And now I'll tell you — it's laughable — I got a half a crown back then. Mostly women then. All kinds but, oh, some top drawer women! Many times outside the caravan there'd be queues. Some would start to come at ten in the morning and people going on till nine or ten at night.

'It was desperately illegal telling fortunes back then. A very serious thing at that time. But anytime that I worked for charity we were never intercepted by the police or anybody. Now once this priest sent for me to do a feat. There was a fortune teller in his constituency and I said, "why come to me?" But a lady says to me "he won't go to her because he's *condemned* it so much in the pulpit". And so I said to her, "well, you go back and tell him that he's not going to make a hypocrite out of me!". I refused. Now in 1937 I got a summons for fortune telling. I was telling fortunes in the yard and this police lady (plain clothes) came. Now you'd come to my caravan and then come up six steps and you'd sit there where you wouldn't be seen from outside. So it was impossible for that women to see money being given to me for reading that crystal. So when she came to me I said, "you haven't come to me to have your fortune done ... why do I see the police in the crystal?" And she says, "how much do you charge?" "I'm not charging anything", I said, "I'll give you a reading but I won't charge you". I told her that she was in love with a married man on the Force but she'd never have him. What I said to her displeased her terribly and she put a half crown on the table and she was gone. In less than five minutes she was back with the policeman. So I was summonsed for fortune telling. Very serious and my husband was very upset. But I went and collected all my recommendations for having worked for charity and even Justice O'Byrne's wife gave me a letter and I went to the court and handed them into the judge and I won the case. It was in the papers for weeks about this attractive young woman — and I'm not flattering myself now — on the dock for fortune telling.

'The majority of women, they'd be young girls wanting to know their future, their husbands, and so forth. And marriage troubles. Years ago it was troubles with raising children or wanting children or success for their children or progress for their husbands. Nowadays, nine out of ten women who come are involved with other men. They're mixed up with the wrong people. They do the wrong things and you try to advise them. The world's gone very bad! With men the trouble is more financial ... business troubles, more success-wise. And politicians come to me. Yes, politicians and all kinds of people come here. And I'm not a doctor but people come here very worried about their health. Some people only want to hear the good and others want to hear both sides. Some people come in *terrible trouble*. A lot of them on the precipice of committing suicide! I was always able to carry these people through. It just comes natural to me. And so many regulars. People will come and say, "if I don't see you today I won't sleep tonight". A lady come here to me the other day and I was only a very young girl when I first met her and so was she. And she said, "there's nothing changed in the whole of my life but what you told me". Those who come to me in serious trouble, I pray for them ... and I worry for them. I get very tired because I see so many people and I've been ill and I've been suffering with depression a lot lately because I've got a lot of worry. I tell them, "come to me, but trust in God and pray".

'Now there has been a lot of people who *claim* to be fortune tellers. Oh, they're down there now around the arcades, but they're not *genuine* at all. I've heard about them. And I'd know immediately if a person doubted me because there's a veil, a dark veil. Some people will come here to me and they pretend — come to see how good you are. And they blow that smoke that's impossible to reach them and that's why I'm able to tell them, "you've only come here to find out if I'm any good. You haven't come here to have your fortune told ... because I can't get near you". And then they're ashamed, you see. Like there came a gentleman here the other day with three ladies and the three ladies had been to me previously and what I had told them was correct. And this gentleman said to them, "I don't *believe a word* of what she's saying but I'll go for curiosity's sake". So curiosity brought him here. When he sat here and I looked at his hands I said, "you haven't come here to have your fortune told. You have come here to see if I'm a *fraud*. But," I said, "if I don't tell you what's in your head then don't you pay me". "Well, good enough", he said. But what I told him ... he went out and *nearly* had a *fit*. "It's *true* what you've said. I'll never disbelieve you again".

'I'm glad I've had the gift and helped people. I had ten children and I've passed the gift on to two of my daughters. They're very good and kind. They got the gift ... they had it.'

Chapter 4

Dealers, Spielers, Vendors and Collectors

MARGARET O'CONNELL — Daisy Market Dealer, Age 73

"It's in your blood", she likes to say, noting that dealing goes back to her grandmother who sold cockles and mussels on Moore Street. At fourteen years of age when her father died she had to take over her mother's stall at the Daisy Market. Back then it was so crammed with people that one had to literally squeeze through the gate to enter. Today she is one of only ten surviving dealers and soon, she attests, "all the Molly Malones will be gone". Each morning she still pushes her antiquated wicker basket through the streets and sells a bit of poultry in the market. But she is visibly saddened by a way of life fading away before her eyes.

'My mother was a dealer and her mother again. They sold everything — vegetables, fruit, fish, geese, rabbits. They used to do the winkles and potted herrings and cockles and mussels. Winkles was a penny a cup. My grandmother sold in Moore Street but my mother was always here. They called it the Daisy Market because daisies grew here on the ground. It's part of old Dublin.

'We just came to the market as little girls and helped our mothers. My mother would get up at five-thirty and go to Carton's Poultry Market and buy poultry and rabbits. They used to kill the chickens and boiling fowl there. The first time I saw it done they were hitting the heads off this bar. Then there was a man named Mick Downes in Carton's and he'd choke the neck, just get his fingers around the neck of the chicken and pull it. Well, she used to buy a few hundred rabbits and I used to skin the rabbits for her with just an ordinary knife. Just chop the paws, skin the rabbit, and skin the head. And we had to get sticks for the rabbits — a skiver (skewer) it was called — to display it properly. They were a sharp stick about six inches long and pine wood. A woman would make them and you'd buy 200 off her. They were a half a crown a hundred. Put the stick in the rabbit to keep them together, to decorate them up. Or if the rabbit had a bruise you could stick it in and hide the bruise. Oh, rabbits was the best dinner of the lot.

'My daddy died when he was only forty-two years old and left nine children. I

103

was the second eldest and had only a week to go till I was fourteen. My mother was on a very small pension of twenty-two and sixpence a week and I did everything and anything I could ... somebody had to do it for her. And with the pension she wasn't allowed to sell herself. So I took over from there. I was very young then and there was about sixty women that sold. They all wore black wraps, coloured shawls and white aprons. And some Irish was spoken. They sold everything then — fish, poultry, vegetables, fruit and all second-hand clothing because people couldn't afford new clothes. You were *glad* to wear second-hand clothes. They had their own stalls and you were under the Corporation. We paid weekly rent here, about a shilling a week then. One lady done a lot of millinery and then the next lady would sell pig's feet. One woman used to sell kippers out there off a board and she used to smoke a white clay pipe — Winnie Talbot ... and she had a grey shawl with the white frill. Sixty women dealers and only one man among us all — Anthony Brassil — and he sold delft. Just one man here.

Three long–time Daisy Market pals (left to right)
Annie Ryan, Margaret O'Connell and Kathleen Reilly

'You'd always bargain, that was part of the trade. Haggle. But there was days that you hadn't got money for your dinner. Everybody had hardship then. Everybody lived in tenements. And large families. Oh, some of them (dealers) had twenty children. And hard times with the men (drinking) and you'd see it in the women's faces. The pawnbroker was important. Women here would pawn their barrows and their irons that you ironed the clothes with. And in them times they had the Jewman, the moneylenders, you could get money off of. He'd lend you ten pounds and used to charge five shillings to the pound and you paid him back by the week. But you could keep on paying the interest *forever* and you'd still owe the money you borrowed. Oh, yes, you made them millionaires, really.

'To earn a bit more money for the family you had to go to the seaside resorts with a bit of fruit. And I used to make fizz drinks to sell. Maybe you'd go on a Sunday. I'd go on the train from Tara Street. Take it in the basket car with three wheels and that'd go in the luggage compartment. The basket cars, you got them from the Blind Institution on Baggot Street. Oh, they're as old as the market is. We can't get them now. These people that made the wheels are all dead. So I'd spend the day at the sea selling and enjoying meself at the one time. And how some women made money was in the black market. We were all rationed at that time and a few of the traders would sell tea and candles and butter on the black market. They might get it from sailors. It was a hush-hush thing.

Colourful and historic Moore Street market

'The dealers here, they were *real* Dubliners. Everybody knew everybody around here and everybody got along well. That was the tradition here. You always got friendship and chat and fun here. We used to go to Mary Fagan's on Capel Street and get the loan of a bike for a shilling and just go off for a Sunday, the whole lot of us, up to the Phoenix Park, down to Ringsend. You always got a good laugh. They were all characters who sold here. And if they'd get a few drinks on them they'd sing. Oh, we'd often sing here. Women would send to the pub for their half-jill or whole jill in their jug. It was a delft jug with a handle on it, like a tankard. Get her jill and she'd have it under her shawl and bring it back here and drink it. Oh, they would. Have a little session and it might end up in a sing-song. You had one lady up here named Biddy McMahon and her friend was Missey Gunne and they used to dress up in old clothes and go around singing and dancing for a bit of fun.

'Women here might argue about little things. Maybe one woman would take another woman's customer and there'd be a row over it. Oh, and if they had a few drinks that would be it! Oh, they'd often have a row ... and more than blows. A real *fight*. Hair pulling and all. Throw off the shawls and that was it. They got into it then. In them times the old women wore those big thick wedding rings. Sometimes they'd get on the ground and you'd see their knickers and all. Oh, we experienced a lot of that. Then they'd forget about it and talk.

'It was very cold here and even now the rain comes in through the roof. No fires and no heating here. But the weather never bothered us. You'd have two cardigans on you and a heavy coat and fur-lined boots and fingerless gloves. And at Christmas time we'd decorate this place ourselves with chains and tinsel and balloons. It was like a fairyland here at Christmas. And, oh, Christmas carols all over the place here. Children from choirs all holding little lanterns. Women would send for their jill and we'd often sing. I remember one woman here and on a Christmas Eve she went off and got a few drinks and fell asleep in a bundle of clothes out there and she was locked in the market. She went very heavy on the drink. And a man going by at night heard her roaring and they had to get the night watchman to let her out.

'The Daisy is nearly on its way out now. They're thinking of closing it down. It's gone run-down. Oh, it'd be very sad to see it go. Oh, we had hundreds of dealers in those days ... lovely traders. There's just ten of us left now. We had a good, happy life. But it's all finishing up now and eventually you're going to see no traders. It'll be all shops. All the Molly Malones will be gone and there will be none of us left. We wouldn't retire. No, it's in your blood and you're too fond of being out in the air and having a chat and meeting people. Oh, we'll still sell outside. Oh, we'll go on the streets ... until God takes us. And Dublin will not be the same.'

ANNIE RYAN — Daisy Market Dealer, Age 67

One of Margaret O'Connell's Daisy "pals" for the past fifty years, Annie is feisty, full of wit and crack and bursts into a spirited jig when the song "Won't You Come Home, Bill Bailey" comes on the radio. Her cohorts laugh uproariously, saying it is just like the "old days" when there was always song and dance among the women dealers. The rest of the morning they share tea and banter away like giddy schoolgirls. But they know their days are numbered as Annie confides that the Daisy is dying and "we'll die with it".

'I was about ten years old when I'd come down here to me aunt. She was like me mother and I took it over from her. Everything was much different in the thirties here. The Daisy was all outside then. It was lovely. Clothing was up at this end and the fruit and poultry down at the other end. Everyone had a little stall. Horses and carts came in from the country and the cabbage was all displayed to be auctioned. It was a beautiful scene. And just outside here was Tyrell's Dairy on East Arran Quay and the milk in the jug used to be hot coming from the cows. She used to have plain butter and buttermilk for baking the cakes. And always piggeries around here. The poultry was kept in steel netting cages on the wall and they could run around in it. There was a girl here, Kathleen Robinson, and she got live fowl. If someone wanted it fresh she'd just go (twist the neck) and kill it. And I remember the chap who used to fillet the fish here. Women would buy the heads and make fish soup. They said there was nourishment in that. And chicken's feet, they'd chop the nails off and boil the feet down into a jelly and made into a chicken broth. That soup was the best cure an invalid could get.

Cumberland Street market, known as "The Hill" to local dwellers

'Now the clothing here, they were second-hand and they often had to take it to the Iveagh to disinfect it. But there was some very good clothes they sold here then. Clothes perfectly clean. See, they'd (tuggers) go from house to house — very well-off ladies' houses — and buy what the wife had. We used to call them "ladies" houses. Oh, there was some lovely clothes sold out here. There was no fitting rooms. You'd guess the sizes and there was a looking glass. See, people weren't ashamed at that time, they'd try it on over their frock. They'd get fur coats in here, muskrat coats, a beige and brown. Even black clothes, black dresses and coats. They were second-hand but you'd be dressed up for a funeral!

'In the olden days people was always pleasant and had time to speak to you. They weren't rude or anything. And you had all creeds here. All the women (dealers) here was Catholic. Protestants was always supposed to be very

107

comfortable people but they were always welcome here, like the Jew. That's one thing about us here, we never criticised, no matter what colour you were, what race, we always made you feel welcome. But there would be some women now and they'd come in to buy clothes and if you met them outside the market they wouldn't even pretend to know you. Oh, yes! A *snob*. And you wouldn't be friendly to them, Kevin. You'd tell them, "I met you and you wouldn't mind us". Then they'd say, "God, I didn't see a bit of you".

'The dealers were always very soft. It was just a tradition. They had time for everybody, especially if anybody was down-and-out or a knockabout or a "poor unfortunate" — that was what we called them. They were prostitutes and they used to call them "unfortunate girls". They'd be up from the country and they'd come here just passing the time. They'd be decent people and we'd give them a few bob. You always had time for them. They were young girls and at that time only got shillings. Mostly country girls but a few from Dublin as well. Years and years ago some were in the Monto. Always very sad. They'd have a hard life, maybe they'd no mother or father that'd worry about them. I always remember me aunt one day here taking off her cardigan and giving it to this poor girl who came in on a winter's day and she was nearly naked. Penny they used to call her. She was putting the cardigan on her to wrap her up cause she'd hardly nothing on her. And after that she'd always come in and say, "how are you, mother?".

'We're the last of the flock ... generations and generations. If you could go back in history it was beautiful. It's an outdoor way of life ... rain and sleet. But you meet nice people. You meet the good and you meet the bad. Ah, we'd really miss it. But the market is going to disappear and we'll disappear with it ... and we'll be digging up the daisies too!'

KATHLEEN MAGUIRE — Daisy Market Dealer, Age 68

One of only four remaining Daisy dealers selling second-hand clothing and shoes, she stands beside a five-foot high mound of assorted garments. From early childhood she accompanied her mother to auctions and "jumble" sales to buy used clothing for re-sale. Once she could make a hundred sales in a day. Today she may not have a single customer. But where else would she go? What else would she do?

'As a child I lived across the road there on East Arran Street on Many Penny Yard, that's what they called it. A big, big yard and there was a few very old white-washed stone cottages. From four o'clock in the morning the horses and carts would be all lined up there with the cabbage and vegetables waiting for the market to open at seven. Me mother sold on Patrick Street before she came here and me granny before her sold there too. Me mother wore a shawl and the women always had the babies in their arms.

'I helped me mother here as long as I can remember. She always went in for bedclothes and ladies things, the kinds of fur coats that was out in them days. And baby's robes and slips, like what a child would be christened in. *Beautiful* lace ones. Clothes was built up from the ground in bundles about four or five feet. You always tied your clothes in bundles then to keep them tidy. And me mother'd sell nice hats and she'd always model the hats for them. People'd always say, "oh, they look lovely on you Mary Ann, but they'd not look as well on us". And the minute she'd put down the hat there'd be four or five of them snapping it up before the other!

Daisy Market clothing dealer Kathleen Maguire beside her heaps of clothing

'The Daisy clothes came from the pawnbrokers' auctions and jumble sales. People'd put clothes into the pawn and if he didn't release them in six months they'd go for auction. We'd go with me mother, bring around the cart and wheel it for her. But you used to get better value at the jumble sales than the auction. At auctions things were sold only one at a time. At jumble sales you bought the lot in a bundle. They were called "jumble" sales cause you wouldn't know what you'd get off them. There'd be *everything*. Clothes and shoes and handbags, hats, hardware, all sold in lots. They put the children's together and the ladies' dresses and men's suits all in different lots. You'd bid. Protestant Halls would always hold a jumble sale. Some Catholic Halls too and the Jews, they'd have one at the synagogue. So you'd just go to the jumble sale and buy and then you'd sell them here. And at a jumble sale you could go and buy a box and you wouldn't know what would be in it. Oh, you'd have to take a chance. You'd get reading glasses and jewelry and all in it … everything. Oh, we'd all go mad to root through them. It was grand. You'd never know what you'd find. If me mother was buying them cheap she'd let you keep a bracelet or a pin. The jumble sales now, they're very few and far between. Now I bought that bundle last week and gave forty-six pounds. That's a lot of money for second-hand clothes.

'Now Kitty Doyle, she was a character here. She'd go on the beer and dress up in clothes. Like some day maybe you wouldn't be selling and you wouldn't be in good humour and Kitty'd come along down this lane all dressed up in old clothes and a hat and a long dress. She was very tall and loved to laugh. Put on an old dress or a wedding dress or an old-fashioned big hat — or dress up in a man's suit — and she'd go across to the pub all dressed up like that for a laugh. And the men would be all *roaring* in laughter in the pub. And there was a woman here that sold new men's underwear. "Maggie-all-wool" we used to call her cause she'd be selling and she'd say, "anyone want the men's drawers ... *all wool* drawers?" And she'd sell rain coats and she'd say, "who wants a man's raining coat?". She wouldn't say *rain* coat, she'd say *raining* coat.

'The old days were better. Ladies used to come in here, *real* ladies. Ah, there's nobody coming in here now. Some days you'll come down and won't get anything. Oh, it used to be *packed*. Everybody was looking for a bargain and everybody *got* a bargain. You wouldn't be able to get through it, I'm telling you. When we'd (children) want to get into me mother's stall we'd have to go under people's legs to get in there. The market would close around three-thirty and the Corporation man that'd sweep the market would have to come around with the bell to get the crowd out. He'd be rattling the keys and keep ringing the bell and you'd always get a few stragglers and he'd be rushing them out ... but he doesn't come around with the bell anymore.'

KATHLEEN HAND — Daisy Market Dealer, Age 70

As a young girl she sat beside her black-shawled mother selling bundles of clothing on Patrick Street. Later she moved to the Daisy Market and auctioned off so many items of clothing that at day's end her throat was sore from crying aloud. She especially delighted in haggling with countrymen who were always big buyers of second-hand clothing and boots.

'My mother sold on Patrick Street, just out on the path. They never had carts or anything, they had bundles. I can remember me Mammy used to tie the clothes in bundles, tied them up in a sheet in four knots and put them on her back. Ah, they were great workers the old people. There were nine children and me mother buried a couple. Then I was here in the Daisy Market with me mother when I was ten, a little girl sitting beside her. It was all just open, out in the rain and everything. She wore a black shawl with a fringe. Some of them used to wear lovely coloured shawls, like kind of a brown with white all going through. They were beautiful really. And an awful lot more people here then. Forty or fifty women (clothing dealers) along here. They're all dead and gone. There's only four of us left now.

'Years ago you wouldn't get into this market it was so packed. Crowds ... packed with people. They sold loads of stuff here. You wouldn't *have* enough for them. The clothes came from the pawn office sales. Heaps of suits, shoes, big skirts, coats with a bit of fur on the collars, dresses from rich people. White dresses and a veil for Confirmation and Communion. And we sold sheets and quilts, pillow slips and loads of men's and women's hats. Some lovely little hats like the Queen wears and men's trilby hats. If you were going to a wedding or a funeral you weren't dressed unless you had a hat. You'd sell the clothes and the whole lot. You'd have to take them up one by one and auction them yourself. Stand up there and hold up your stuff selling it. Hold it up and say, "will you take it for fifteen shillings?" and a woman would say, "I'll give you ten for it". And I'd say, "now give me twelve shillings for it" and that's the way it's going all day long. It was hard work. You'd be shouting all the time and you'd go home with your throat (sore) and you'd be sucking something sweet or an orange. And people were great here ... you'd have more laughing when they'd be selling. They had lovely sayings and all. Selling nighties they'd say, "now girls, you can sit up in the Coombe in your nice nightie there". Customers used to take the clothes home in newspapers. We used to buy the *Heralds* for a penny a bag. We always had a big pile of newspapers.

Daisy Market clothing dealers Kathleen Hand (left) and Kathleen Maguire

'The countrymen used to come in and buy big bundles to sell in the country. Oh, when they'd see the countryman come in they'd all flush around him, be delighted to get the money off him. He'd buy all the coats and trousers and the big boots. He'd come in nearly every fortnight. You knew you were going to get a good few pounds off him. Oh, he'd bargain and haggle with the women. And he'd walk off, walk out. Then he'd put his head in and he'd come in again. And out again and in again. He'd keep coming in and out to see whether you were

111

going to change your mind. Oh, it was a bluff. "I'm *really* going this time", he'd say. We'd let him go off. Then he'd come and take it.'

NANNY FARRELL — Daisy Market Dealer, Age 84

At eighty-four years of age she is the doyen of Daisy dealers. Other traders refer to her reverentially as "a legend here". At age seven while helping her mother sell fruit on the street she was wounded during the 1916 Rebellion. During girlhood she hawked fruit outside the old Mayro Picture House. But most of her life has been spent behind her wooden Daisy stall wrapped in her shawl. Today she sits in silence, almost motionless, with an expression of saintly countenance. When an old loyal customer shows up she smiles softly and sits more erectly to make the sale. Says Nanny, "I sold to their mothers before them". So many memories.

'Me mother was a dealer, had two stalls there in the market. She had fruits and cabbage and turnips and everything. Oh, I sold all the stuff for her. I'm here since I was seven. She had twelve of us and we were let sell there at the Mary's Street Picture House. We had a tall box like an onion box and put a tray on top of it. I sold fruit. I had a little wrap and you'd get used to the cold weather when you were out in it. It was a *beautiful* picture house and a lovely crowd went into it. Now I have a bad arm, you see, and I got that when I was only seven years old crossing Grafton Street during the Rebellion and was knocked down by a car. Oh, hundreds of people was there ... and they called it the Rebellion. They were all coming up along from Capel Street Bridge from the Castle there. Oh, people had to lie on the ground, frightened they were. People lifted me up. I wasn't taken to a hospital ... brought back home I was, on Church Street. I've no elbow bone.

'Me mother died when we were very young. I used to sit there and sell the stuff with her and she left me the stall altogether. She knew I'd never work (because of the bad arm). I sold fruits and vegetables. Oh, the old days here were grand. The people weren't like now, they were better. More enjoyable and everything. They were grand times and you'd see them all be dancing and singing. There was a girl down there who was a scream, a beautiful singer. Mrs. Dunne was her name. She's years dead. A *beautiful* singer. And she'd dance and everything. She knew *every* song ... "I walked down the strand with my gloves on my hand" ... oh, she was a howler. Very comical. They'd be coming in here just to see her. And now that girl who was there — and she's over eighty now — she used to take a few pints and she'd be dancing and singing to her heart's content. She's alive yet. She'd be dancing and singing all day, same as this Mrs. Dunne. They were a good laugh. They kept everyone alive. Two howls they were. It was grand. Oh, I could listen to them all day ... two devils they were.

'I have thirteen children meself. There was a fella used to fillet the fish here and he was mad after one of my girls but she was going then with another chap from a very comfortable family. And she'd say to me, "Mammy, they're too rich for us". I buried her at twenty-three years of age. She was always kind of frail, but never really sick. She was twenty-three when she died on me ... and I nearly died. It broke me up bad. I buried her. And one baby I buried young, a lovely little boy called after me husband. He was only a few months. Then when me husband

Eighty-four year old Nanny Farrell, doyen of the Daisy Market dealers

died I was left on me own. I'm living on me own now. Very lonely. But I couldn't be lazy. I like it here mixing with the girls. And lovely customers. I sold to that girl's mother when I was only a young one. It's gone very bad here now ... some people straggling in. It was a good market but this is gone, really.'

IDA LAHIFFE — Iveagh Market Dealer, Age 64

One of thirteen children, her father was a dealer in the old Iveagh Market and her mother was a "tugger" working the streets for second-hand clothing and oddments. As a child she began helping her father sell hair cream, pot scrubs and buttons and eventually inherited his stall. One of about a dozen remaining dealers in the market, she accepts that the Iveagh is nearing its end, reminisces about its past colourful characters and historical significance, then adds ... "but it's still alive".

'My father worked in the market here and my mother sold in the Daisy Market and then she come over here in her latter years. There were thirteen children and we lived in Carman's Hall. My mother was a tugger and used to go all over with the basket car. A tugger was the person who done the roads. They went out with the basket car and knocked at doors and bought clothes, shoes, odd household goods — anything she'd see a few bob in. The basket car's wheels was like horse and cart wheels. They were a marvellous thing, they'd last forever. Me mother used to bring delft out and bring the clothes back to the Daisy. I used to stand in the Daisy with her and sell it when I was about eight or nine.

'It was great here in the old days. The market would be packed. About seventy or eighty dealers here. Every stall was full. There was great variety — mostly clothing and footwear, hardware, pots and pans and strainers, jewelry and toys and ornaments for Christmas. And second-hand furniture sold down at the end. My father owned this stall here and I used to help him. You never had to have a licence, you just paid your weekly rent here. He used to sell hair cream and Brilliantine and all them bottles of things. And he sold olive oil and pot scrubs and buttons. Sold loads of loose buttons. You could find almost anything you wanted if you came in here. Maggie, she was very old, she sold rosaries and medals and bits of jewelry. There was Mr. Condon with a big stall and used to sell all second-hand tools ... *everything*. Years ago Mary Warren, an old woman, used to have loads and loads of hats all tied up in that corner. A shilling each. And then there was a woman that sold only second-hand shoes and she'd have them all polished in rows. Sit there all day polishing each one herself. And this woman, her name was Kate, used to hold up new curtains and say, "here's a bit of sugar for the bird" ... saying that it was a nice piece of curtain. I always remember that as a child.

114

'Clothes used to have to be disinfected outside. There was a big disinfectant place and the Corporation did that as part of your rent. Chemicals of some description was used for the fumigating. They wouldn't let you into the market without having the clothes disinfected. Oh, no. Disinfect them first and then bring them into here. See, an awful lot of lice and bugs and fleas and hoppers back then years ago. And down at the end of that lane there was a laundry. Anybody could use that. You'd pay sixpence and do your own laundry. Bring the clothes in and wash them and then you'd spin them in big spinners and dry them on what was called a "horse". The clothes was auctioned and they'd come down in price. And sometimes rows when one customer would have it first before another. Very often. That was a regular thing. Oh, yeah ... "she took that out of my hand!" ... "I seen that *first!*". And then the *price* would go up! But they used to be dressed out of here with good stuff. If you had a little bit of a wage you could come over here and dress the kids. Sure, there was often special stalls with all the Communion and Confirmation stuff hanging up.

Iveagh Market dealer Ida Lahiffe (right) behind the stall she inherited from her father

'Some of the dealers had bad husbands and they held the families together, no doubt about that. Men would drink the household money but the women would always get a few quid. We all got on great here. Still do! There was always a bit of crack. If there wasn't much selling they'd dress up for a bit of a laugh. Dress up like they were somebody else. And tea all the time. And some used to go out and have a drink at Frank Doyle's Pub. That was the most popular because there was little snugs and women didn't go into pubs much.

'The market was lovely back then with all the people ... great here in the old days. It got people through the hard times. Ah, you'd hear a lot of people coming in here saying, "Oh, I reared me family out of here". It's not a source of money now, that's for sure. I think it's fifteen years since it's been painted here. It's ridiculous. It's gone so bad now that it's hard to keep it clean. The Iveagh, it has an awful lot of historical significance, but it's nearly finished.'

Women dealers preparing morning tea at old Iveagh Market in the Liberties

LIZZY BYRNE — Moore Street Dealer, Age 82

"All of us on this street were reared in a basket ... or a banana box", she is fond of saying. At eighty-two, she is one of the genuine "old crowd" of Moore Street dealers. Indeed, she goes back to the days when there were no stalls and women wearing black shawls stood with their baskets on the ground. One of fifteen children, she was out on Henry Street next to the G.P.O. when the Rebellion erupted in 1916. A small woman of spry disposition, she stands before her huge display of colourful flowers and proclaims, "we never get tired here". At closing time Lizzy can be heard merrily humming away and anticipating her well-deserved pint.

'I was born in 1908. My mother was a trader before me and me grandmother. All of us on this street were reared in a basket ... or a banana box. That's the way it used to be years ago. And we all followed the trade. It carries down. Oh, it's in the blood, definitely.

'I'd come out and help me mother. I done that for love. It was all in baskets then, it wouldn't be a stall. The baskets were down on the ground and we always stood. It's only going back about sixty years that we started getting stalls. The street was all cobblestones and the old lamplighter used to come along and light the lamps. And all the deliveries for the shops was by horse and cart. This corner here (Moore Street and Henry Street) used to be a rank with jarveys and hackney cars, or a jaunting car we used to call them. And I remember the Rebellion … 1916. I was playing on Henry Street when that happened, beside the Post Office. We didn't know what it was, we were too young. We heard the shouting and people got all excited. They were afraid for their life! We locked ourselves up for nearly a week. You'd be afraid to come out. It was only fighting between two certain crowds, you know. But we let them go on with it and it only lasted for about a week.

Eighty–two year old Moore Street trader Lizzy Byrne setting out her flowers

'I guess that there was about twenty traders when I started out. It's over eighty of us now. We're all licensed traders here. The thirties were hard times and people worked very hard for very little. People had hard times. There was one trader here had twenty-one children. Me own mother had fifteen. And we never gave up … came out in hail, rain and snow. Oh, God, when it was cold we'd put plenty of clothing on. Three coats maybe. And covered up the babies in the baskets. We'd have the rugs over them and all, keep the rain off. They were all right, don't you worry! And I'll tell you, the women long ago were fine, big women. Hefty, big women maybe fifteen or sixteen stone. And the women were *tough*. You don't see a fine, big woman now. Look at me (about five feet) for instance! And they had big hearts. Oh, their hearts were as big as themselves. They never let one another down. We all helped one another and up to the present day we're still doing that. Nobody ever went hungry. We always got by. We're all like one big family here.'

MAY MOONEY — Moore Street Dealer, Age 72

*She has been out on the street selling for more than sixty years and her
dealer friends say they have never known her to be cantankerous, even
during the hardest times. She arranges her pyramids of fruit in perfect
form and calculates the price of a sale in her mind — scribbling figures
on paper just interrupts the flow of good chat. At the end of a warm
summer's day she tidies up her stall, removes her apron and treats
herself to an ice cream sundae, explaining that it soothes the throat
after hours of selling and socialising.*

'Me mother sold and me two aunties sold and me grandmother sold. I was in it
from a child. The women who were dealers, their daughters took over from
them. It was tradition. The generations ... tradition, tradition. Now me mother
only used to get seven and sixpence (government allowance) for eight of us and
then they found out she was selling and they took it back off her. My father was
very God-fearing and he *told them!* Ah, me mother used to call him "Honest
John". But we survived. And we had an old horse and cart and we used to sell
ice cream and all at Portmarnock on Sundays. But I was with me grandmother on
the street since I was about ten. She sold fish and I used to sell for her, and we
sold poultry and rabbits. They were dead. Skin the rabbits on the street and we'd
sell the skins to the Jewman and he'd make the fur coats, gloves or whatnot.

May Mooney (left) who has been selling on Moore Street for over sixty years

'Dealers back then all lived in the city centre, like Cole's Lane and Denmark Street, all little tenement rooms. And it was a woman's job. No men dealers. Never. The poor women was the breadwinners cause there was little work. People had to live on what they earned, come rain or snow or all weather. We used to be freezing but we had to put up with it. Every day. We'd survive. I used to wear a shawl. Used to get them off the Jewman. Cost twenty-six shillings. We used to get them for a shilling a week. Now the women were huge and had ten and twelve children each. They'd have their baby and then be out on the street. Bring the babies with them and put them in a banana box. And people were more close then. Each one would help one another. Years ago if you were finished selling your stuff you'd go over to sell for the others. And the women, very charitable. Now supposing someone — a passer-by or a poor customer buying — lost their purse. Well, they'd make up a collection for them. They'd send a bag around amongst the dealers and they'd make up a few pounds for them. Very nice like that.

A bit of early morning chat along Thomas Street

'In the war years there was a lot of black market around, like teas and that. We didn't sell it but it was around and anyone could buy it. And stuff wasn't coming in and we'd nothing to sell. Some Irish stuff but very little foreign stuff coming in. We only depended on the Irish stuff. No fruit at all. For about four years there was no bananas. Bananas hadn't been on the scene for about four years and when they come in children didn't know what they were!

'They couldn't close Moore Street up … it's marvellous. There's some old crowd left but nowadays it's all the offspring, the daughters. Once you're used to it, it's your *life*. I couldn't change it even if I got a millionaire. I'd go on.'

MARY DUNNE — Thomas Street Dealer, Age 54

At twelve years of age she was out helping her mother who "reared nine of us out of Thomas Street". She fondly remembers having to sit up all the night before Hallowe'en in Mulligan's Lane to protect the family pitch. Today she still pushes her mother's old wicker three-wheeled basket car through the streets laden with vegetables. Despite generous offers from persistent antique dealers, she refuses to sell the family relic.

'My mother was on Thomas Street, where you met me, and her mother sold further up on the same street. Selling fruit and veg the same as me. There was money to be made dealing back then. I mean, my mother reared *nine of us* out of Thomas Street. You wouldn't rear nine out of it today! My mother used to sell ten bags of cabbage where I'm only selling three now. In my mother's time they were out every day of the week — not Sundays. It was that good. We only go out on a Friday and Saturday now, it's gone so bad on the street. Oh, me mother was the longest on Thomas Street and never went on a holiday. No, never. But she was happy. *That* was her holiday, Thomas Street. Oh, she loved Thomas Street. She was out in tough weather and she took sick and died when she was seventy-six. When me mother died they brought Mass cards and attended the funeral. Now I have me mother's customers.

'I got up and sold on that street when I was twelve years old. You got nothing for it. You had to do it. When we were children we had *nothing*. And all tenement houses. The youngest in the family would be brought down on the street in the pram with a bottle. Some breast fed. They'd no privacy so they'd just go up Mulligan's Lane there. And some just took the child under the shawl and no one knew what was going on. It was all shawls back then. Women had a black one for working and a grey one was the good one for Sundays. Like a big paisley shawl all decorated and flowers. They were a lovely article. Used to be second-hand clothes. They'd get them at the Iveagh Market. Women used to go around with a pram door to door tugging the clothes. Go out to well-off people. Oh, they'd go miles. *Miles.* They'd walk to Blackrock … you name it. Well, if those tuggers came across a shawl the dealers would buy it from them. And nearly every dealer had a pram. There was *oceans* of prams. If you had an old pram you didn't want you'd give it to the dealers and they'd give you a bit of fruit for it. Ah, a good old pram would last long enough. Now that basket car there was me mother's. They're (antique dealers) always asking for it. Oh, I wouldn't part with it … she'd turn in her grave.

'Now in Francis Street we used to go to the Tivoli Picture House and it was four pence. That was our enjoyment. But you had to *earn* it. We went door to door collecting slop — that'd be the leavings of all the dinners, the cabbage water — and we sold it to a man for his pigs and he gave us fourpence a bucket. Then we

Saturday morning clothing sale at Cumberland Street market

went to the Bayno and that was our free enjoyment. The Bayno was a big hall that was run by Guinness's. You had all different children's games and when you'd go in you'd have to sing, "Good evening to you, good evening, Lady Guinness". Oh, you always had to sing that. And we'd gather in at Hallowe'en and Christmas for parties. At Christmas we got no dolls or toys. You only got rubbish, very little … a Christmas stocking. Sure, Easter was the same. I mean, you look at the children now and it's twelve, thirteen and fourteen eggs they're getting. We got *none*. All we got was a fried egg on an Easter. When I tell my children that they'll be laughing at me. But that's the *truth*. We never seen a fried egg until Easter and that's as true as God.

'Now I remember when I was a child on Hallowe'en and me mother and all of us stayed up all the night (before) to watch that no one went into your pitch on Thomas Street. Oh, yes, we stayed up all night. On Hallowe'en if someone tried to get in on your pitch there'd be a row. Oh, you had to protect your spot. We sat in Mulligan's Lane and had cans for carrying down tea from the house. At Hallowe'en the oranges and nuts was a traditional thing. Mixed nuts and monkey nuts. Monkey nuts were like a white shell and there's two peanuts in it. They'd sell better for the simple reason they were cheaper than the mixed nuts. It was only on Hallowe'en they'd ask for them.

'In me mother's time there was about sixteen dealers in Thomas Street. That's all. There's about sixty dealers today. That's how it's gone so bad. But now they're from the northside and all trading here. We call them "runner-ins". We don't like it but there's nothing we can do about it if they get their licence. But they're inclined to take over. They think they owned the street. You have your pitch and you pledge to the Corporation. It's classed as a permit. That does you for the twelve months. In my mother's time it was five shillings for fruit and veg. It's now sixty pounds. From five shillings to sixty pounds! And on Thomas Street there should never been clothes allowed to sell there. In my mother.s time any clothes that was to be sold was sold in the Iveagh Market. About ten years ago clothes came in and now there's more clothes than anything else. Shouldn't have allowed clothes into it ... no way.

'Now my sister beside me (on the street), she's saying that in years to come there'll be no dealers the way the street's going. "I can see it happening", she says. Whether she's right or wrong I don't know. It wouldn't be the same. You enjoy doing it. You get a bit of laugh. I'd go mad if I couldn't go anymore. I would, I'd go mad. Stay up in a four walls? Not at all.'

JIMMY OWENS — Thomas Street Dealer, Age 66

He is one of only a handful of men street traders. Born into the tenement poverty of the Coombe, life was an upward struggle. For at least three generations, street trading provided the only means of survival for his family. At the tender age of thirteen, upon the untimely death of his father, he had to go out on the streets in the cold and snow of winter selling hairnets for a penny apiece. Later, he graduated into stall-type selling and hawking fruit and candy at sports matches. Of his fifty-eight years of street dealing he proclaims simply, "it was hard earned money".

'I was born and reared in a tenement house in sixteen Coombe Street. My father was a stoker on a boat around the time of the Titanic and me mother was a fruit dealer on Thomas Street, and her mother before her. I had six sisters and two brothers and a brother that died. Very hard times. It was all poverty then. Me mother sold flowers and fish and poultry, cabbage, potatoes, onions. She had her pitch and we're there ever since. The permit cost a shilling a year in me mother's time. Now at that time they weren't allowed to sell off a board, off a table. See, the law in them days was to only sell out of a basket with a pole underneath it. That was the rule, but they never done that. See, it was very awkward to have a basket around you selling stuff. So they ignored it and just put up a board and a table for to sell off of. And when they see the man (guard) coming up along they'd put the pole there. But the guards got used to it and never minded.

'I was on the street since I was eight years old and I didn't get much education. And school was very bitter. A hard, hard school. Hundreds of children went to school in their bare feet walking on nails and lumps of glass cutting their feet.

And I was often half hungry going to school. The Christian Brothers were hard. If you were a minute late you'd get a hiding. The *minute* that bell would strike. A load of us used to be lined up on a cold morning to get a few leathers. I had to come out of school when I was thirteen cause me father died and me and me brother had to provide for them. So I was a little boy and I sold women's hairnets on the street for a penny each. I was out in the *freezing* cold and the snow. Some days you'd go out and hardly earn. Then I sold cabbage and potatoes and fruit and vegetables. If you earned ten shillings a week it was a lot of money in the 1930's.

'Thomas Street was the *heart* of the Liberties — that and Meath Street. The streets were cobblestoned cause the horses had to grip if it was a bit of a hill. I often seen a horse fall but they'd unyoke it and lift it up again. And the number twenty-one tram was on Thomas Street. And there was a penny bank there — a *penny* bank — for to save up money. They called it a penny bank cause it was a poverty-stricken area. When I was a boy there was fifteen or sixteen women dealers on the street and two or three men dealers. I learned an awful lot from looking at what went on. The majority of husbands was unemployed and the women had to go out and bring in the money. The trading women always had *something*. And nothing ever went to waste. In them days bananas and pears and oranges used to come in wooden boxes. You'd use the boxes to put a breadboard on and sometimes you'd break up the wooden boxes for firewood. And there used to be a rope on the boxes and we'd cut that for the hank onions and they'd never go rotten.

'The women dealers, all shawls they'd wear. And they'd wear the button boot and lace it up. They used to wear white smocks and a bib and in the summertime they'd wear black wraps. And put the child in a basket or box, same as Moore street. She'd have to go into a hall to breast feed cause they were very modest in them days. And when the women needed a toilet they'd go to a tenement yard cause there was no women's toilets in the public houses in them days. The women were all friendly and they'd go in and have a couple of bottles of stout at the heel of the evening ... and they'd have a gargle at the weekend. Then they'd go in and maybe buy a pig's cheek and a couple of pig's feet to make a feed for the family. The shawls disappeared in the fifties ... they felt old-fashioned in their shawls then.

'On a Sunday I'd go to a football match at Croke Park and push me fruit on a two-wheeled handcart. I used to hire it for a shilling a day from a handcart place in Granby Place. Ah, they had a couple of hundred. I was about fourteen then. At Croke Park there'd be loads of people. Now the police would stop you, they didn't let you into Croke Park. But you'd still get in (sneaking) over the stiles and hand the stuff over the wall. One fella'd throw it over the wall to the other and we'd catch it and then go and sell it. Great fun ... great crowds. And then I went to race meetings and the point-to-point races and sold fruit and chocolate. The point-to-point race is in the country and the field is hired off a farmer by the hunt. Oh, you'd sell plenty of stuff but, I'll tell you, it was *hard earned money*. I handed the money to me Ma. I was delighted to give it to her for to buy food. And I'd get fourpence back for the pictures and I was *delighted* with it.

String of vegetable stands along Thomas Street

'About 1942 me brother and me travelled with a woman named Mrs. Quinn of Benburb Street. Travelled all over the country. She had a little lorry and we used to sit up on the back and go to different counties every Sunday whenever a match would be playing. She'd be selling her own stuff and I'd be selling me own fruit and chocolate and lemonade and pears and apples. She was a very kind person to us. See, she'd set up a stall and we'd put the basket around our neck and go around to all the crowd hawking and we'd sell. If it was a long journey, like to Killarney, we'd go on a Saturday and stay overnight. Then you'd be fresh the next morning. And like for the Munster Final you might earn ten or fifteen pounds! Now that was an awful lot of money for that day. Then we'd come back and say to our mother, "there's the money!". Oh, they were good times ... great times.

'I love going to Thomas Street, love going over to the market and love trading. It'll never leave me. Every customer that comes over to Thomas Street, they all know me. Some of them goes back sixty years. You know their background and their family and everything. I love it. It's a *gift* ... a thing that you have to be *born into it*. We're a special breed of people. If I won the lottery I'd *still* go out. Even me family loves it and follows on from me. My mother took it up from me grandmother and I took it up from me mother and my family's taking it up from me. And me children will continue in it. Traders just go on and go on and go on.'

ELLEN PRESTON — Henry Street Dealer, Age 62

Every morning she can be seen pushing her rickety pram through streets broad and narrow from her home on North William Street to Henry Street, animatedly chatting away with other dealers along the way. Street trading goes back a full century in her family and she has been at it for nearly fifty years. She takes great pride in having raised twelve children from street dealing. It meant working up to the day of births and returning to the street a few days later. As she puts it, there was "no choice ... they were very, very hard times". Her children and grandchildren are openly devoted to her, understanding the sacrifices she has made for them.

'I'm part of the history of the street life ... yes, I am. See, my grandmother and my mother and my two sisters and my brothers, they all sold on the street. Trading goes well back in my family, over a hundred years. My father used to go out to Howth and get the fish on an old horse and cart and me grandmother'd sell it on Parnell Street. And the Black and Tans even held them up when they used to go to Howth on the cart.

'I was born on Gardiner's Lane and my mother had fourteen of us. Times were hard then. We had no electricity or gas and we had an oil lamp. And you'd have a fire and bellows and cook on the fire. We used to make carrot tea out of carrots. Me mother and grandmother sold vegetables and fruit and fish on Parnell Street. It used to be great up there years ago. Oh, there were loads of street traders there. All had large families. Mrs. Boyle, she had seventeen. All wore shawls with babies in their arms. I was about twelve when I started selling up there with me sister. Selling fruit and potatoes and then flowers. When I was young when we'd be finished we'd push one another up and down the street in the prams for a laugh.

'I got married when I was nineteen. Then the children started coming along and things were very hard — I've had twelve children. Parnell Street was starting to die out and there was nothing down there anymore. So on a Monday I said to meself, "I'll just go off by meself and sell off me pram". And I went off to Henry Street and I've been there ever since. There was only eight of us then selling fruit and flowers. We didn't go near Moore Street cause the street traders there had their stuff and we wouldn't go in front of them. Henry Street was a great street. God, you wouldn't be able to walk through it! Five shillings, that was a *great day* for me. See, if you got five shillings from the pram in them days that'd get you loads of bread and butter and milk to feed them. I was earning a living. But you were just making ends meet. This street is what we're all reared out of.

'Every day I pushed me pram on the road in the traffic. *Every day.* There was horses and cars and we'd be walking through them. Keep walking. And we had to push the prams over the cobblestones and it was really very hard it was. I got a pram back then used for maybe two, three shillings. If you were bringing down (heavy) bananas or oranges the pram wouldn't last two months. I must have had sixty prams in my lifetime! Some days was miserable. I often came home with the rain beating off me. You'd be drowned but you *had* to do it. I remember one day — and it's as true as I'm drinking this (tea) — and I went out to sell and it was snowing and I remember the snow getting into me shoes and I was expecting one of the babies at the time and I brought me little parcel with me and I went straight to the hospital and had me baby. And I was out on the street again then in a week.

Thriving street trading scene along Thomas Street

'They were very, very hard times. They really were. It was the women who really made it. There was no work for the men. The women traders, they held the families together. They were the whole upkeep because they *had* to go out. I used to go out on the street, come back home about five and do all the meals for the whole lot of them — and I'd have to do different dinners for some of them — and I didn't get away from cooking till nine at night. Then I'd clean up, do the washing and all me housework and fall into bed. And I'd be up for seven Mass the next morning. It was very rough but you just got used to it. I always made sure that the children had food and got dressed and had a clean bed. With Confirmations and Communions you had to manage. One year I remember when Liam (son featured elsewhere in book) made his Communion and we were very badly off — had *nothing* at all — and Sister Louise up in the convent came down and gave me a suit and pair of shoes for him. And I tried to keep the children in school as long as I could. That's why I really went out selling. I remember once, when I was about thirty-six, I was brought into court for trading (without a licence) and this judge said to me, "how many children have you?" and I said I had nine at the time. So he said, "I'll only fine you half a crown. Just go home and make sure you keep them at school". I never did let them run the street.

Henry Street trader Ellen Preston who raised a family of twelve children from the street

'When the strawberries would come in we'd get loads and go over to Grafton Street with our carts. It used to be quality (people) up there at that time and they'd buy the strawberries. Used to push our carts over there by the Gaiety and Maureen Potter and Jimmy O'Dea used to come out and buy strawberries off us. We'd end up on O'Connell Bridge about eight at night trying to sell the strawberries. We went up there one day and the police chased us all the way up to Meath Street. And when there'd be an All-Ireland match on at Croke Park we'd be on O'Connell Bridge selling loads of peaches and grapes. All the countrymen used to come in … and loads of Belfast lads. And when I was younger we used to get into the Croke Park matches and sell apples. See, you wouldn't be let in to sell so we used to just duck under the stiles. Just sneak in, run in under the stiles. Then we'd put the basket and stuff up over the wall and go around selling it. And people were very gentle at that time, not like now.

'I loved Christmas. Oh, God, when you'd walk into Henry Street you'd really know it was Christmas. They had tinsels and decorations and there were choirs. Christmas used to be a very good time for us. We used to sell Christmas trees and mistletoe and holly. And little pianos and small toys and Cheeky Charlies. Oh, very, very busy years ago. Now for Christmas month there was a five shilling licence and we used to have to go and sleep outside in Henry Street the night before to get your place. We'd go down the night before about ten. We'd all sit there with our boxes in place waiting for the next morning. We'd relieve each other for an hour and then go back again. But one family member would always be there. All sit there and send for a few chips and have tea and a bit of laugh, a bit of crack, and we didn't feel the cold. Once it was morning then you just put your board out and that was it. That place was yours for the whole month and nobody touched it.

'Anybody that's out on Moore Street or Henry Street, they all work very hard. All out in hail, rain, frost and snow. Oh, but it was great to be part of it. We're the old crowd ... the *real* old ones left. It's part of the history of Dublin. As long as I'm able I'll go out. I never get bored. Every day is different. I couldn't stick this (inside) kind of life. I'd miss it. The women street traders, they feel that they must stay out there ... or it's finished. It's over with if you sit in. I have twenty-six grandchildren and I'd like to see them doing well. Now if one of them could go to college I'd work the nails off me bones for to get them there. I *would* ... I'd really do that.'

LIAM PRESTON — Street Spieler, Age 35

The son of street dealer Ellen Preston, he is incontestably Henry Street's premier spieler. Born on Sean McDermott Street into a poor family of seasoned street traders, he instinctively had the knack for selling. Spieling proved a highly specialised and challenging form of street dealing and no one has mastered the art better. He begins by thrashing down his black case on the pavement with the loudest possible bang to attract the attention of passers-by. Then he squats down, opens the case and spreads out gold chains enticingly displayed on velvet and begins his well-rehearsed and finely tuned spiel. It is delivered in a non-stop, rapid-fire staccato flow, creating an atmosphere of carnivalesque excitement. He masterfully draws and holds an audience with his glib tongue, joking chatter and dramatic hand gestures. Soon a huge human circle forms around him in the centre of Henry Street. Unlike some spielers who seem shifty and aggressive, Liam is observably sincere and affable, offering an honest product at a fair price.

A portion of his spiel, as recorded on Henry Street in July of 1988, is as follows:

There is only one *question you have to ask yourself. What would you get this morning in the city of Dublin for three pounds? For that set of chains my price today, just pay me three pounds. That's the long gold chain, your twisting rope chain and right back down to a choker chain. My price for the whole set –* forget *about ten,* forget *about five — pay me* three pounds! *There's no fancy box, there are no fancy bloody prices. Show me the colour of your money, I'll show you the biggest bargain of the day … for the price of a hamburger and a cup of tea. If you love your wife you'll buy her one … if you happen to love someone else's wife you'll buy bloody* two *of them! A lady asked me this morning, "where's you get them from? How can you sell them so cheap?".* "Mind your own bloody business*!". I don't ask you where you get your money, don't ask me where I get the jewelry. Watch this … there's one, there's two, there's three gold chains. Pay me just* three pounds! *They're all brand new. They haven't seen daylight or nightlight …they haven't even seen a bloody Israelite! Come right in, don't be shy …if you're not too proud to buy off a briefcase. No fancy box, no fancy price … pay me just three pounds … and when they're gone there'll be* no more. *Sorry, Love, when the guards come* I have to go.

'I lived down there on Sean McDermott Street and we were really very, very poor. I mean, there was poverty. It was really bad here years ago. And the only thing we could do was go out selling. Ah, me mother's sister sold and all her brothers sold. Everyone sold. It's in our blood all the way down … really in the blood. Me mother has twelve children and six of us are in street trading at some stage. When I was six years old I used to go with the pram in the morning and wheel it down to the market and buy fruit to sell around Ha'penny Bridge or O'Connell Bridge. Selling from baskets at age six or seven. I'm thirty-five years old now and I've been at selling for the best part of twenty-eight years.

'In the inner-city area of Dublin the mothers hold the families together. Me mother, she really stood by us. You wouldn't believe how hard things were, really hard. I seen me mother having a baby and she was out three days after on Henry Street selling and it was a really bad year snowing and all. And on a Monday morning me father's good suit would go into the pawn. And me mother used to sell black market tickets into the cinemas all along O'Connell Street. She'd borrow money off somebody first and go down on a Saturday and buy, say, ten tickets for, say, twenty pounds. Then she'd go down on a Sunday night to the theatre about four and sell the tickets for thirty pounds cause the cinemas would be all booked out. It was called "black market" tickets. It was illegal but all the traders done it. It used to be an awful struggle for me mother. But there was food on the table.

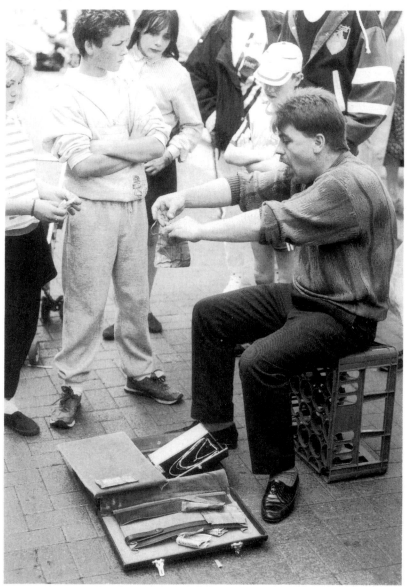

Henry Street spieler Liam Preston enticing crowd with his polished pitch and gold chains

'I started off first selling apples and oranges from a cart. Then I graded meself up to flowers and strawberries. And from flowers I went up to balloons. Then I went into whatever was available, like socks. And in October here we do fireworks. They're illegal here in Ireland, you see, but we'd sell them and the guards allow it. The whole month of October thousands of people will buy fireworks for Hallowe'en — bangers, rockets, flares. This goes way back. See, we used to get a train from Dublin to Belfast (to buy fireworks) and when it was coming back — just before they'd get into Dublin station — they'd throw it all out. You'd get a line of prams going up that night to meet the train around the East Wall area. A certain train would be passing by a certain spot and toss the bags off and then the people'd get the bags and put them into the prams.

Henry Street spieler Liam Preston skillfully gathering a crowd

'Then I decided I'd go into jewelry like Bimbo (another spieler). I seen him doing it and he was making a few bob. So I says, "I'll try that". Jewelry is good to sell. It's small, it's compact. I mean, in my little case I could go around with hundreds of pounds of jewelry. At first I just watched him for a while. Ah, he knew I was doing it. But an *awful* lot tried and failed. Anyway, I went out on Saturdays and just started doing what he was doing, saying the same things. And on my first four Saturdays I didn't sell one. Not *one!* I was just kind of shaking. I used to have to go in and get a pint or two before I'd go out ... to strengthen my feelings. Even now, you still get nervous the first thing in the morning. So I was nearly giving up but I said, "I'll try once more". And I started using me *own* few sayings. And I went out and sold forty of them (sets of gold chains), two pound sets at that time. So I took eighty pounds home. My confidence went *zooom!*

'I'm a spieler. We "spiel" them. Spieling means to get out and actually do it differently than just standing there selling ... to give a speech, a good line of speech. Like on Moore Street anyone can just go out with a pram and just let the wares sell themselves. But if we just put out gold chains on a board people'd just walk by us. Unless it's forced upon them or put in front of them in a certain way.

Make 'em think "it's too good to be true" — three gold chains for only three pounds! You've got to get them to stop first ... with the noise. And then *hold them.* See, they'll hear the noise of the case when I'm slapping it on the ground. Then they'll stop. Curiosity! They'll want to have a look. But just let them see a little bit at a time cause then other people will see them looking at something and *they'll* stop. And eventually you'll build up a certain amount of people. Oh, I wouldn't give a price until you have enough people there.

'I watch the people and I have to also watch for the police as well ... look left and right. And when the people see you doing it it's like they think you're doing something illegal. Like *they're* even doing something illegal, buying stolen property — although it's *not.* But the *psychology* of them thinking it's stolen, they'll jump at that ... "it *must* be a bargain, how could he be selling it so cheap?". And when one sees one buying you'll normally get a group of people following right in. I think people themselves are like sheep really, they want to be led. And you'll always get people who'll take out their money but haven't got the confidence to walk into the pitch in front of the people and buy it. I know they've got the money in their hand cause I can see it. That's why I say, "if you're not too proud to buy off the street come in, don't be shy". Some people will send their child in to buy it. Or wait until I'm closing up to come up and buy. Some people just don't have the confidence to actually walk up in front of a stage of people, cause it is a stage. That's a *stage* there. Last Christmas I had a good crowd and there was one gent there and here I was calling him in saying "come in now, don't be shy" — and he was a plain clothes guard!

'Some days *I really love it.* You'd get some pitches now and it wouldn't be the money you're taking in, it'd be the great crowd and you'd get laughs, really good laughs. Ah, I see meself as a performer. I have jokes and all. Much more personal relationship with people than in a store. I can communicate with people a hell of a lot more with humour. Before I even talk about jewelry I give them a few laughs first because it brightens up their day. They seem to relax. And now when the country people come in here you can tell most of them right away. Just by looking. Cause it's mostly new to them, a novelty to them.

'Psychologically it's hard. It's something you have to psyche yourself up for from the time you get out of bed, as soon as you're awake. It's all in the *mind.* There's no doubt about that. If you go out there and say to yourself, "I'm going to *sell*", you'll *do it.* But if you go out with a few doubts in your mind, if you've got a doubt, *go home!* I really believe that if you have the confidence to sell, you will. Anything. *Anything.* I can get along with people but if you stop talking at all, you lose. You just have to keep going. The summer season for me starts in June and then I go up until Christmas. I normally work between eleven till two on Saturdays and other days I sometimes stay out till four or five. I enjoy meself more if it's a good day's work. If I done fifty sales in a day it's good. At Christmas time a good day would be a hundred. One day, about two years ago, I sold 300 in one day! After Christmas I take a break. What happens at Christmas is your throat is so badly damaged from the whole month cause it's twenty-four days non-stop, Sunday included. And then in June, after months off, it's very hard to get back into it again. Your timing is all wrong. It takes a while for you to get back to the right rhythm again.

Horse cart deliveries are still part of Moore Street life

'You have to have somebody watching for the guards. My son keeps an eye out because the police *do come*. Now some of the guards are all right. Some will just pass me by. Most of the guards is great. Most of them, by making themselves be seen, will give you a chance to go. But they get pressure from their boss and obviously they've a job to do as well. I mean, it can be a bother if you get down on the pitch and shout your lungs out and you've a good crowd and you're just about ready to take the money and a guard comes along and says you've got to get up. Ah, it gets discouraging. And positioning in the street is important. It's always best to keep in the middle of the street where I have less chance of getting caught. If I'm too close to one corner police could come around. Saturday is a worry because they put the plain clothes men on. No way to guard against it. They'd just walk in and nick you. So on Saturdays I just take the chance.

'Police, they're much harder on the men. It's generally known that they'll pass by most of the prams. Holding women, it's just a thing they don't do. They'll overlook the older traders, like me mother, if they haven't got their permits for Henry Street. Cause she's one of the originals. So they'll pass by most of the prams to get to me. I was often caught. See, normally when you're caught you've got three charges — obstructing, trading without a licence, and trading in a non-designed or non-trading area. The middle of the street is a non-trading area. What happens to you depends on who gets you. I often seen a judge just giving two or three pounds fine or just dismissing the case. But sometimes you'll get a cranky one that'll hit you with a sixty pound fine. That's a very heavy one. So you go to court and you get a fine. You just plead guilty and the fine now ranges from £1,000 down to two pounds. The judge is mostly O.K. But one guy put me into a cell and locked me in a cell, just for selling on the street. I was put in the Store Street Police Station for five hours and, ah, the *smells* in those cells. Oh, it was the worst five hours I've ever spent, it really was. Oh, that was a terrible experience to be locked up ... just for street selling.

'I work very hard. It's a good, honest wage. Sometimes I get tired of it. And I wouldn't want to do it for me whole life. But I'll always stay in selling. Definitely in selling. If you're no good you're out ... a lot of people have tried it. The people, they say who's the best, who's top. And I think I'm the best ... I'm *convinced* I am.'

CHRISTY MURRAY — Newspaper Seller, Age 83

Christy is one of the storied barefoot Dublin newsboys of a past era. In 1918 he sold papers on Westmoreland Street outside Bewley's. When the manager was not around soft-hearted women would bring the lad out a cup of hot tea to combat the chill. The dreaded Black and Tans would barge up to his pitch, grab his papers and placard reading "Big Raid" to display on the back of their tender as they drove arrogantly around the city. When he moved his pitch to Meath Street he found the Liberties folk the "loveliest people in the world". Kindly women would give him a bit of dinner when he was hungry. It was just their "nature", he says. After nearly seventy years of street selling his legs finally wore out and he reluctantly retired.

'My father worked on the docks but my brothers, Dinny and Jack, they were older than me and used to do papers. They brought me onto the papers. At eight I was selling papers outside of Bewley's in Westmoreland Street where there was an awful lot of newsboys, about ten. Oh, you had competition, all right. And there was a girl newspaper seller, Mary Clark. She was like a tomboy. Used to crop her hair like a boy and she could play football and fight and box and everything. You can put that in your book!

'You had to have a half crown licence. You'd get it at the police station. It was like a piece of tin and a strap and had a number and you had to wear it on your wrist. Once you had that badge, that was your licence. If you had a place you'd make a pitch of it and no one else could stand there. If someone tried he'd be in trouble he would. He'd get murdered. Oh, there was often boxing matches over fellas claiming pitches. When I was about sixteen years of age I wouldn't pay the five shillings for the licence. I said "no" ... because we weren't earning that much money then. And I got four days in the "Joy" (Mountjoy Prison) over the licence.

134

I went back on the papers again but I had to get the licence or they might give me maybe a month then, and I didn't want that.

*Eighty-three year old Christy Murray who sold newspapers barefoot along
Westmoreland Street during the days of the Black and Tans*

'I done the evening papers, the *Mail* and the *Telegraph* and the *Herald*. Ramble down and pick 'em up and put them under your arms, a couple of dozen. And if you sold 'em you'd go back for more. You were young and you'd fly down and back with them. And I used to jump up onto the trams to sell the papers. Used to go up to the Nelson's Pillar. Just hop on. I'd jump on and dash upstairs to see who wanted a paper and then hop off and then onto another tram. I was young and like a hare and I'd dodge the horses and traffic. The conductor might say "no" and put you off. But if he was all right he'd let you jump on and sell the papers. They cost eight pence a dozen and I'd sell them for twelve pence. A penny apiece and you'd earn four pence. On a good morning you'd earn a couple of bob. I'd give all that money to me mother. There was eight of us in the house and all we used to get for dinner was potatoes and bread.

'It was a poor life. You were very poor. You had to struggle to exist. We were so poor I made me Holy Communion in the police clothes that you got free. Oh, I sold in snow and walked in snow in me bare feet when I was small. Sure, I don't think I wore boots till I was fourteen. And I was often very, very cold. Your fingers would be *freezing*. But people in them days was great and sometimes when I'd go around with the papers I'd get fed. I used to get me dinner up on Earl Street from a Mrs. Riley. She'd give me a bit of ribs and cabbage and potatoes. It was her *nature*. And at Christmas time you'd get loaves and cakes from shopkeepers and customers. And there was a fella named McKenzie, a broker, and he used to go into Bewley's for his coffee. He took an awful liking to me and used to give me two shillings for the paper every day. And my brother Dinny, he got a sovereign off a gentleman on a tram one day. He said, "go and buy boots for yourself". Gave him a sovereign to buy boots. *That* was a gentleman. I'll always remember that.

'At the time of the Troubles here, that was a mad time with the Tans here. They was released prisoners out of England ... murderers and robbers sent over here. They used to go around in tenders and netting all around it cause of the bombs thrown. The Tans often bought papers off me. And when they made a raid they'd take the placard (large newspaper advertisement poster) off you and put it on the back of the tender and off around town they'd show it. It was to show off. Like it might say, "Big Raid on so-and-so a place". And I was out on the street when they were at the Lord Edward Public House firing up at the Christchurch belfry cause there was snipers in it. People'd always say to me, "get away, you'll get killed, get out of there". I was very curious about things when I was young.

'When I left Westmoreland I went up on Thomas and Meath Streets. I was there for forty years. And I met the loveliest people in the world in the Liberties. Oh, Lord, in them days with no T.V. and when there was no wireless the papers was the only way of getting the news. They'd read them inside out. Bring the paper home and the family would read it and give it to an old person they knew. And when the *Sports Mail* came out it had football and racing results from England and all over. Out into the street I'd run like a hare — fly — and people on the street would all be waiting with their money in their hands to give it to you. You could sell them in a half an hour. You could earn five or ten bob off them. But I often got bad money. They'd stick you. You'd be in such a hurry that maybe they'd give you a coin and you'd run off and later be counting your money and find it. And the *News of the World* came in here a good few years back. Had the sex in it and all ... the first dirty newspaper. They (sellers) were all saying, "oh, I'm not going to take that filthy paper". This is before it started to come out. But the way it was, you'd sell anything you'd get. The first time I had them I was standing on Meath Street one Sunday morning and as soon as the Mass was over I couldn't have *enough* of them! They just folded it up and brought it home.

Socialization among womenfolk along Moore Street

'I've only been off the street now for five years. I got crippled in the legs. The bad weather will cripple you. The old times are gone. A paper now, it's thirteen shillings in old money — sixty-five pence. And they pay nearly a pound for the *Financial Times* and *Economist*. The pound in my time was a *pound!* I used to get a pint for seven "P". If I had a pound I could go out on a bus to Howth bonafiding it ... and come back with a few bob the following morning. Now you can't go into a pub with a pound and get a pint. Dublin is finished I'd say ... nearly.'

BILL CREGAN — Newspaper Seller, Age 67

His newspaper stall is at the corner of O'Connell and Abbey Street — a prime pitch. The trade was passed down from his grandfather as he began selling papers for a penny in the days when people were hungry for news of world events and war. He'll always remember the evening when the crowds swarmed out of the late cinemas to snatch up his papers and read about J.F.K.'s assassination — then stood about the

streets stunned with grief. From his strategic corner perch he has
witnessed every imaginable type of humanity and inhumanity.

'My grandfather sold papers up on Hanlon's Corner and my father was in it. I was thirteen when I started out. You just done what you were told. There was thirteen of us in the family. You had to get a five shilling licence back then from the police station. You got a badge to strap on your arm and there was a number on it. They had a badge man going around to check on you and if you hadn't got a licence he'd put you off the streets. Some vendors didn't have a corner, they just kept going around. Selling papers you were classed as very low. But we have a code among ourselves — unwritten — that I wouldn't stand over there and he wouldn't stand over here. We just sort of knew each other.

'There was just the *Herald* and the *Mail* then. They sold for one penny. If I sold a couple a hundred a night, made a few shillings, I was doing well. I was at Hanlon's Corner and used to do North King Street. Just carry the newspapers under your arm like that, a hundred at least. And you had to carry them even in bad weather. It'd be lashing rain and wind but you'd still have to come out. Every day. Oh, I'd get colds but I'd still come out coughing and sneezing. Get lemon and glycerine and honey and drink that. And in the cold in winter time my hands would split here … it's frostbite or something. Never wore gloves. Couldn't work with them on. Then I got an old bike and a sack on my back. Or you could put the papers on the handlebars and walk it. I delivered to houses and you'd give them credit. You put it in your book and collected your money on a Saturday night. You knocked and they often came to the door and said, "me mother said she's not in". The mother would be there but she mightn't have the money … but you'd get it. Then I used to stand on Parnell Street and a Mr. McDermott used to be here on this corner at that time. He was very fragile and he asked me to come with him to help him out. I was with him for years. Then he died, the Lord have mercy on him. He gave it to me and I'll hand it down to my son now.

'Donkey's years ago this (O'Connell) was a great street. Old trams going up and down and horses. The bread men and the milk and coal men, they all had horses. And the old horse-drawn cabs, the hacks. And everybody had an old bike. The trams was better than the buses. When the trams went, ah, the city changed. I remember them taking up the tram lines here and putting this street down. There was about thirty horses with tar buckets and fellas on their knees spreading it. And I remember I came down one morning and the Pillar (Nelson's) was gone. There was a shock! It was really a landmark, a terminal for all the trams. I'll tell you, it changed the street.

'This city was nice back then. The Metropole was there and plenty of cinemas and you'd stay out late and nobody'd bother you. Forty years ago on a good day I could sell 500 papers, just *evening* papers. Everybody lived in the city. Oh, you'd get loads of people. See, it was no outskirts then, it was all city. You had plenty of work in the city then, all dockers and factories. Dominick Street there was full of big houses and maybe ten families in the one house. No Ballyfermot, no Tallaght, no schemes on the outskirts. And during the war there was no television and you were well off if you had a wireless. Loads of war news and so people depended on the papers. Cause it was only one penny. But this street's *gone ... finished.* No business in it at all now. Only cafes and bloody banks. There's nobody working now. These days I can't even sell 200 evening papers. It's not the *city* anymore. The city is in Cabra, Blanchardstown, Donoghmede, where all these big shopping centres is. The heart of the city has gone out to the suburbs.

Newspaper seller Bill Cregan at his prime pitch along O'Connell Street

'Oh, it seen lots of coming and going. You have to put your heart into it, have to love what you're doing every day or you couldn't do it. And you always have to have a smile, even if you're down in the dumps. You don't see too many smiles now. Life is took too seriously now ... everybody is grumpy. Oh, but I couldn't stay indoors. It'd kill me altogether. I'm as well known as anybody, like a landmark. Even if I was to retire I'd still have to come down to O'Connell Street and knock about, have a walk around. I couldn't stay in the house. Sure, you'd go off your head.'

JIMMY BYRNE — "Rag and Bones" Scrap Collector, Age 67

He began as a lad picking through the Dublin dump sites for items of scrap to sell. At twenty years of age he began working for the legendary northside Jewman Harry Lipman whom he refers to as the "Godfather of Dublin Jews". His apprenticeship as a "rag and bones" collector under the master Lipman was rigorous but he learned the street trade better than any of his rivals. In old age, Lipman turned the business over to Jimmy, a gentile, in violation of his synagogue's rules. After nearly fifty years of combing the streets for scrap items he is content to hang around his shop on North King Street. Out front are displayed used toilets, wash basins, doors, brass and copper items, almost anything of value. In earlier days he may have been a "rag and bones" collector but today he is a "waste merchant".

'Harry Lipman ... ah, he was the biggest Jewman around here. He was on George's Lane. Always known as "Harry Lipman the ragman". He was the Godfather of all the Jews in Dublin. He started in 1900. It was only an old scrap store with bottles and rags and jars and that. I was twenty when I started working for Mr. Lipman. I was on the dumps out in Tallaght picking up stuff and selling it. See, there were dumps where the Corporation dumped all their stuff and we used to drag it in. We got it on handcarts and a horse and cart. So I went to work for him. He collected everything — rags, bottles, jars, tin milk cans, bean tins, scrap boards and beds and furniture. A lot of Jewmen would have you slaving for little or nothing. But Lipman was a decent old sort. Oh, he was a millionaire. Sure, he used to send away lots of money to Israel for the cause. And he used to preach in O'Connell Street. Stood up on a box and preached religion and everything. Ah, he was a *legend.*

Scrap merchant Jimmy Byrne (white shirt) with customer in front of his shop on North King Street

'People used to go around collecting with these basket cars they'd get from him. Lipman used to get them made down at the Blind Institution on O'Connell Street. They were big basket prams made out of cane with a wooden handle and two wheels and a wheel in front. They'd bring in old sacks of rags and bottles. Now some people wouldn't collect stuff, they'd go and pawn his car on him! So he had his name stamped on all the hand cars. But the pawn *still* used to take them! And I'd have to go to the pawn and release them. And there was kids used to come down and rob the stuff off him and sell it back to him to get their picture money.

'We got *everything* in there. See, people'd maybe be wanting a cup of tea or the price of their dinner and they'd gather up rags in their house, sell furniture and everything to get money. And when people died they'd want the house cleared out, like furniture. We always had a horse and cart. We got antique stuff but in them days antiques wasn't that good (a business). At that time I used to break up brass beds. You wouldn't even get a fiver or three pounds — for a lovely brass bed. Ah, today you could get 500 quid for a brass bed. There was no money in them times. Ah, I often think back and say, "Jesus, if I had them now I'd be a *millionaire*. Today now even old postcards is valuable. Ah, and there were some *characters* around. There was a woman who would be out collecting stuff all day and when she'd be half jarred she'd be putting rubbish and everything on the scales. See, when bags of rags were brought in they were just weighed and paid for. Now there was this woman who was about twelve stone and her husband put her into the bale of rags and had it put on the scales and weighed. He said he come in from the dumps and had the bale of rags on a lorry. And he had his wife in one of the bales! Weighed her on the scale! We found out he was doing this.

'Lipman'd get a load of rags — old coats and trousers — and he used to employ women for tearing all the linings out. Places wouldn't take them with the linings in them. He was giving them four shillings a hundredweight for cleaning the linings out. They had knives for cutting and stones for sharpening them. A heap of rags could be ten or fifteen feet high and they'd be sitting up on the top. They'd start at the top because they'd be loose. To start at the bottom, then pull them out, would be too awkward. Then they'd clean them and pack them in bales. And there were women down there washing jars for him in the yard. He had a big metal boiler that was placed up on a block and you'd just heap the timber up underneath and light the fire and the women would just stand up on each side of it with brushes and there was a cage for the jars and bottles and they'd wash them. Even if they were working out there in the winter and there was snow it wasn't cold there. And the girls in his yard washing jars used to sing a song. It had a little few words but they'd repeat it all the time ... "Down in Harry Lipman's old yard, where the girls are working so hard, we don't give a damn, we get money for jam, down in Harry Lipman's old yard". They used to always repeat that.

'I'll tell you about Lipman. He always worked. Never had a holiday. He used to *work* the holidays. Now the Jews was supposed to be home on the holidays but he was at work with the gates shut ... working behind the doors. You'd get

141

people that'd talk bad about him. But he wasn't a moneylender. But if someone died he'd lend them the money to bury whoever died. And I could go into him and say I have a young one for Confirmation or Communion and he'd lend me the money. He was decent enough in that way. Some fellas that worked for him hated him ... the money was no good. And he was abrupt and he'd argue with you and get annoyed with you at times. But I understood him. He was an honest fella.

*One of Dublin's last "tuggers", commonly still seen along Meath Street in
the Liberties*

'In the long run I got the place off him. Now when a Jew retired or wanted to get out of it he was always supposed to go up to the synagogue on North Circular Road and put it for someone to get the business — see that another Jew gets it. But he just gave it to me. See, it never happened before that a Jew would give it to an ordinary Christian. The synagogue was angry but there was nothing they could do about it. He must have been about eighty. The rabbi came to his house and another (Jewish) scrap fella, but he says, "it's *my* place". And he gave it to *me*. When I took over the business I hadn't got the stores in it. He cleared it out. And I hadn't the money to buy the stuff. So I said to him, "will you lend me 500 quid to buy the stuff?". And he said to me, "look, when I started here I had nothing. I had to work meself up. You do the same or otherwise that place is no good to you". I had seven kids but I pawned everything in the house. Pawned all the furniture, all the clothes to get money. I had seven kids and it was hard for me even feeding the horse in the stable. And I worked meself up.

'When he was dying in the hospital I went up to see him. He was lying in the bed and he said to me, "listen here, Byrne, what are we going to do with all these beds?" They all had patients in them. Here he thought we were after *buying all these beds* in the ward ... and he wants to know where I'm going to put them and how I paid for them! I went up to see him this Sunday and he was just lying there, not talking or anything. I could only see two white balls in his eyes. His eyes had gone to the back of his head. And I said, "I have to go, I'll see you, I'm going off". And the funny part about it is that he waves to me like that ... but still he looked to me like he was unconscious with no eyes. He *knew* I was there. And I'd only gone down the stairs when he died. He was decent to me.

'I moved down here (North King Street) about twenty years ago. There's no rags or bottles in here now. It's brass and copper, old washbasins, toilets, prams and doors and that. I still struggle through life. But I reared seven children. As long as I'm able to live I don't mind. If you're happy in the old place it's all right.'

DENIS McCABE — "Rag and Bones" Collector, Age 76

From an early age he earned a living from the streets. At fourteen he began plying the tenement rows with his ass and cart selling coal blocks. Then he became a "rag and bones" man, rambling the roads with his pushcart offering delft for old rags. When plastics replaced bottles and the demand for second-hand clothing declined his peripatetic scavenging trade became obsolete. A hapless victim of modernisation, "Dinny" turned to the dole for subsistence. But he was getting too old for the roads anyway.

'I'm a Liberty boy, born in 1916 and reared on Ashe Street. Me father was a fruit dealer. He used to go around to private houses, carry a basket with an oval-shaped handle with a cloth covering the fruit. I come out of school when I was fourteen and I had an ass and cart. It was me mother's. Oh, he was a good ass. I used to go down on the North Wall and get a quarter ton of coal blocks. It was ten and sixpence. There was twenty-one dozen in a quarter of a ton and I sold them at eight pence a dozen. I'd start out at about eight in the morning. I'd go off Meath Street, Gray Street, up to Pimlico and then up to Marrowbone Lane, up to James' Street. All tenement houses. I had me own customers and I used to shout "coal blocks! coal blocks!" outside the old tenement houses. And people'd look out the window and say, "bring up half a dozen". The coal blocks was square and I used to carry a dozen on me arm. I'd finish up about two and then I went home to me mother and got a cup of tea and bread and butter.

'I sold the ass around 1941 when I joined the Irish army for seven years. When I come out I went out collecting rags and bottles and jam jars. Only had a hand car for that. It was a boxcar, two wheels. A Jewman, Harry Sive, used to lend them

Denis McCabe, one of the real "rag and bones" collectors from the Liberties

out where we sold our rags and bottles. He didn't charge us for the handcar cause we brought rags and bottles and jam jars in to him. He had dozens of fellas like me collecting for him. He paid you in cash every day. He was a good man. At Christmas time he'd give you a pound because you brought the stuff in the whole year for him. He's dead and gone now, but he was a multi-millionaire when he died. He was!

'I'd start off around Whitehall and then go up to Cabra. Oh, miles I'd be going. I'd buy delft, only cups and saucers, and it was white and I'd go around calling out "rags for delft! rags for delft!". I had the delft in a little wooden box in the handcar packed in hay so it wouldn't break. Now I'll tell you, I had to look at the rags first. If I thought they were valuable enough for a cup I'd give them a cup. Oh, there was some good clothes. Like a lady might say "there's a suit. Me husband died and it might suit you". I'd give her a couple of cups and saucers for it. Sometimes it'd fit me but more times it wouldn't. So I'd take it around to the Iveagh market and sell it. But the rags you took to the Jewman. Knitters and wools were the best to get. Men's jackets were called "cloth" and shirts were "wipers". He had women used to weigh the rags on scales. And Jewmen got women to cut out all the linings and collars and buttons and that'd be what they

Woman newspaper seller on Henry Street

called clean cloth. He'd make them into a bale and get five pounds for a half a hundredweight. The wipers was used for machinery work, you know, for wiping the hands. He'd sell them to factories.

'I collected stout bottles. I never went to the dumps. Got them from people's houses where they were clean. I'd take them back and sell them to the Jewman. You were paid a penny a bottle. He'd pile them up and any publican (who) wanted bottles he used to ring them up. And jam jars were a ha'penny or a penny for a large one. If they were dirty it didn't matter, he used to sell them to the jam factory. Oh, you'd put 'em on top of your load, on top of your rags. And I'd get behind me handcar and just pushed it on. Cobblestones was hard and maybe you'd have to go up a hill. Or maybe over a bridge. Going down you'd have to put the wheel into the curb to stop it. But I was happy as a lad when I got me load on.'

Chapter 5

Transport and Vehicles Men

JOHN REARDEN — Jarvey and Cabbie, Age 86

He was born in 1906 on Railway Street into a family of jarveys going back three generations. At seventeen years of age he took up the whip and handled horses and jaunting cars as well as any man. Business was booming at the docks, railway stations and with horse funerals. But coping with trams was a damned nuisance. As horses faded from the streets he switched to the newfangled motor cabs and worked up until 1981. After fifty-eight years on the streets "Johnny" is something of a legend in Dublin cabbie circles.

'My father was a jarvey, too, and back to me grandfather. I lived in Railway Street and we kept pigs and a cow with six horses. A jarvey was sort of a handed-down job if your father was in it. I started me apprenticeship driving an ass and cart lugging feed for the pigs. I was in school at the time. They allowed you to get a licence at seventeen. There was no test in regards to driving the horse but you had to go to Pearse Street Police Station to have a test to know the city. We didn't really have to study up because Dublin was a small place at that time. Oh, they'd only ask you about a half dozen places off the main streets. You had a licence for yourself and a licence for the vehicle. It cost a shilling for your driver's badge and a pound a year for the vehicle licence. The badge was a sort of aluminium and some were brass and had the crest of the British Crown on it. A man was supposed to wear that on his breast. The Carriage Office inspected jarveys on the hazard. They'd check the condition of the vehicle — see that it was clean and safe — and even the horse and harness. You wouldn't know they were coming. And if you weren't wearing your badge that was an offence. You'd be summoned and brought to court and it was a fine.

'The horse, he was *one of the family!* He was the main ingredient in the game and you had to look after him. And you'd talk to him. I think that's what made a good horseman, talking to the horse. Oh, there was a real relationship there. He'd be well fed and there were water troughs around the city then for horse cab drivers ... and any horses in the city. And the horses would smell them too! And you'd have to look after his feet in the summertime. You'd put manure on his feet for to cool the hoof. And brush him, keep him clean and healthy. You could get eight or ten years out of a horse in the city. Some men got their horses from Cooper's of Queen Street but my father believed in going to the fairs in the country and buying his own horses. If the horse was unbroken, wasn't used to the harness, you had to break him yourself and get him used to all the things. Like they'd shy away from the electric trams, especially when they'd give a flash.

'Men took pride in their vehicles. Oh, some of them were able to buy a better horse and rig. Oh, there was some fine vehicles. And you had silver-mounted harness and brass-mounted harness. At that time there was a hackney car, but they called it a side-car. And there were cabs like a carriage, a four-seater, and completely covered over. It was a four-wheeled vehicle with four passengers inside and the driver outside and carried heavy luggage on the roof. They were made by firms here in Dublin like Sanderson's of Dominick Street. I think they cost around one hundred pounds. In the early years the men liked the outside and preferred the hackney car but the ladies would sooner have the carriage. And horse vehicles had special candles — carriage candles — in a lamp. They were short but very thick. You just put your candle in the lamp and lit it and it wouldn't go out.

'It was up to yourself what you wore. Most wore a soft hat or a bowler hat and a tie. The tie wasn't compulsory but you had to keep yourself reasonably well dressed ... like the jacket I have on now. Out in the weather they nearly all wore a blue menton coat over their jacket and some had real oilskins. Side cars were open and we always carried rugs, heavy blankets. So passengers would be covered with a rug, but nothing overhead. And everybody had a whip. Most of the harness makers made whips. Just a piece of cane, a cane handle, with a piece of lash on it composed of leather strips. But there was some steel-lined whips. Whips was part of the equipment whether you used them or not. It was mostly for show.

'I started in 1923. When you got your licence you were appointed to a certain ground to work around where you lived. We had a hazard at the North Wall where the Holyhead boat come in and the Scotch boat. And you had the Northern Railway and all of O'Connell Street. The docks was busy in the mornings with the arrival of the cross-channel steamers. But there was enough jarveys ... *hundreds*. There wasn't many motor vehicles. And the taxis come on a little later. There wasn't a great rush of bicycles in the very early years but they came in afterward and it was like China! There was no traffic signals but the trams dictated it because they were in the centre of the road. And they were faster too. Oh, the streets were alive night and day. There was a lot of night life in Dublin with the theatres and cinemas. And we'd go to Donnybrook Fair or Strawberry Beds or Lucan. There was the Phoenix Park races and races at Baldoyle, Leopardstown. You might get twenty or thirty going out (together) and it was sort of an agreement that you wouldn't be passing one another ... but you'd see some of them doing it. I did trips twelve and thirteen miles out to the mountains up around Enniskerry. And I done the racing at Punchestown and that's about twenty-three miles out with the horse. It was good work for a horseman.

'Sometimes you'd get up to twenty horse vehicles on a funeral. It was the custom in them times that the remains would be brought down to where he worked and around his residence and then back to the cemetery. And it was a regular thing to stop at a public house. Oh, that was the custom to have a drink. It could be *hours* ... according to their financial position. And you'd be asked in with them. They'd buy the drink for you. Jarveys done their share of drinking. Some characters was known for their capacity to drink, others for to tell stories. The police could interfere with the jarvey if he'd been drinking and take him and the horse to the police station. It didn't happen often because the policeman didn't like handling the *horse*. And if he'd had too much to drink the horse would bring him home.

'The horses was starting to fall away and then the taxi came in the twenties. There was (at first) what we called private-hire taxis that could be hired from the garages. There was no opposition to that. Then this man Wilson from Clontarf brought in six of the old London taxis and used the horse hazards. Oh, the older men had a lot of opposition and wouldn't let them into the hazards. Horsemen kept them off as well as they could. You could fill it up cause it was only for a certain amount of vacancies. So the taxi man couldn't get in. Ah, there were some heavy words exchanged. But they didn't resort to violence. The older jarveys worried about it but the like of me, only starting, saw that there was a life with the taxi. I thought it was for me own benefit. But me father was working the horse till he died. Some of them did make the switch, but he couldn't. He *tried* it. He got into the car with me, got in behind the wheel, but that lasted just one day. He kept the horse to the 1950's.

'When I went to the taxi the same licence done me but you had to get a driver's licence. Just filled in the form — no driving test. My first taxi was an old Unic, a French car. I paid ninety quid for it. Carried four passengers inside sitting face to face. I had a crank and you had to get it going yourself. Oh, no self-starter in them times. You just got out and wound it up in front. You could set the trunk beside the driver. See, there was no door on the lefthand side. You got the weather! It had a half windscreen and no windscreen wipers. You'd get wet. You were driving faster against the elements and they came in. Some days you'd be sitting drenching wet. And no electric lights. There was two oil lamps and a tail light and an acetylene headlight you filled up with a mixture of carbide and water. And the tail lights worked with paraffin oil. And in the early days when you went into the country there was no petrol pumps. So you'd have to provide your own petrol. Cars had a running board and a square plate, a case, where the two-gallon tin sat. You got your petrol from the BP (British Petroleum) down at the docks or in garages. They had it in two-gallon tins that was sealed for two shillings. And when the motor cars come in they was rather mature people driving and there was a certain code in it. It was very nice to drive in that period because if you were in trouble and stuck for petrol or anything there was nobody that would pass you by.

'At the 1932 Congress people came in from all over the world. Oh, there was plenty of business. Then during the war there was no petrol and no private cars allowed. I got one gallon of petrol a day. You had to apply for coupons from the Department of Supply. And there was certain restrictions on you, like you couldn't go to a race meeting or sports meeting of any kind. So horses was revived. Some men drifted back to the horse and there was a lot of men that came into it with horses that was never in it before the war. They went all through the country trying to resurrect horse vehicles of all descriptions. Anything went!

'I retired at the end of 1981. I saw the end of one period and the start of another. It was in the blood ... with me father and his father before him. And I liked the open air, too. Oh, Dublin was more colourful with the horses. It was a romantic period. Oh, Dublin was a grand old spot at that time.'

MICKEY SHERIDAN — Jarvey, Age 68

When his father, one of Dublin's best-loved jarveys died and left behind a family of twelve, Mickey had to take over the job. Though he was only fourteen, authorities agreed to "fiddle the record", as he puts it, to get him a jarvey's licence under the required age. It made him the youngest jarvey in the city. He still becomes emotionally choked and teary-eyed when telling of how the old jarveys "adopted" him. He quickly became a tough horseman and during the horse revival of the war years held his own against the rough crowd of "bowsy" jarvey interlopers. He held on part-time into the 1960's, one of Dublin's last jarveys.

'Me father, me grandfather, me mother's people even, going way, way back, were jarveys. We kept sixteen horses and two yokes in a yard on St. Anthony's Lane. And we used to keep pigs as a sideline. I was reared in young and used to give me father a hand with the horse. The breeding is in you. And in me father's time a jarvey's son married a jarvey's daughter. The girl's father would give him a wedding present of a horse, hackney car and harness. That'd be all brand new. My father died in 1938 when I was fourteen and there was ten boys and two girls. Now you had to be sixteen to get a licence but me mother appealed for me in the Carriage Office on account of me being the old jarvey's son and they fiddled my certificate. And I was the youngest among them. You had to apply for a licence and have two householders go security for you and a publican or priest. The badge was a shilling a year and you used to hang it on the button of your coat. The licence, the plate, was twenty-one shillings and they'd inspect your yoke and horse harness. Very strict at that time.

'You had a side-car — a hack we called it — that's what you see in Killarney, a two-wheel yoke. They carried five passengers, two each side and one on the back dickey and yourself on the front. The hack car had no protection against the weather and I used to carry three rugs, one on each side and one for yourself. The rug that you'd be using used to go over the horse's back when you'd be standing. But the ones that you'd put on the passengers, they were fancy rugs. And you'd nearly have to guard them during the war because clothing was hard to be got and women at that time, if they seen a good rug they'd pinch it and get a coat made out of it. That *did* happen if you'd leave your horse standing somewhere. It was very hard to pack luggage on a hack car because there was no real place to put it. We used to have a net tied underneath the car and we'd shove the cases into that. And I'd strap cases to the back dickey rail. But some passengers had to carry the cases on their laps.

One of the "resurrected" jarveys now catering to tourists in St. Stephen's Green

'Our horses were three-quarter bloods. They were better horses. But they'd come in from the country and weren't used to the noise of Dublin. The man you'd be buying horses off of, one of his stable hands would drive him around town for a couple of days. They had a special yoke called a "brake" to put them into to drive him around to find out whether the horse was proper to drive in the city. Horses coming from the country, some would go mad with the noise. It took lots of them a long time to get used to it, particularly the trams because they were very noisy. A tram would come behind a horse that wouldn't be used to it and he'd take off. Oh, many a horse run away and broke up the yoke. You *had* to

151

have a whip because of the trams. Going down O'Connell Street you might be in between two trams and the old horse might shy and you'd give him a clap of the whip to straighten him up in the reins, to let him know that you were *driving* him. There used to be an old man used to make a holly handle whip, a cheap old whip from the holly tree. And he'd cut up an old felt hat to make the handle. That'd cost two and sixpence. And they made a Mullingar cane whip with a good lash and a bit of gut on the end for three and sixpence. But we used to buy the steel-lined whip made in England. They were like a fishing rod, tapered out with silver or brass and the lash made out of pigskin and a bit of catgut on the end ... beautiful. That would have cost about seven and sixpence in them years. And when you went in to buy a whip you brought the whip out into the street and held the whip by the handle and if the lash was heavier than the handle you didn't take that whip. You must have a whip that was balanced.

'Some jarveys used to wear top coats down to their ankles. Me father always had a frieze coat with a black velvet collar with ivory buttons, with a hard hat. I tried to keep myself very clean and it always paid off. Oh, you had to have a clean shirt and tie. And you could be summonsed if there was some horse manure on your boots. Oh, God, yes. And I'd two trilby hats, soft hats. I'd a spare in the boot for a wet night. And you had your Sunday gear. And when you'd be going to the races on a Saturday you'd wear your good gear cause you'd feel like you'd have to be as good as the race crowd because they were the moneyed people. Like we drove lords and ladies, that's no joke ... it was a romantic period. I drove Lord Longford when he'd come out of the Gate Theatre at night and he'd give you six bob for to take him home. And I used to go over to the old flower woman on O'Connell Street that used to stand on the Pillar and she used to give me one of those carnations and I'd put that in me coat. And at Christmas time I'd put a bit of holly in the top of the winkers on the horse and maybe stick a bit of holly in my coat or maybe on the rim of my hat.

'The location of your hazard — taximen calls them a rank now — was according to the neighbourhood you lived in. But when the war broke out it was a free-for-all! Because there wouldn't be enough yokes. Cars were off the road and taximen was under petrol rationing and banned from going to any race meetings or sports. So, some of the old hands (jarveys) come back, and their sons. But in the war years you'd meet the bowsies, the blaggards, the men only coming into the job. They were a rougher crowd and rougher on their horses than the old jarveys. They were a different grade. They hadn't got the same *class*. They gave decent jarveys a bad name. And you'd be coming from a race meeting and they'd want to pass you out. But a *decent* cab man would *never* pass another because that was making little of his horse if he had a fare in the cab.

'During the war years there'd be 500 to 600 jarveys. All types of horse-drawn vehicles started to come back onto the hazards. And you'd know where the good work was. You'd have to know all the times of the trains and you had the B&I boat every morning and two Scotch boats a week. Or you might chance the docks. All our hazards was took up between horse cabs and taxis. In the war years I seen maybe *seventy* yokes on the hazard. See, the cars was off the roads and there was that many people travelling. There was an awful lot of people coming in. Sure, half of Ireland was in England! And I found the North of Ireland people very generous. See, during the war years the North was getting bombed and the only place that was safe was to go to bed was here. And you were sure of a good feed here. And I got twelve pounds a day to go to Punchestown with the race crowd. Punchestown would be fifty miles there and back and taking four people. They were North of Ireland people and used to give me a fiver for myself. Twelve pounds a day! I think a man working at any manual work had two pounds a week at that time. During the good times we *did* earn money, but where it ever went to we don't know ... we drank it.

'I'll tell you, the jarveys did drink. Wherever there was a hazard there was a pub and the publicans got plenty of money. It was porter they drank at that time. Oh, sometimes the horse brought the jarveys home! There were some great old characters. And jarveys had nicknames like "Dicer" Lynch, "Gilly" Keogh, "Banker" Walsh, "Codger" Hynes, "Redpole" Walsh, "St. Anthony" Walsh and "Take Down the Bed". Some great old characters. This one old jarvey had his horse trained to lift his foreleg and shake hands with you. He used to have a few sweets in his pocket. And one old chap, Barney Doherty, had a big old heavy horse under the cab. It should have been under a *plough* and not under a cab. He wasn't a smart-going horse. So the fare he had in the cab put his head out and says, "hey, jarvey, will you put on the lashes? I can walk quicker!". And he'd three articles with him. So Barney opened the door and says, "if you can walk quicker there's the path ... and there's your three articles of luggage to keep you from breaking into a gallop!" Oh, they were characters.

'During the war we found it very hard to get frost nails for the horses cause they were from England. So we were buying size 8 nails and beating them out with a hammer until you put an edge on them and we'd put them on the horse if it was frosty. If a horse was going to fall he'd go down with you. Oh, God, they were great people and they'd run and help you. And everybody had a fire at that time and on hard, frosty winter mornings the people would bring out their ashbins and make a track for the breadman's horse, the milkman, the coal men, to give a bit of footing cause you had deliveries in the early morning. Anyway, one night I was in the bad weather outside the Gresham on O'Connell Street and there was about 350 people at this dance. And all the boys (jarveys) was outside beating out the nails on the tram tracks and putting the nails into the horses. And didn't Joe the night porter come over and he says, "you'll have to stop the noise, the guests in the hotel is ringing down to me". He got no satisfaction cause we kept working away. So he went for the police and the sergeant says, "this'll have to stop. There's a big lot of guests staying in the hotel". So there's an old jarvey, Mickey "Dribbles" we used to call him, and he says, "Sergeant, the people that's making the complaints is in their bed, but there's 350 in that dance and they have to go home to *their beds!*" They got back in their police car and drove off. They could say not more.

'Many jarveys went off the road before the war. Some jarveys died out. But in 1945, after the war, taxis started getting the petrol. It started to die out. Too much competition. But I still held onto the cab. I *loved* the job. And I stood on Amiens Street station for three days at twelve hours a day and never got a fare off it. That'll tell you how bad it went. I got married in 1945 and I had to sell me good mare to get a suit of clothes to get married in. I stopped full-time about 1947 but I stuck it out into the sixties only part-time.

'I'm very, very proud of being a jarvey. And I was often lying on the bed at night and your mind starts going back and I could shut me eyes and see all these old lads — I know they're all dead and gone — and before I go to sleep I say to myself, "I hope to God you'se are all in Heaven" and I say a few prayers in me own mind for them ... because they were *gentlemen* to me. I lost me father when I was fourteen and me mother died three years after me father, of a broken heart. Had one father and lost him when I was fourteen but I had a *hundred* after him because me father was very well liked and them men treated me as if I was their own son. They looked after me.'

PADDY LYNCH — Tram Driver, Age 80

From childhood his dream was to follow in his father's footsteps and become a tram driver. In the early 1930's he got his wish and became one of the best on the track. His face absolutely beams when recalling the exhilaration of racing along the Dalkey Road with the tram open full-throttle on the ninth notch. As he gushes, then you were really "flying". But coping with fog, frosty rails, scutting children and belligerent horsemen tried one's patience. Worst were the careless motorists who would sometimes dart recklessly between two approaching trams and risk being "sliced in two". Nonetheless, driving trams was the "happiest time of my life ... the end of an era".

'I was born in 1912 ... as Dublin as can be. My father was a tram driver. So was my wife's father. I *always* wanted to drive a tram. In fact, when I was little I went in and out from Inchicore with my mother on the tram to College Green. And I always went upstairs and would stand on the foot of the tram and imagine that I was driving. Ah, and I was always criticising the driver, the slow fella and fellas that jarred it. Oh, when I found out I could be a driver I was over the moon!

'I started at fourteen years of age on the trams as a ticket-picker. My father was five years dead. I had one brother and three sisters and I had to help out. I got fifteen shillings a week. Now Nelson's Pillar was the terminus for most of the trams in Dublin and it was a meeting point for *everybody*, young and old, lover and the whole lot ... "I'll meet you at the Pillar!". That was the meeting point, the focal point, of every blooming thing. So when the tram would come to the terminus I'd jump onto it and with your bare hands you'd pick up all the tickets that people'd throw around so it'd be cleaned up before the tram went back on its next journey.

'In the thirties when I started it wasn't a closed trade but they'd give preference to a tram driver's son. I had six weeks training to be a tram driver. Now driving a tram was much different to driving any other type of vehicle because you couldn't get out of anybody's way. You had to *read ahead,* what you're going into. Every situation. In a motor car you can brake real hard or swerve, but in a tram you can't. When I started, trams were the ones with four wheels. Double-deck trams, open on top, with two motors, one at the back and one front. See, the back was the same as the front. When the tram would come to the terminus the driver would change and go to the other end. There was no turn-tables. The compartment with the driver was completely sealed off by a sliding door and there was stairs going up behind him to the top. And you were standing driving the tram. You stood all day long, never sat down. And no heating at all and you'd be cold. We used to wear very narrow trousers, we called them "drainpipers", and a single-breasted jacket. And, oh, you had to go in polished up — shoes polished and straps and all your brass buttons shined.

'There was a motor and this big control handle with notches on it. You'd push it forward one notch and it'd click in same as you put your foot down on the accelerator on a motor car. Put it on the next notch and more speed comes in. Oh, there was an art in being able to judge how long to stay on each notch to get it to the top as fast as you could. It took skill because if you put it in too fast from one notch to another a big safety switch would go "bang" and the current cut off immediately. A good tram driver got his notches right. Otherwise he'd be roasted, especially in the summer. See, if you stayed too long on any of the notches you'd have resistance and pressure and it'd heat up. Now you could run the tram all day long on the fifth notch if you wanted to go that slow cause you were just driving on the one engine. Now when you went from the fifth to the sixth notch the *two* motors were driving it and you could go till you got to the top notch, the ninth. And there was a saying, when he was on the ninth notch "he was flying".

'Trams were always in the middle of the road and there were two tram lines. And in those days there were horses on the road and horse-drawn vehicles like the bread van and coal and turf and vegetables. Horses was one of the biggest problems. You'd know a horse that was flighty, you could see his ears wagging. We were trained to knock off the current so you can go by them. And there'd be plenty of arguments between the tram drivers and the men with horses, especially the coal men. The type of people they were, you know ... tough. Sometimes they'd leave their cart out where you couldn't get by and another tram would be catching up on you and you'd be delayed. They'd just dump it there and go in and get a pack of cigarettes or something.

'Oh, you couldn't take your eyes off the road. In frosty weather the tracks would be kind of frozen with frost early in the morning and you wouldn't have the stopping power and you'd slide. Very seldom a tram could get off the track under its own power but it could if there was something on the track like a big ball bearing or big bolt. It *did happen.* Now when you're stopping a tram you had to be careful. There was a handbrake mounted on the righthand side and it had a chain on the end of it and when you'd turn it it would tighten the chain and that pulled the brakes on to the brake wheel. You'd want to be strong ... the stronger you were, the more turns you'd get into it. If it was an emergency stop there's a pedal in front of you with this thing of sand and a pipe going down. A split second before you put on the brakes you'd get the sand out on the rail when you wanted to stop. And, of course, there was a cloud of dust goes up.

Horse traffic is still a common sight around vegetable markets

'There were accidents. You had to learn the different bell rules. One bell was to stop, two bells to go, three bells the tram was full and in case of an emergency there was four or more rings. Maybe a trolley coming off. If the trolley jumped off the wire it could do untold damage. This particular man was on top of the tram and the trolley came off the wire and hit him in the face and he got a disease and he got hundreds of pounds compensation. And one time there was a mother getting off with her parcels and the conductor gave the bells (to go) and they heard a child cry and the driver stopped. The child had crept under the tram. Killed. And children might get it into their head to do scutting. They'd do it when we'd be moving off, hold on to the back of the rail. And all around the front of the tram there was a big iron buffer and they used to sit on that, hang on to that. Oh, you'd have to stop immediately and hunt them off cause they'd get killed falling off. The hardest part of the job was lights at night time. Honest to God, you'd be more frightened going out at night. There was one bulb on the front of the tram but it wouldn't go any further than about ten or twelve feet. And we'd no wipers when there'd be wet on the window. We tried all sorts of things. Some people used to break a cigarette and rub the tobacco on the window to clear it. It worked ... for a while. And then some people used to slice a potato in two and rub the window with the potato. Oh, they'd bring one for that. Now another one is a little bit vulgar. Did you ever hear of goboil? It's an Irish name. Well, we'd do that (put some spit or saliva) on the glass.

'The tram I was on most of the time was to Dalkey, a luxury tram. Double-decked, covered-in trams and they had eight wheels instead of four. Luxury trams were lovely, with more upholstery on the seat. Oh, much smoother and double the speed. The four-wheel trams used to kind of sway and passengers could get sick on them. When the trams were full it was called a "swinger" because it'd swing or sway. But the luxury trams used to do up to forty-eight miles an hour and that was quick now for a tram. You'd get spells on the Dalkey Road, a straight stretch, on the ninth notch. Now on the Dalkey road parts used to come out real wide and then they'd come in narrow again. It used to confuse motorists very much and the new trams going so fast also used to disillusion them. They were so used to trams going so slow everywhere else they'd be misjudging and the next thing they'd get sandwiched in between trams going that way and the other way. There was only two or three feet between the trams. See, they'd be trying to overtake you and the trams would be going so quick ... and the motor cars used to be sliced in two. Ah, there was one there that I come across and there was people lying all over the place and blood everywhere. Now once I had to make an emergency stop. Now you had no driving mirrors on a tram, so you couldn't see what was coming behind you. But I had pretty good hearing and I heard this and I knew it was a motor car trying to overtake me. I heard him and I saw the other tram coming down and I went down on the sand and went down to the last on the brake and he *just got through by that!* Just missed. I nearly got sick.

'Oh, on a nice fine day you couldn't keep people off the top of the tram. It would be magnificent on the top. Dalkey was a beautiful place and you'd get parties of people. In those days you'd know nearly half the people on the tram and they'd say "good morning" to you. Very friendly. And passengers could carry a bicycle on the tram and the dealers on Moore Street, well, they'd come out to the seaside places with their baskets full of oranges and fruit to sell to the people on the strand. Ordinary big baskets with two handles and some of them had a small barrow with three wheels on it. They'd fit on the back of the tram. We always helped them on and off. Tram drivers were gentlemen, really gentlemen, compared to a lot of bus drivers. Because the bus drivers at that time thought they were God Almighty. Oh, they did. And very often they'd say nasty things to the people getting in and out. But tram drivers were *gentlemen*.

'Trams died away when the buses came on the roads. People liked them because they were quicker and much more convenient to their homes. People that heretofore had to walk for a distance to get the tram into town could walk out their door and get the bus. The time I was driving the tram was the happiest time I had in all my years. I was very attached to trams … it was the end of an era. I was fifty-one years in C.I.E., from fourteen years of age to sixty-five. When I was going out they gave me a bit of paper telling me that "no longer do we need your services … we thank you for your long and dutiful service". That was it. There's only one or two others of us tram drivers left.'

TOM REDMOND — Tram Driver, Age 77

Tom was the last tram driver in all Ireland. He commanded the famous Hill of Howth tram, one of the most popular features of Dublin life in the first half of this century. It was, he believed, the "best job in the whole, wide world". There seems no end to the tales he can recount from that civil, romantic age. He speaks with such description and passion that the listener can almost feel the gentle sway of the tram as it wends its way around the scenic hill. It was his ship and he was the captain. Thus, when the tram was terminated and he was demoted to city bus conductor he was emotionally devastated.

'I was the eldest of nine, born in 1915. My father knew the manager of the Great Northern Railway and sooner than having me running the roads at age fourteen he puts me onto the railway as a boy porter on Sutton Platform. Cleaning the platform, closing the doors of the trains. My wages was seven shillings a week and I worked fifty-four hours for that! I was taken on as an electrician's mate at sixteen. I was a few years at that and then I was transferred to Sutton tram depot. Now tram men were a sort of family knitted-in job, a closed shop. But I suggested, "train me to drive a tram". So I started to drive a tram at twelve on a Saturday morning. I got four hours training and on Monday I started off as a tram driver. That's true. Believe you me, I wasn't what you'd call confident in myself but I took it on. I had an old chap by the name of Bob Connor, he was the senior driver at the time. And old Bob, he was a grand old chap. So he gave me the controls and showed me what to do and what not to do and says, "I'll be behind your back and watching you".

'Now the Hill of Howth tram which I operated started in 1901. It was an open-topper. It left Sutton Station and you went right around the Hill of Howth to Howth Station, approximately five miles. Your running time was about twenty-three minutes because you were pulling against a terrible gradient. The tram (motor handle) had eight notches on it and if you were giving it more power too quick you'd blow the electric currents off. There was an art to that. And operating the hand brake was treacherous because there was a ratchet and you were pulling the handle clockwise and if that slipped it would knock you completely unconscious! Oh, it'd be about six or seven hundred pounds with the brake handle flying back and it'd knock your brains out. It happened to me a few times. You had to wear an old glove or a piece of sock and it'd give you a grip because the brake handle was copper. Our major problem was in the autumn when leaves would fall onto the track and the sap would stick to either the wheel or the brake shoe. The problem was your brakes were locked and you needed the good sense and knowledge to release your hand brake.

Tom Redmond, the last tram driver in Ireland

'We were a staffing of twelve men, six drivers and six conductors. Each driver had his own conductor and very rarely did we switch. Now you had to do eight hours without a stop. And I was standing all the time and exposed to the weather. You got no meal break at any time. Drivers' wives would have to bring you a few sandwiches and what we called a "tommie can" of tea, a small can that'd hold about a pint. And you'd be drinking out of the can and eating the sandwiches driving along. There was central heating in the tram and long seats on each side and people faced each other. Then on the upper deck in the open they were wooden seats you could shove forward or back. Your seating capacity was seventy-nine but I often had as much as 150 and 160 on it ... and I often saw 200 passengers. They'd be up around me ears and me neck and up and down the stairs and everywhere. You wouldn't ask them to get off. The old tram would take them and the bigger load she got the better she went, she was more steady.

'We knew our passengers so well. Everybody knew everybody and everybody knew everything *about* everybody. There were no secrets. See, the Great Northern Railway owned the trams and paid the staffing their wages, but we were moreless governed and controlled by the *residents* of the Hill of Howth. What they said was law to the railway. It was mainly what we called the gentry of this country — the Jameson's, the whiskey people, and Guinness's and all the various big people. They classified us and brought us to their level. There was no class distinction. They all had their cars, Rolls Royces and everything, but they travelled by *tram*. Conor Cruise O'Brien lived up here and took the tram and he christened us the "Black Gestapo" with our dark blue uniforms and polished shoes and polished buttons. And Mr. Jameson would get on the tram in the morning and say, "good morning, Redmond, there's a little power, Redmond, to keep her going until I'm coming home". And he'd hand you a bottle of whiskey. And coming home in the evening time he'd hand you *another one!*

'In my day you carried *everything* and *everybody* and you stopped *everywhere*. We took *pride* in it. We brought prams, bicycles, dogs, cats — you name it. We delivered their paper every morning on the lawn or gateway as we were going by. The conductor would be doing one side and I'd be doing the other. And in the wintertime if we didn't see light in your house when we were going by with the first tram at half past six either myself or my conductor would go over and kick your door down! So's we'd have you up and out of bed to pick you up going back. Oh, we done that. And the good lady of the house she'd say, "Tom, would you call to the druggist in Howth and collect a parcel there for me?". Or the butcher or the grocery. *We done all the shopping!* And we looked after their kiddies, we brought them to school, we lifted them. We were sort of nursemaid, delivery boys, you name it ... we were it. And during the last war when things were rationed there was a power station where the tram was depoted and we used to rob the coal in the bags and give it to the poor people, like maybe the lady going to work for some of the big people on the Hill. Oh, we done that.

'At Christmas the tram would be decorated with all the bunting and flowers and a Christmas tree in the centre down below and lights and everything was put on. And people would sing Christmas carols. A week before Christmas a bank manager and manageress would circularise all the residents of the Hill of Howth for the Christmas present for the drivers and conductors. That was routine. They would bring in the money to their bank and four days before Christmas each member of the staff would get his Christmas present from the residents. You got their names — who they were and who they *weren't* — but not the amount of cash. And it would be a very bad Christmas if we didn't get seventy or eighty pounds a man — the *whole staff.*

'In the summertime it was a *marvellous* job. You were out in the open air and the open country. The conductor, he'd be alert — in surveillance — in the danger of maybe a cow running across or maybe a horse after breaking out of a field. And you'd watch for sheep in the fields. Often we'd see a sheep maybe upside-down on his back laying in a ditch and we'd stop the tram and the two of us would go out and get him by the four legs to lift him up because he couldn't get out of it himself. Ah, we done all those things. But when it came to winter you were exposed to the bad weather. Where the driver was standing it was spitting rain or snow and it was all coming down your back. And in bad weather along Strand Road you were exposed to the sea and the sea wall. And in heavy tide you'd get a splash and it'd come in and you'd be drenched. Oh, you'd be floating.

'Now that electrical storm in 1949, My God, I won't forget that, believe you me. This particular Sunday afternoon a terrible electric storm come along. I had a full tram and as I gave the first notch to move off a sheet of lightening came along the trolley and glued me to the controller ... for a split second. I got the shock of me life. Oh, I thought it was my end, no doubt in the world about it. The passengers panicked with the lightening. All came below. Now I proceeded on because the last thing I should do was make panic. And as I was coming in there was a tram just ahead of me by about two hundred yards, going the same way as me. I can see it as clear today as I did then. He had just thrown his power off to cruise in and apply his brakes to stop and a flash of lightening came right along the trolley wire and cut the back completely out of the tram in front of me. Just cut the back *completely out of it*. Just the same as you got an acetylene burner and burned it right off. But there was no one injured.

'The 31st of May, 1959, was my last run. The trams came off on a Sunday night and the following morning we had to be transferred into Clontarf Bus Depot to become bus men. I was demoted from a tram driver to bus conductor when C.I.E. took over. To do city work on the buses. It was really dreadful. You were dealing with different types of people. I mean, you go from being a tram driver — where you were on the front, your own boss ... just the same as the captain of a ship — and then you have to go to the back of buses looking for fares. The people (on trams) *respected* you. Everyone was civil, everyone was social. Civility in our day cost nothing. That has *completely changed.*

'There were tears for the last old tram. The residents were very sad and the drivers and conductors were very sad. We had wedding parties and we used to bring thousands of courting couples out on the trams on weekends, particularly in the summertime, getting up on top of the tram to get the sun and sea breeze. It's *history gone*. A way of life. I'd be the happiest man in the world if I'd be in front of that tram again. I'm built into the history of it. Oh, there's no doubt about it, I was the last tram driver in Ireland. Definitely ... I'm the last link.'

GEORGE DORAN — Busman and Cabbie, Age 93

He is one of the true pioneers of Dublin's modern transport age. Born in 1898, he began his apprenticeship as a motor car mechanic at fourteen years of age, learning to drive the novel contraptions in Phoenix Park. At twenty-one he began driving one of the city's first privately-owned buses, known as a char-a-banc. Taking passengers for outings to Glendalough with solid rubber tyres on the bumpy, dusty roads was an adventurous excursion. And he had to navigate Dublin's streets dodging the notorious renegade "pirate" buses that darted dangerously in and out of traffic. In 1925 he switched to motor taxis and stayed behind the wheel until 1977. He is proud that his son and grandson have taken up the job after him.

'The school I went to was St. Gabriel's and at fourteen years of age you were *out*. It was a Friday and I come home and me father says, "you're going to work on Monday, going to serve your time as an apprentice mechanic". I was an apprentice mechanic at Keaton's of Abbey Street for the old-time motor cars — Humbers and Model-T's. You had to do seven years. In I went and got nothing me first year. No money, no wages. Second year I got a shilling a week. After we done a job on a car we'd take it out of our garage up to the park (Phoenix) to test it. The mechanics always put me behind the wheel. That's how I learned to drive. There was nothing there, only horses, and twenty miles an hour was your speed limit. Then the Rebellion broke out in Abbey Street in 1916 and the place was blew down. Burned down. So then I got a job at a private car hire driving around to different race meetings. If you wanted to hire a car for a day or a week you'd just ring up. Hackney cars they were called … hacks. There was no metres on them, they were private. No motor taxis on the roads then, just horses and trams. No buses even. So I done four years of that.

'In 1921 when the Tans was here I was a hostage. I was walking down O'Connell Street, passing the Gresham, and four of them come out, Tans, and says, "c'mon, get in there", with a gun. I got into the car and this fella had this (revolver) at me head. I was frightened. Out at the Baldoyle races I was walked around with them, between two of them at the front and two at the back. They said, "you *stay with us* — anything happens to us will happen to you". They did that to save themselves. Oh, that was regular. If anything happened to them I was gone! Everyone was looking at me. They knew what I was. And they'd go around making bets and have a drink. After it was over back to the Gresham and they said, "come in and have a drink" and I said, "I don't drink". I had a lemonade, that's all. And then they said, "go and have a f— good day for yourself" and they give me a pound. After that I met a few of me pals and we *drank* the pound!

'When I was twenty-one I went on char-a-banc work. That was a single-decker bus, an open bus, with no roof. One man owned it. No top, but if it rained you could pull up the hood. There was about twenty-five or thirty of them char-a-bancs around Dublin then. They were Leylands and they were good. Had four cylinders and up to forty horsepower. And solid rubber tyres. Ah, they'd last a long time. No punctures but you'd get all the bad bumps. Oh, the roads were very bad. Bad bumps and cobblestones and potholes everywhere. And, ah, you'd *smother* in dust on a fine day. Years ago if you just went up to the Phoenix Park your car would be white from all the dust. Even here in Dublin there used to be watering cars going around keeping down the dust, the horse pulling the water car and spraying out the water. It was that dusty. The Corporation did that. There was a horse cart and a man sitting up on it and he'd put on the thing and it'd spray out like a watering can to keep the dust down on O'Connell Street. And children'd take off their shoes and stockings and run behind it in their bare feet.

'We used to go on a day's outing. Go to Glendalough on a Sunday. They paid me fifteen shillings for the day. They'd ramble around the lakes and had their lunch. Oh, they'd be singing and dancing … a great outing. You started out around eleven and fifteen miles an hour, that's all you were allowed. And a char-a-banc, it had no window wipers. You used to have to do it with your driving hand. You could use a raw potato on the outside of the glass. And you had a horn with a rubber end and it was compulsory to blow it coming to a crossroads. And there was a code that we'd never pass one another. You always carried tools with you and sparking plugs. And always a fanbelt. Them big tanks at that time took about eight gallons of water but she boiled up like hell. They'd just get out and have a bit of a sing-song and bit of a dance. Coming home we'd always stop in Bray to get a drink. You'd be there until may three in the morning. Oh, you'd get as much drink as you wanted. And tipping, they used to go around with a cap and maybe get thirty bob at the end of the day. I was driving the char-a-banc for four years and enjoyed every bit of it.

'Then I went to driving taxis in 1925. I broke in first in O'Connell Street. There was no driving exam but you had to get a badge from the police. You had to get two households to sign for you and a letter from your parish priest. And if you had been up in court for breaking a window or mitching or anything when you were young you got no licence — now *anyone* can walk in and get a licence. The police ran it and you'd have an inspection every year. Inspected your car mechanically and everything else. Oh, yes, if you had a dirty car you'd get a summons. We wore a suit and you must have a collar and tie, that was compulsory. And the police, they'd check your shoes and if you weren't shaved they'd tell you to go and shave. Back then there were pubs by the hazards and we'd go in and have a drink and chat. And there was an awful lot of nicknames. "Eye-opener" was one. "Show me the ropes" was another. And "The Mystery Man" and "Johnny Growing Pains" and "Snowy" and "Raffles" and "The Dummy" and "Follow Me Tail Lights". And "Screw me down" … see, he'd be out late and he'd be in the cab like that (laying down), like he was dead or something, like he was in a coffin. And I was known as "The Devil".

'Cars had cranks and you had to swing them. Mostly forty horsepower with six cylinders and about twelve miles a gallon. They had a roof rail for the big old American trunks. You had the Unic and the Byrdmore, Daimler, Humber, the Buicks, Dodge, Chrysler. And I always carried a couple of tins of petrol on the running board and a spare wheel. And a two-gallon tin of water in case she'd boil up. The first car I drove was a French car, a Chadron. No gates and acetylene and oil lamps. The tail lamps and two side lamps was paraffin oil. On the acetylene lamps you used carbide and a little tank and you turned on the water dripping in and then the gas would come through the tubes. The more water you gave it the more gas you got and a big blaze would come up. But you'd only need a glimmer. And when you were going along if you hit a heavy bump it'd go out. Then get out, light a match, and light it again.

'Now I once had an old Dodge I bought and there was a radio in it and I'm going from Amiens Street to Kingsbridge and I had it switched on nice and low. It was around the thirties and I think only another two cars had radios in them. And your man was sitting in the back and the partition was open and they were playing all old ballads. And when he was paying me he says, "I'd like to bring you down to the country for a hooley some night, you're a great old ballad singer … where'd you learn all them old ballads?" He thought *I* was singing them! I said nothing. I couldn't believe it. "Oh, yes", he said, "I'd love to have you down there to sing them old ballads".

'In them days there was no traffic signals and you had guards on point duty. But then at six in the evening they finished and then you just took your chance and blew your horn. And at that time the Independent buses, the "pirate" buses, used to go around to all different routes. They were privately owned. It was only a one-man bus and you'd pay the driver. They were twenty-two seaters. Oh, they could go anywhere they liked. They weren't confined to the one route — a free-for-all! There was no bus stops, anybody could just put up their hand and stop you anywhere. They had different names like the Silver Queen and the Silver King, the Pilot Bus, the Savoy, the Contemptibles. Blue and white and red and grey, all different colours. They'd cut one another's throat. They'd make out a route and maybe another fella'd come on it. So they just got away quick on it and got back. They were trying to get a crowd in and get away and then take a short cut back to beat him to that place to start off again. Oh, they'd cut one another's throat they would.

'When the motor cars come out the horse men felt very sick about it, especially the old horse cab men. They didn't like us pulling onto a hazard. Tried to keep us out. They'd put the amount of horses (allowed) on the hazard, like when it was a eight-horse hazard on the street. Well, when there was eight horses cars couldn't pull onto it. Sometimes there was rows. Then they started to learn how to drive and they started to buy taxis. They'd switch over. Like on O'Connell Street we were mixing with the jarveys and by degrees you could see them fading away. But some of the jarveys couldn't take up taxis. Just couldn't take it up. Their heart wasn't in it ... no, it was with the horse. One fella, when he was in a motor car learning to drive he'd be saying, "c'mon ... yup, yup! ... whoa! whoa!". Oh, it was no use with him.

Second-hand furniture being delivered to old Iveagh Market for re-sale

'I was on Amiens Street for fifty-two years and the trains then was very good coming down from the North. And it used to be great going down to the docks in the morning with the B&I boat. And the big hotels then were the Gresham and the Shelbourne, the Ivanhoe, the Royal Hibernian, the Standard and Jury's. Horse Show week was the best. You had people coming in by boat from everywhere. Hotels would be booked out and you got them sight-seeing around the city. And the 1932 Congress, that was a great time. But in the war years it was a gallon a day (allowance) and you done about twelve miles a gallon and you were finished. I used to draw seven gallons (weekly) and work two nights or two days with it. The regular price was five shillings. But you could get more on the black market — a pound a gallon. Certain garages that you knew had it and they'd give you two gallons for two quid. When I first started in Keaton's petrol was eleven pence a gallon and sixpence for a pint of Castrol oil!

'I retired in 1977. I got to know the public and I never had a row with a fare. My taxi badge — number 126 — when I was handing it in the sergeant says, "keep it, George, for a souvenir". Well, me eldest son has been at it for thirty years and now his eldest son is at it and when he started taxi work I got me badge transferred to him. So now he has my badge.'

HENRY "GINGER" KELLY — Bike and Car Parker, Age 80

Car parkers on the northside, themselves in their sixties, advise that if
you want to talk to a real "old timer" you should seek out "Ginger" Kelly
who can be found most days at the Parnell Lounge. Still tough and
crusty, he is a survivor — both of Dunkirk and the streets of Dublin.
After starting out in 1927 parking crank-type cars in front of Wynn's
Hotel on Abbey Street he claimed a prize pitch in front of the posh
Gresham Hotel on O'Connell Street. He rightfully calls himself one of the
"pioneers of the early motor car age" in Dublin.

'I was born in 1910 on Cook's Street. Me father went away in the First World War
and then was a bit of a carpenter. Me mother died when I was eight years old
and I had one brother and one sister. My aunt couldn't keep us cause she was
married with a house full of kids and she put us into a convent. When I come
out of the convent I went into another place called Artane run by the Christian
Brothers. Then when I was sixteen I was sold to a farmer for two bob a week
down in Roscommon. Rough, rough ... he used to kick me and belt me and I run
away from him. Come up to Dublin and I hadn't a crust of bread and I had to
mind bikes and cars. Oh, and in the last war I was chased out of Dunkirk by
Hitler. Now I'll tell you the whole story.

'I started minding bikes and cars at Wynn's Hotel on Abbey Street in 1927 for
tuppence and thruppence. They'd give me anything ... apples, oranges, maybe a
packet of fags. Anyone could mind bicycles, just an ordinary fella looking for a
living. Bicycles used to be parked all in the middle of Abbey Street and
O'Connell Street and ordinary blokes minding them. It used to be packed. You
could watch forty or fifty bikes. Just stick a ticket on the handle bar or saddle and
give them the original. If one was stolen you'd have to put up with the
consequences. Oh, the police would be on you. And if a bike was left you had to
take it home. There was three of us on Abbey Street, just looking for a living.
Standing there maybe for six or seven or eight hours a day for four bob in
copper.

'Now when I started minding cars over at the Gresham you had to be made
"official". Had to go over to the Commissioner (Police) at Dublin Castle or
College Green Police Station and he gave you a badge and a licence and then no
one could touch you. There was only about twenty-five of us all over Dublin ...
"official". On O'Connell Street there was seven or eight of us out. They had their
own pitches. Oh, O'Connell Street used to be black with cars. I worked in front
of the Gresham and it used to be *packed* in the middle of the road. I had me cap
and badge and a badge on me arm. Ah, it made a good living, that pitch. I
worked evenings from about four to eleven and there'd be night balls and horse
show balls and all the posh ladies in their gowns out till maybe three in the

morning. Up at the Gresham I had de Valera and Jim Larkin, the great union man, and Gene Autry. We'd see that they were safe in and safe out. Walk all up and down and watch the cars, look after them. They all knew me as "Ginger".

'When I started all the motor cars had a handle. You'd have to swing it and there's a back-kick with the big brass handle ... big bull-nosed Armstrongs and

Rough and ready Henry "Ginger" Kelly, one of Dublin's pioneer bicycle and car parkers

Model-T Fords. Sometimes you'd get a rough looking bloke and he'd swing it himself. But nine times out of ten you'd have to swing it. The men were generally very sedate and delicate and if you cranked it for them you'd be lucky if you got tuppence. Women drove cars very little back then, very little. As a matter of fact, when I was at Wynn's if I seen three a week ... and they was all *ladies*. And hail, rain, snow in winter, it didn't matter — there was always cars. Now you'd sometimes get a bit of jealousy. See, it was "dog 'et dog", that's what went on. There'd be a fight. Now I'll give you an idea. Back at Wynn's Hotel if a well-off man come in and he'd give you a half crown, well, there was three men working with me and as soon as you'd see him coming in they'd try to claim him. And there'd be a boxing. At that time I used to go home with about four or five shillings in copper and it got us stew for the seven kids. Christmas time people would open up a bit more. Instead of thruppence they'd give you maybe two bob. And then in the Eucharistic Congress of 1932 I made a bloody fortune! Dark Bishops, Chinese Bishops, visitors from all over the place and all big posh American cars. They come from everywhere — bishops and priests and clergymen, nuns, everyone. Oh, for God's sake, man, you never *seen* such style! I got a pound off a foreign priest.

'So I was out on O'Connell Street and all I'd get was four or five shillings a day for seven kids and so my wife says to me, "you're going to join the army". Fourteen shillings a week to go to war and I nearly *got killed!* I went to Belfast and joined up, was dressed out, sworn in, and shipped over to France. Hitler was coming and we had to be fast. We arrived in Le Havre and went up to Belgium riding in cattle trucks. Full marching orders and nothing, only a tin of salty sausages and a tin of dog biscuits. True as God! And you know the water that comes out the side of the train, the pipe, we were making tea with that. A dispatcher pulls in on a motor bike and says Hitler is about three miles away with about 500 tanks ... *back on the cattle trucks* and all the way to Dunkirk this time. Ah, for God's sake, there was chaos. About a quarter of a million on the beach — British, French, Poles. No rifles, no uniforms, in their bare feet some of them. And these bombers coming over every half hour blasting Dunkirk. The Gerries are coming over in the planes so low with their goggles looking out at me ... laughing. Honest to God. I was scared ... I'm no hero. And refugees on the road — women and children — and he mows them all down. And we had to bury the lot of them ... kids, girls and boys, twelve, fourteen. Eighty, ninety or 150 in a grave. An old blanket around them and slop them in, a few prayers, and the bulldozer covers them over. Ah, but what could you do? War is a cruel thing ... a very cruel thing.

'Anyway, we got back over to Ramsgate and the English people were all waiting there with tea and sandwiches and cigarettes. Ah, fair play to them. Fifteen of my company was all I could see come back — out of eighty-seven. Anyway, I got a pension out of it. Fourteen pounds a week. And it's all changed now. Today parkers are getting a pound and two a car. And I was getting tuppence and apples and oranges! On a match day they get forty-fifty quid and off to a pub as soon as the people go into the match. We wouldn't walk off. No way. Minding cars you had to be conscientious. And civility and sociability I always used and it got me through life. I *worked me heart out*, believe me I did. And got very little thanks for it. But honest work and I tried to please. We led the way ... the early pioneers of the motor car. There's not many of us left.'

CHARLIE DILLON — Bike and Car Parker, Age 72

Nearly sixty years ago he began helping his father park bikes at Dollymount. A few years later he staked out his own pitch on O'Connell Street where he minded Model-T Fords. On more than one occasion he had to engage in fisticuffs to hold his turf. In the 1940's he was one of the "official" members of the Car Parker Attendants' Union. Today on match Sundays he can still be found at Mountjoy Square proudly wearing his old "M.C.A." cap badge from an earlier era and skilfully guiding cars to safe haven.

'Oh, I seen the street life. I'm fifty-seven years at it. My father used to drive a horse and lorry but work was slack and he was unemployed and then he started going to the matches parking bikes. I was about ten and I used to go along with him. I remember the first match was in Dollymount between the Bohemians and Shamrock Rovers. When I was about eighteen there was a big match this Sunday at Dollymount and I went up and made a pitch there. I asked a woman at the house, "can I park the bikes along the railings?". If I got permission I'd put them up against the railing three deep. Or if the house might say "no", well, I could put them on the road cause at that time there was no cars to bother you.

'I was nearly all bicycles at that time. Ah, *thousands* of bikes. You couldn't cross the road with the bicycles. At a Cup Final match you had hundreds of bikes and it was threepence a bike, three old pennies. Now threepence a bike, that was *great* money at that time — it was only seven pence a pint! And some of them might throw you sixpence, say, if their team won ... "here's a shilling". See, a person would come in and I'd mark the bike with chalk, the number on the saddle. And you had a double ticket and you'd stick one into the handlebars and give one to the person. See, in case it was raining the number would sometimes get washed off the saddle and you wouldn't know whose bike it is, but the ticket would stay on. But with the rain even the ticket could double up and the number fade off it. Then you'd have to just say, "pick out your own bike". There was some confusion, all right. And if a man didn't come back I'd have to take his bike to the police station. Bring them down and hand them to the police. And in them years there was so many bikes getting robbed the police would go around to the football matches and we'd all the bikes parked there and they'd look at the numbers. See, bicycles had registration numbers under the frame where the saddle was. They had the missing bike's numbers on their book and they'd say to me, "don't say anything to this fella coming down".

'If there was a match on and you weren't there (early) someone would be in quick and they'd say, "you weren't here and I'm taking it over". And there'd be a fistfight. Oh, you had to hold your pitch. I seen a row down alongside Lansdowne Road, two brothers against three other fellas. I had to fight three fellas. I was in a row with one fella trying to take my pitch and so I fought him around the back lane and I busted his two eyes and he went off to get the policeman. And when the police came they said (to him) "move on", they moved him away, cause they knew I was there. Or a policeman would say, "fix it up between yourselves".

'Then I done the middle of O'Connell Street where there used to be the Metropole. The horse cabs and side cars used to park in the middle of the road. Oh, but you couldn't cross the road with the bicycles … it was as disaster. And then there was no traffic lights at all, it was "go" all the time. You nearly had to walk from one end of O'Connell Street down to the other to cross over where you'd get a safer place to cross. You'd put up your hands and they'd stop. Oh, bikes in front of the Gresham and the pictures, the Savoy and the Carleton. With the cinema crowd you'd be there till half-ten or eleven at night. And on a Sunday I used to be at Croke Park. I could get fifty or sixty bikes in a laneway or up at the Ballybough end.

'I started doing cars when the bikes was slackening off. That was after the Congress (1932). First I did cars at Dollymount and on Lansdowne Road at the rugby matches and at the Horse Show and the Spring Show. Then I went to get a pitch on O'Connell Street. Now on O'Connell Street there was Mr. Crosby and his two sons, Mixter and Smokey, and a son-in-law there too. See, there was nicknames like "Battler" McCann and "Smokey" Crosby and "Kit" Crosby and a fella called "Bullhead". Now the Crosby's held the pitch from the Pillar up to Clery's. Oh, no one could get near them or there'd be a row, a digging match. Mr. Crosby, he might slip off for a drink and his wife used to come down and stand there with a shawl on her parking. Well, I went over to Inspector McDermott to get a pitch in the middle of O'Connell Street. I got a licence and a badge and then you were the "official" man. You had a cap badge with "M.C.A." — Motor Car Attendant — and I used to have the hand band, a brass badge with a strap on it, just put it on your arm there. You had to get your own cap. We used to go to the bus station and get an old cap. And we used to have a green band around the cap. You were "official"! So Mr. Crosby says, "you take half that pitch". We divided it between us. So me wife would bring me down a can of tea and a few sandwiches and you'd be out in the weather. Wintertime was hard. You'd wear an oil skin cloak, a cape, and pull-ups and big rubber boots and big woolly gloves and a rain hat.

'Now there was a union. Mr. Crosby and "Battler" McCann formed a union. They wanted a union cause of other men coming in. See, you'd have all casual parkers coming up near your pitch. And they'd get a few bob. They just had an ordinary cap, no badges. So Inspector McDermott said, "I'll give you permission to form a union". So parkers paid a shilling a week to Crosby and McCann and they gave you a union card. There'd only be about twenty or thirty of us union men. And if

Seventy-two year old car parker Charlie Dillon, still at work around Mountjoy Square

there was a detail going on, like the R.D.S., Inspector McDermott would give them a police list of the names of whoever (parkers) was going out on it.

'People with cars then, you called them a "gentleman". Cause at that time it was great to have a car. They'd cost two or three hundred pounds, a lot of money. And if you seen a *good* car — three or four hundred pounds — you'd say, "oh, that's Lord so-and-so". You had to let your customers know how clean you are, especially on O'Connell Street when the people would all be going to the cinema and they'd be all made up themselves. Cars then all had a crank handle on the front. You had to choke it and crank it. Ah, that was terrible hard. And you might have to give your man a push to get going. And you'd have to take what they'd give you. Tuppence or thruppence. Some of them were respectful. Ah, from some you'd get a half a crown or two shillings. Once I got a pound note! Got it off a publican.

'Now where I was on Sunday (Mountjoy Square), I'm there for the past thirty years. There wasn't many cars coming from the country at that time to Croke Park. They used to all come by train. I started there with only about ten cars and then it was increasing every match day. Country people are better … the Wexford people, Tipperary, Kilkenny and Offaly people. Nowadays you'll get a pound off the country people, all right, but from a Dublin person you're lucky to get fifty pence. Oh, I respected me clients, the people that'd come to me. I'd look after their property, stayed till the end of the match. And they'd know that. I have a great reputation up there. Oh, everybody around the whole square knows me.'

FRANKIE FARRELLY — Car Parker, Age 62

Unlike the "official" union men, Frankie was a "bluffer", a runner-in car parker. He took his chances and punched it out when necessary. He went on to win a coveted pitch on St. Stephen's Green directly in front of the Shelbourne Hotel. Dealing with upper-crust society, he is among the top-echelon of the car parking pack. Dressed respectably in coat and tie, he has a gift for witty chat and crack — good for tips. In recent years a few bold young intruders have invaded his turf but he has courageously held his ground.

'I started when I was about twenty. At that time there was official car parkers. They used to belong to a union and had to have badges. But I was a "bluffer", that's unofficial. But I'd have me cap and put a green ribbon on it, to let people see that you're a car parker. I never worked Croke Park because there's a gang there and it was mostly inherited in the family going back to the bike days. See, a son, he'd be taking over his father's pitch. I started out at the old Jury's Hotel, for maybe six years. There was many a scrap over pitches. Oh, I was in a couple meself. It would be over tips and "this is *my* pitch — buzz off!" and such. It'd be a couple of digs but you wouldn't do any harm. And it'd be all forgotten. But if a man was tough they wouldn't touch him at all, wouldn't get near him for their life. Ah, but car parkers stuck together. We were all friends and happy and singing a song, having a few old pints. Sometimes car parkers get barred from pubs cause some are mouthy and shouty. But all the old car parkers used to go into Uncle Joe O'Dwyer's Pub on Leeson Street. We were always allowed in there to have a few old jars. Oh, there was some big drinkers ... most are now dead, or oldy or mouldy.

'Stephen's Green is the best pitch, all right. There's great style there at the Shelbourne. That's my pitch since 1953. I'm the senior there now. They *love* the car parkers there. It's the way you speak to people — "Yes, Sir. Thank you, Sir". It means a lot, you know? Manners. And people love an old joke. You can get rich people and you'll crack an old joke and they'll break their heart laughing and that puts them in good form. Cause some come in so serious, you know. Some aren't happy anyway. All the people that comes in knows me, and I mean hundreds and hundreds. Oh, I'm very popular, well liked. Even the doorman (Shelbourne Head Porter), Mr. Dixon, he gives me a tip every weekend. He might give you a fiver. And the English are good tippers. The biggest tip I ever got was from a Chinese lad. He gave me twenty pounds and I says to him, "Sir, that's too much money". "No, it's not too much money", says he, "cause I come up the *hard way*, like you". That was very nice of him, wasn't it? A twenty pound note. He *understood* me.

'I put me heart into this. And it's not for the sake of their money. The thing is that they *like you*. If you respect them, they'll respect you. They're decent people. Ah, people even buy me pints. At the age I am now I'm the senior there and that's supposed to be my pitch. But there's two rowdies on it now and they want every bob and that's upsetting me. They're younger men. Two raw individuals that shouldn't be there at all and they get ratty. If they weren't there things would be more happier.'

HUGH MAGUIRE — Bus Conductor, Age 64

He started out at fourteen years of age as a ticket picker on the trams at Nelson's Pillar. At seventeen he graduated to C.I.E. messenger boy wheeling handcarts of correspondence down O'Connell Street. By the 1940's he was a full-fledged conductor on one of the old fifty-five seater double-decker buses. In his day the conductor was undisputed boss of the bus with full responsibility for handling passengers. Much of his life was spent standing on the open rear platform supervising loading and unloading, as mischievous lads would pelt him with snowballs. Innocent pranks by today's standards.

'I started off in 1942 on the trams as what they call a ticket boy. I was fourteen. I'd get onto the tram at Nelson's Pillar and pick up all the tickets off the floor. I had to do an examination and they had very high standards in those days because there was very little employment. *Gross* unemployment at that time sticks in my mind. A senior ticket boy brought you out and told you what to do. I had a uniform as a junior ticket boy and I was very proud that I had a job, very proud. And I remember distinctly walking down the road on which I lived and the woman that had two sons my age *pointing me out* to her sons as an example. *"There's* a fella with a job ... how well you couldn't go out and get a job?". My wages were eleven shillings and sixpence. Nine shillings went to my mother and father and two and sixpence for myself.

'I spent four years in that job and then a job as messenger became vacant on Aston Quay. C.I.E. had depots around the country and on the buses they'd bring in correspondence and money enclosed in black boxes. When they arrived in Dublin it was my job to bring those black boxes up to the head office. I did this when I was seventeen. I had a little handcart and I wheeled it up along O'Connell Street every morning at nine. The black boxes were metal, about eighteen inches long by about twelve inches wide. There would be an accumulation and I'd carry up to twenty on the little handcart. Oh, it would be heavy. Then at nineteen I became eligible to apply for the job as conductor. I was sent to work on the Dalkey-Dublin trams for eighteen months. Now I enjoyed the job of conductor but I lived in Whitehall and had to bicycle in at five in the morning. Oh, you'd be riding in the darkness. If you were late you'd be sent home and lose a day's pay. I was *so tired* at the end of every day's work.

'Back then very few people had their own car and public transport — trams and buses — was *essential*. And there was a lot of horse-drawn traffic and that was a problem. If there was a horse and cart in front of you you had to wait until he got out of the way. Then during the Emergency there was a big influx of people riding bicycles. It was a cheaper form of transport. An awful lot of people resurrected old bikes. There weren't many traffic lights at that time and the bikes created a terrible hazard, particularly in the winter time. The buses and everything else would all come up to the traffic light and be stopped there waiting for the lights to change and all the bicycles would go up in the *front* of them. And if the roads were slippery in the winter time ... "zoom"! ... they'd be going in all directions!

'In 1949 when the trams came off Dalkey they put people that were working on the trams on the buses. Many of them didn't like that ... it was an emotional break. Cause they'd spent their whole life with the trams, you see. I was transferred to the city bus services. They had a double-decker bus at that time known as the "R" Series. It was a fifty-five seater and was much more compact than the present double-decker that holds seventy-four. This was smaller, had steeper stairs to go up, and they were faster. They weren't heated and the platform on the rear was open. See, they got on and off at the back. The conductor had to stand at the back and in the winter time the rain would be belting in on top of you and the snow. And kids would be throwing snowballs at you because you had to stand there, you know.

'You went around the bus to collect fares and supervise the loading. Our shoes were polished and you were shaved and a clean shirt. We were pretty smart at collecting our fares. We had a bell punch in those days, a little silver square thing with an aperture in the top for putting in the ticket. You pulled a little thing and the bell rang and there was a hole in the ticket at the stage at which the person got on. And there was a great relationship between conductors and passengers, a great *respect* built up. And if a man was sitting down and an old lady got on he would stand up straight away and give her his seat. Now on Sunday mornings they'd put on early Mass buses. I worked the Mass bus in Clontarf. Now breakfast in Dublin on a Sunday morning is a big thing and in every area where a Mass bus operated there was always a lady who'd come out for the bus crew with tea in a can and maybe some sausages on bread as well. I'm delighted that I was alive at the time ... a *great amount* of respect.

'There was a manufactured difference in wage between drivers and conductors. Drivers got a shilling more per week. It was meant to divide the loyalties of the men if it came to a situation where everybody should vote. There was absolutely nothing to *merit* that shilling. It caused some resentment. The conductor had *more* responsibility for safety on the bus, to see that the bus was started and stopped at the proper signal. You have one bell to the driver to stop and two bells to go. The conductor was only allowed to give the signal from downstairs because upstairs he couldn't see that the platform was clear. You were always there to hit the bell. But there were certain conductors who were so slow collecting the fares that the driver would wait a reasonable length of time, look in his mirror, decide he wasn't going to get a bell, and he'd move off. Which was against the regulations.

'There was a pub in Parnell Street called the Shakespeare that was a known pub for transport men. There was another one on Gardiner Street called the Rat Hut that was a notorious place for busmen. Busmen weren't big drinkers — they couldn't *afford* to be. What really appealed to me was at night time when we'd tell the stories of humorous things that happened during the day. Like the time we were handicapped with fog at Phoenix Park and there was an old driver that many people said had lost his birth certificate. "Sherlock Holmes" we used to call him — Holmes was his name. I was working with him this particular day and the fog got very bad and I decided that I'd walk in front of the bus waving my handkerchief to get him into the depot. So we got over to around Fitzwilliam Square and he blew his horn repeatedly at me and I thought he must be able to go on on his own now. So I got back on the bus and said, "are you all right now? Can you continue?" "Come in out of that", he says, "I can't even see *you!*" But we made it eventually.

'We always had characters, real characters, in the company. People who were larger than life and were quoted for their actions and humour. I remember this Johnny Kennedy who worked on the trams and the buses. This particular day in a place called The Washerwoman's Hill in Glasnevin — and it's a steep hill — the driver wasn't around and he went down to the controls of the tram and started fooling around with them. And didn't the tram take off! Oh, this is the truth. The tram took off and he didn't know what to do. Didn't know how to control it or reduce the speed. And it was fairly early in the morning. When it got down to the bottom of Washerwoman's Hill it overturned into a lady's garden. And the lady comes out in her night attire and said to Johnny, "what's this going on here?" And he says, "it's door-to-door service, Ma'am, are you coming?"'

Chapter 6

Animal Dealers, Drovers and Fanciers

CHRISTY "DILLER" DELANEY — Drover and Horse Dealer, Age 65

At eleven years of age he began helping his father drive cattle and sheep in from the fields in the dead of night during the most frightful weather. Then he would put down his ash stick, clean the dung off his hob-nail boots and head for school. Living the life of a drover he mixed and sometimes tangled with tough men in a world of hard drinking and brutal fighting. But what he most feared were the "wild" cattle that would tear "hammers out of hell" down the street leaving death and destruction in their wake. One of the most respected animal handlers in Dublin, and known to all as "Diller", he resurrected the old Smithfield horse fair in 1981 after nearly twenty years of dormancy.

'I was born in number thirty Blackhall Street. My father was a drover at the cattle market. My mother wore a shawl, fed pigs and sold vegetables up around Oxmantown. It was a difficult life. Most drovers' families was all born in one (tenement) room. Like meself, I was born in one room … ten of us. As a boy at age eleven I'd go out in the fields with me father in the night time in the dark. I was reared up to it. We walked from Blackhall Street to Dunsink, about three miles, in the darkness. I'd have me leggins and hob-nail boots on. You'd leave at twelve and be out in the fields at one. No matter what the weather, you had to be there. You'd have maybe 300 or 400 cattle in the field and maybe 500 sheep. You brought the sheep in first and then back out for the cattle. And you'd get in quicker with the cattle — easier to handle. We used dogs for both cattle and sheep. We had great dogs. Trained them ourselves. So you'd do your night's work bringing in the sheep and cattle and I went to school the next morning! I went to Brunswick School and had to be in at nine. And I had to be spotless clean as well. I left school at fourteen.

'When you brought the cattle and sheep into the market you'd use your stick as a prod. I had me ash stick. Most good drovers always cut their own plant, around January, when the sap comes up. You cut them from the roots, just young plants, and you dressed the root. And for droving cattle you'd put a prod in the stick, a screw, and you filed the head off it which left it a little proddy at the top. The humane people (Humane Society) thought it was very severe. They thought it was ill treatment. Now a little before my time, before we started pulling up our own plants and cutting them, they come from London. They were called a "London pole". See, English cattle men brought them over and they were varnished and everything. They'd give them to the drovers for nothing, just throw a bunch of them into the offices at the market.

Highly respected former drover and horse dealer Christy "Diller" Delaney at Smithfield horse fair

'There was very little clothing to cover ourself with at that time. Me father'd get us hob-nail boots — they were the greasy leather — for five bob. All the *real* drovers and their sons wore them. And the leggins was two and sixpence and we had to wear them whether we liked them or not — those were the father's orders. We wore a cap and you'd tie a hankie around your neck when you'd be very wet. See, we used Brilliantine to keep our hair down and it was great for the water to run off your hair as well. That's why you tied the hankie around your neck. Now when you'd go into the market sorting sheep on a wet night the sheep would be very wet and you'd be really saturated. What we used to do, we used to cut the sleeves out of a sales master's old trenchcoat. When they'd get too raggedy and shaggy at the bottoms the sleeves would still be good. So we used to cut the sleeves out and make pull-ups out of them for over your legs. Just put a string around it and tie it up to your suspenders. They were really the first pull-ups that was ever wore in the market.

'When the French, the Dutch, the Germans and the Belgians started coming into the market we judged the cattle for them. You were really only a drover but he'd

178

buy on our judgement. The dealers, they'd have five or six hundred pounds from the tips of their fingers up to their shoulders. Walk around with the money and nobody'd touch it. Deals was made and they'd spit in their hands. By the end of the day you're exhausted and up to the waist in muck and cow dung. There was boot blacks around and most of the cattlemen and sheepmen always had two or three pairs of boots and they always got their boots done by the blackies. But no drovers ever done that. Most of the bootblacks come from down on Sean McDermott Street and Linen Hall Street. One was a coloured man, funny thing. So the men'd have their boots cleaned and polished and shined and if it was a day they didn't wear pull-ups they'd have their trousers scraped and brushed and cleaned. Mostly only from the knee down. See, the blackie would use his special type knife and he'd scrape all the splashes off and he'd have a clothes brush. It was sixpence for the boots and trousers.

'The cattle, when they'd get going from the market to the boats you went in batches of fifty. There was three men with fifty cattle (allowed) and you'd have to let them run to loosen themself out. But you knew your job. As you crossed the city the front man was the main man and then the two men at the back. Cattle'd go up the side roads and that's where you used the dogs to bring them back. But some cattle, when we'd get them up here in Dublin they were so *wild* that they'd run hammers out of hell down the street. Breaking up shops and breaking up bicycles. And, you know, a bike was a man's motor car nearly at that time. They'd get into a bike and it'd go a quarter of a mile on their feet and it'd be in bits, finished. Now when they'd go into shops if you could just get the people to stay quiet you knew your job. You'd just walk quietly around them and get their head and you wouldn't bash them. You'd just tip the head with the stick and turned them and then you'd just catch their tail and give it a twist and he'd fly out. But some would run like hammers out of hell and come down on the quays with a woman or man on their head! Killed. Dead! Ah, it happened many times. I remember this one occasion we turned down Queen Street and this old woman was crossing and this heifer collided with her and she was up on his head. She was dead.

'Droving was recognised as a very poor job. And there was a certain lot of drovers that were rough, but a lot of them of very respectable type. You'd see them on Friday morning — as hard as they worked all the day and night Thursday — dressed up with a collar and tie at Hanlon's Corner at the top of Prussia Street. And they always wore what we called the dust-coat. Some with a velvet collar. They'd just stand around. Work two days a week and stand around the rest, that was their routine. If you done a day's work it was twenty-six shillings ... and you done a good few drives to the quays. The English and Germans was great, maybe tip you an English ten shilling note. But drovers never saved money. Drovers were all heavy drinkers, very heavy drinkers. They'd all get very drunk at the end of the day. Pubs opened at six in the morning and drovers was always down to have their coffee. Actually, I think that's where Irish coffee came from cause they'd have a coffee when it was so bitter and cold and they started putting the glass of malt into the coffee. The glasses would be hot, heated, and put some treacle in. That would be a great thing when you'd be very wet.

'Some, they'd fight when they got drunk. Some very rough. Fight with sticks they would. Serious injuries. Very good, some of them, with their sticks. There was cow men which didn't like the bullock men. When the beef drover would be fighting the cowman sticks would be getting used on the head and across the shoulders. And the beef drover, he'd *hock* him! See, if a beast was getting away from you in the street you hocked him ... left him on three legs. That's why you had the root of the plant. There was a way of doing it. You hocked him in one of the hind legs and he'd hit the ground immediately. Then you'd get your knee on his neck and hold him down. It was painful but it had to be done cause he was a danger to the public. But the cowman never could do that, you know. So the beef drover'd hock him right under the ankle bone there and that finished him. That was the end of the fight. I done it meself! And I wasn't a fighting man much.

Smithfield horse fair held every first Sunday of the month on the old cobblestones

'By the time I was in my twenties I was interested in horses. I lived in Smithfield and had horses in my yard. We had great horse fairs and pony fairs. And the Tinkers (Itinerants) was great donkey dealers, selling donkeys in batches. Now the Joyce's are Tinkers. They were the chimney sweeps, the tinsmiths and all. And the Joyce's would fight the Wards — every Thursday. Both Tinker families.

They fought in Smithfield here after the horse fair every Thursday. Real anger. Seen it meself. See, the two of them would start off after drinking at Paddy Egan's pub at the corner. He was the only one that'd serve them. And they'd fight with the fists. Happened *every* Thursday. Big crowds. And when the fighting would get really rough they'd draw their sally sticks, big long seasoned sally sticks roughly ten feet long. They used them for chimney sweeping. Both the Wards and the Joyce's used them. They'd have them on their flat carts and along the handlebars of their bikes. They'd end up then with their sally sticks and there'd be ten, twelve, fifteen of them all lying around Smithfield in bits. *Bleeding* bits! And up Red Cow Lane. And with any type of carts you'd have you'd take them up there to the old Richmond Hospital. Just throw them on the steps and the nurses and doctors would carry them up. Every Thursday.

'The horse fair here in Smithfield was stopped for almost twenty years. Trade went off around 1963. I restarted the horse fair here seven years ago. I lived in Smithfield and had eleven horses in me yard. So we arranged to start the fair and keep it going every first Sunday. It went slow at the beginning, about fifty or sixty horses. Here last week we had 250 to 300 horses! Good work horses and pleasure horses. And two hackney cars sold. Deals are made here in the traditional way, the clapping of the hands. It gives great life to the area.'

CHRISTY DONOGHUE — Drover, Age 73

"Ah, the wild west had nothing on us", he likes to boast, recalling the havoc of driving unruly beasts down the North Circular Road to the docks. He still curses the motorists and tram drivers who, for sheer devilment, would stampede his herds. Equally exasperating were stubborn bulls that would simply halt dead in the street centre for a bit of a siesta in the afternoon heat. Nonetheless, he contends that life back then was altogether more exciting. Today he frequents the same pubs around Smithfield sometimes sitting next to younger patrons who admit that they're not certain what a drover was years ago. He just smiles and sips away.

'Me father worked at the cattle all his life. We were all bred to that. We'd nothing else. I was about twelve when I started at it, mitching from school going out. My father was working for an Englishman shipping cattle. We used to take them off the train up on the Cabra Railway and bring them down and put them on the boats. There could be up to 8,000 cattle on a shipping day. And thousands of sheep. Ah, and there was a lot of pig men up there too.

'Thursday was the market day and then they switched it over to Wednesday. Buyers would stay in the City Arms Hotel and guesthouses all around the North Circular Road. Ah, they'd have the best of everything. The market opened at three in the morning and cattle used to be waiting outside from one for the gates to be opened. At night you had to go and get the cattle out of the fields and put them into the market. The fields was all out around Cabra and Finglas. You went out at twelve in the night and you weren't finished till six the next night. And it was mostly bad weather all the time. You had gear like pull-ups and boots and a cap. In the summer it was hot ... cruel. Then in the winter you were drownded between the snow and whatever. You used to put brown paper underneath your clothes to prevent you from getting wet. Everyone had their own (animal) brand, different dots of blue and green. You'd know your own cattle and sheep. But if they got mixed you had to sort them out. That's the best place I ever heard curses. There were curses *invented* up there in the market. Oh, the drovers, we were all rough and ready. The ordinary drover just drank the pints. And hot whiskey in the winter with a squeeze of lemon in it.

'Now there was a little French nun in the market up there for over forty years. She was some French Order. Collecting money for the poor. She'd be there at eight in the morning and wouldn't leave there till one. And she always had a little smile. All the Englishmen would drop money into her bag. Englishmen were *outstanding* in putting money in that bag. Very kind. They wouldn't pass that nun. Just to see here there alone and the job she was doing. And she wasn't afraid of the cattle either! She used to wave her umbrella. Oh, it was something to see the way she'd shake that umbrella at the cattle.

'There was different ways you could work the cattle going down to the North Wall. The best way was straight down the (North) Circular Road cause it was a straight run, about two-mile of a run stretch. You could have about 500 cattle being let out together going down at one time. Ah, the wild west wasn't up with us! Not on a Wednesday up there. And you'd see the cattle going right behind the sheep and you'd have to turn the sheep off and let the cattle go down cause the cattle would be walking on top of them. Ah, it was murder — *murder* — going down that North Circular Road. I often went down it five and six times in the day. Get the bus back up to the market and run down again with another herd. It was ten bob for the driving down and the more that we was bringing down the more money it was. Money was very low at that time and you was only working two days, don't forget that.

'Now a dog was a great thing. Ah, there were great dogs, for sheep mostly. See, sheep wouldn't drive without dogs, they'd keep going around in circles. But dogs would go up on their back and keep 'em going in front. Nearly everyone had a dog in the market. And a drover always had to have a stick, an ordinary ashplant. They had great bend in them but would never break. A lot of men would put a screw in the end, to prod the cattle with. But it was cruel and used to damage the hides. It was *wrong*. You were better off if you had a flat head just to give them a bit of a jab.

'You were allowed five cattle to one man, anything up to twenty cattle with two men, and after that fifty cattle with three. And there was a policeman down there at the Five Lamps and he'd count 'em right there if he thought you had over your number. You could drive down ten sheep with one man and it was no bother. And you could drive down fifty or sixty with two men and he wouldn't mind. Oh, but if you told him *lies!* If you were over your number you were summonsed

182

and had to go to court and you were fined. And if there was a heavy frost the Corporation had to sand the roads for the cattle cause they'd break their leg. So, say two in the morning the Corporation would throw sand on the roads down to the boats, two or three horse-drawn wagons with men just shovelling it out. And the Corporation had to clean the streets … there was plenty of mess, all right.

'Going down the North Circular Road there you had people coming up the paths. Oh, they were afraid for their life! Oh, you had to keep them off the pathways. People used to be looking out the windows and used to get out of the buses for to look. And trams was in the middle of the road and they used to make it very awkward for you. Trams, they were a nuisance. Some of them clowns in the trams were always ringing their bells. They'd do it just for devilment. It'd break your heart and they'd be laughing. So if he was a hardjaw we'd get back at him. What we'd do when we had a cranky fella, we used to keep the cattle in front of him. We'd slow the tram up. There was nothing he could do. Oh, they'd be cursing! And the people on the tram, they were enjoying what was going on. See, they did that just for devilment and we said, "we'll put a stop to him!" And he never done any more hooting.

'And some fellas in their motor cars used to be stampeding them. They'd do it out of devilment too. There was always those that'd do it, especially busmen, to get them out of their way. Oh, they were devils! Run them down and it'd be breaking your heart cause you had to keep up with them. Ah, they'd run their hearts out all the way down the Circular Road. They could easily get out of control. Sure, we were going over a stone bridge down at Sheriff Street and the (train) engines would go underneath. Your man hooted the engine and the steam come up and the cattle stampeded all over the place. I seen one beast jumping over a car and he couldn't manage to get over it and he hit the engine and it fell on the ground. Didn't do any damage to the person, it just knocked the engine out of the car on the ground. And you know the spikes on these garden railings? Oh, they'd jump over the low railings into a garden. I seen one bullock going over and it went straight up through him. We had to get underneath and saw the railings to get him off.

'Oh, you had to be very careful bringing down big, heavy bulls. One bull at a time. Sometimes you wouldn't know how to handle them and he'd face you and give you a lick. And if they seen a bit of paper or anything on the road blowing they'd jump. And in the warm weather you'd get a bull that'd sit down cause he was *exhausted*. Ah, he'd just sit down there in the road and you could do nothing about it. You had to put up with it. "Just giving him a breather", we used to call it. You'd give him an odd stick but you couldn't cod him too much because there was people watching for cruelism and they'd say, "let him take his time". And cattle often walked into shops. But you had to have a cool head, I'll tell you, cause no matter what went wrong you were the drover and you were to blame and that's it. I seen them walking into shops and glass all over the place. And then trying to get them out of that shop! You'd have to try and back 'em out cause if he'd be turned around he broke everything. It's a very hard thing. Oh, if you'd try pulling his tail he'd give you a kick and you'd go flying. So you'd tip him on the forehead, keep tipping him and he'd keep going back, back. It was a *miracle* to get him out. I think it was just God up there that got him out.

'There's no walking the cattle at all down the Circular Road now. No walking at all now. It's all going down by lorries. It's the best thing in a sense, cause it was only hardship.'

JOHN MANNION — Horse Dealer, Age 70

He is, by unchallenged consensus among Dublin's horsey set, the premier horse dealer in the city over the past half century. As the loyal top-hand for the Cooper family of Queen Street, he dominated the heavy horse dealing trade in the city. Back in the forties when a labouring man was fortunate to bring home four pounds at week's end, John commonly had thirty or forty pounds in his pocket. He chose living the high life and the money evaporated. If only he had stashed away a portion of it he could have been a wealthy man today — old cronies swear it is true. No horse dealer was as tough and canny when it came to negotiating a price. Even rivals respected him for his expertise and honesty. Today as he strolls through the crowd at the Smithfield horse fair, he is treated with a certain awe by the old horse men. And occasionally he still even makes a deal as a crowd gathers around to watch an old master at work.

'My father was always in the horse business and my grandfather. Oh, I'd be the fourth generation in it. My grandfather in County Roscommon had a mail coach with two horses for delivering letters in little villages, like the Pony Express you had in America. My father and my three uncles worked for a man in Clones buying work horses on commission. The first time I was ever with him buying horses was at Claremorris and I'd be about ten. Oh, sure it was a grand event for me. See, there'd be the cattle fair, the pig fair and the horse fair the one day and you'd see hundreds of dealers. We went to every town in Ireland for the whole year around, getting on trains and sleeping on them, going all the time. I was learning at ten years old and he'd say to me, "listen, John, the secret of success is to always know your opposition". Now the first horse I ever bought was in Ballinasloe, the famous horse fair, and I was about fifteen. I had the brains and bought a lovely little mare for twenty pounds and made a five pound profit.

'My brother Patsy was a leading horse man in Dublin buying work horses from the farmers for the city. He'd sell them to dairies. Well, about fifty years ago he come down to the Westport Fair and bought fourteen horses and he asked me if I'd mind going to Dublin with the horses by road. I was never in Dublin and leaving the country was a big thing to do. We had what we called a Belfast Flat, a little two-wheel yoke with rubber tyres and one horse pulled it and you'd bring the other horses behind it tied by rope. So I come to Dublin when I was about sixteen and Dublin was all horses then. You couldn't cross the road. Five hundred horses lining up on O'Connell Street in the morning. That's *unbelievable*. Oh, yes, jarveys, C.I.E., bakeries, very big work on the docks with horses. In the *heart* of Dublin. And Dublin people kept a horse and cart in little lanes. Everywhere you'd look there were horses.

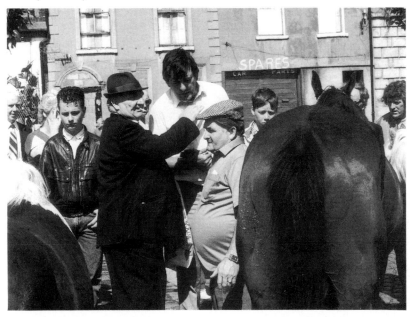

John Mannion (dark hat), Dublin's most famed horse dealer, closing a deal
with the traditional slap of the hand in Smithfield market

'Now my brother bought this car off a priest in Westport and he used to bring a lot of the horse dealers to fairs. There was often ten and twenty men up on top of her going to fairs. They'd be sitting on the car *everywhere* but there was no traffic on the roads anyhow. Now if you had a horse in the country and you got him to *Dublin*, that was the secret of success. If you put a horse on a train it'd take days to get him to Dublin but if you bought him fifty or sixty miles away you'd ride him home to Dublin and sell him that night. My brother had two yards, one on Bow Street and one in North King Street. We could hold about thirty or forty horses in one yard and about twenty in the other. And when the war started people would be knocking at your gates. See, at that time you *had* to get a horse (because of petrol rationing). It was like gold dust. There'd be no bread delivered, no letters delivered, no coal delivered.

'Anyway, I had a row with me brother and I got in with the famous Cooper's of Queen Street. I suppose they were the biggest family in the world in the strong horse business. Now Thomas Cooper was the father, a very strict man, top man in his business. He had Guinness's, C.I.E., all the bakeries. We had *queues* for horses. So I started buying horses at fairs for them. Mr. Cooper, he had two or three cars and his sons would drive me to every part of Ireland. So I always had a chauffeur and I could sleep in the back seat going to fairs. It suited me. Fairs at

185

that time was on for two or three in the morning. I'd be dressed clearly as a dealer. I always wore a nice blue suit and the best of shoes and a hat. If you hadn't a hat years ago you weren't a dealer. I done business fair and honest and I was in every town in Ireland. There wasn't many farmers in the country that knew anything about dealing. But I always gave farmers a fair chance and you get known for that. Now the seller could change his mind at any time but the dealer *couldn't* — that's the funny law. And all that slapping and spitting in your hand when you'd buy a horse, that was a great tradition. And when I'd buy a horse I'd put my name on him with a red raddle, like lipstick in a tube but twice as big.

'Horse dealers always carried only cash. Working for the Cooper's I could carry £10,000 in cash. No trouble. Oh, in 1955 I had £20,000 on me! And there was terrible jealousy between horse dealers. The slang word for horse dealers in them days was "razor blades" cause they used to cut one another's throat in the opposition. And at a horse fair another fella he'd be trying to "sharp" you — a slang word — trying to "get inside" you. But if you were a clever man you'd never let the opposition get in. Now a good strong horse in the forties or fifties would cost about seventy-five to a hundred pounds. I was paid two pounds a horse commission. Oh, I'd make fifty or sixty pounds and spend it that night. Ah, there was days when I'd take twenty drinks ... a small gin and a drop of peppermint and a glass of cider. Oh, no bother ... and I could go out and do my work as well. But you'd be drunk that night and you'd have to be in a different town *every* day. Mr. Cooper said to me one time that if I'd bought some property for the money he was giving me I'd be a millionaire before I'd be fifty. And he was *perfectly right*.

'When you'd bring a country horse to the city to work you'd yoke it up for a couple of days, put it into a cart or a gig or a trap and drive it around the city. And you'd have to have a man with you in case it became flighty with the trams. Now there was what's called a "nagsman", a man for breaking-in horses. Like my friend, Tucker Cole, he was a genius at that. He broke in thousands of horses in Dublin. He'd break-in horses in Smithfield, running 'em up and down. He'd do what was called "moulding" them. Put a soft bit, a rubber bit, in their mouth and a bridle and winkers and two big ropes or reins and walk them up and down. Then, to get them used to the cart you'd put a bag on his back and on both sides. At night you'd leave that tack on him and put two bags of cement on his back to get him used to the weight. That was for breaking him in to go for the cart. There was a certain kind of horse that was good for the city — patience and temperament. He had to *stop* when you asked him and walk on when you asked him. Oh, during the war a man that could handle his horse was terrible valuable. Cause there would have been *no Dublin*, only for the horses and the horse men. That's an awful thing to say, but that is *true*.

'On hard frosty mornings you'd have to put frost nails on the horse's shoes to stop them from slipping. We used the McLoughlin Brothers farriers, they done all the Cooper's horses. See, the way it was when you'd go into a blacksmith's forge in the morning time there'd be a hundred horses in front of you. And they would be taken out of the way and Mr. Cooper's horses would be brought up. That's right. He was the *king* of the business. And the Jewman would come around to Cooper's and buy the horse hair. And there was a difference between the horse hair off the mane and the horse hair off the tail. The tail is best. It was used for putting into horse's collars and you might get sixpence a pound for that. The horse hair from the mane they'd put into mattresses and they wouldn't give you much for that. Cause feathers was very scarce, you see, during the war.

'Now all that strong commercial horse business, that stopped just after the war. The next thing, after the war, a Frenchman called Major Madeaux came here and he wanted 200 breeding mares every week landed at the boat — at fifty-eight pounds each. After the war we could buy them, no bother, from thirty to forty pounds. So we got that job for five or six years. In the meantime we got business for pit ponies in Belgium. Then in the fifties we got an order from the Belgium Government for *seven hundred horses a week*. At thirty pounds apiece. Now at that time you couldn't *give* a horse away in Ireland ... couldn't get a shilling for a horse. No one wanted 'em. Horses, they was running wild some of them. Seven hundred horses a week between Limerick and Dublin and, oh, I was making a lot of money. But, as I told you, I was *spending* it ... gambling and drinking.

'After that I moved to professional men in the blood business and bought famous showjumpers. In my profession I was the top. Oh, *no doubt* about it. There's no one had the mind and brain I had. I wouldn't change me life in Dublin cause everybody still knows me. I never missed the horse fair in Smithfield. All the horse dealers would go to Smithfield to a very old pub, Peter Donoghue's, and talk horses, make deals, have drink and have a good bit of crack. I'm telling you, the great ruination of Ireland was to take horses off the street. Oh, the horse age is dying out in Dublin ... but there's still plenty of horsemen around Dublin.'

ANTOINETTE COOPER HEALY — Horse Dealer, Age 50

The "Coopers of Queen Street" have been known as Dublin's premier horse trading family for the past century. As a pretty female in a rough man's world, Antoinette established her own identity and gained respect as an expert on horse flesh. As a young girl she was attending horse fairs, dealing and even driving horses down to the North Wall docks with the men drovers. No man dared to call her bluff or challenge her word. Today she lives along Manor Street next to Smithfield where she still stables a horse and has a gig for taking jaunts around nearby Phoenix Park.

'From the time I was knee-high I remember nothing else but going around buying horses, selling horses, all over Ireland. It was just in the blood. I was the youngest of eleven children and I was *born* with horses. Horses and cattle and pigs flying about the streets, it was a familiar sight in Dublin when the cattle market was open up there. It was just part of the street life of Dublin. And I could handle the horses as well as a man could. I took as many horses down to the North Wall for export as the average man would take. I took four on my own. I did that as a young girl, at about eleven. Leading our horses down to the docks you started at three in the morning walking down the back streets. You always had to use a stick when you were driving horses. I had an ashplant. You *had* to have a stick to wave and check them back and keep them in line.

'Both my great grandfather and grandfather were property owners here in Dublin and got into the horse business. My grandfather owned most of Queen Street on the Smithfield side, some tenements and private houses and shops. He started dealing in horses and became very famous ... an honest horse dealer. The stables on Queen Street would have been about a half an acre. I've seen up to a hundred horses in that yard. During the Civil War when the English came in they took over our yard for a livery stable. When there was shooting our stable boys would stay overnight and sleep in the harness room. The British soldiers would share their food with them, give them bully beef, which was a spice beef, and their dog biscuits which were hard biscuits packed for going to war. On one wall in the yard there was all bullet marks from the guns from the Troubled Times but everything was intact.

'My father was born in 1900, born with horses. My father and my three brothers, they were all *geniuses* at it. Eat, drank and slept it. Horses! He started going to horse fairs with his father around 1916 by train at that time and covered the twenty-six counties. He supplied most of the firms here in Dublin. We had Guinness's, C.I.E., the B&I, the Gas Company, coal firms, bakeries, all the main dairies. He had the undertakers and the cab men (jarveys). We had the *whole lot.* He had the *name* and an honest reputation. My father's policy was when he'd sell a person a horse there was a trial period to see how the horse would go for a fortnight. Like to carry crates of milk and glass bottles you'd have to have a very placid type of animal, one that would fall in line. So if the animal was too strong or too fresh for the job my father would always give a replacement.

'Now when our business was really at its peak (1940's) — that was when my brothers came into it — we had three cars on the road. And later my sister and I drove. Going to fairs it was horse talk non-stop — breakfast, dinner and tea. We might be gone for two or three days when there'd be fairs in one part of Ireland. Stay in good hotels and eat well. My father never believed in living any other way. His business was so vast that he had to have other people buying for him. They were "tanglers" (see book section previous on John Mannion). A tangler is a person that would have gone out before you and spotted the type of animals you'd be interested in and have this man (seller) ready to take up with you. And he would make the deal. That would be called "tangling", making a price. The tangler was working to bring off a deal, working for the buyer and paid by him. It was all cash at that time and they'd slap hands. Deals could be made in the open or they could revert back to the pubs, depending on if there was persuasion needed. Like maybe if they had a drink they'd come to terms. My father was always fair. Always fair.

'The horses were brought back to Dublin by train or lorry. When they got to the station we had stable men and they'd tie them together by interlinking the rope and lead them just by walking. And we also had a pony and trap and you could take a couple of horses behind the trap. You might be bringing twenty horses with the stable men walking them. It would be early in the morning. Despite them being a work horse my father treated them well and we knew all the cures and didn't need a vet. The stable boys and my brothers would break-in the horses out in the training paddock in Queen Street. You put a long rein on your horse and send him around in a ring for to get the freshness out of him. Then introduce weights onto the horse or put a saddle or set of harness on him. Then they'd yoke him maybe in a cart and let him rip away to get used to the feel of pulling a vehicle behind him. Then he'd be taken out on what you call a brake, introducing him to the road generally. Then he'd be ready for sale.

'During the war years when there was no petrol horses came back in vogue more so than ever. You *had* to have a horse here. People who had lorries and tractors, there was nothing to run them with. When the petrol shortage came *everybody* was looking for horses. There was a horse revival. The demand was there. Our business really just *rocketed* at that stage. During the war — and even after the war when we went into a very poor period here — it was cheaper to keep a horse than it was to keep a car. It was easy to stable a horse because you had all the back lanes in Dublin and you had the Haymarket in Smithfield and all these factors who sold oats and bran cheap. And you didn't need a mechanic. So it was cheaper to run a horse than it was to run a car. This was well into the fifties and into the sixties. In Dublin here we were always a little bit behind.

'Oh, Dublin street life was better then. There were horses everywhere, on every street corner there was a horse coming around it. You can never bring the grace of a horse to a car. I still jump up to the window when I hear the clopetty-clop sound of a horse going by. I guess you could say my father was a legend in his own lifetime. Everybody knew us. There's nobody there now to do what we did and there's no demand for it. Horses nearly went off the street altogether, but the nostalgia won't die. I was the end of the originals.'

JIMMY RILEY — Pig Raiser, Age 50

Were it not for the squeals and pungent smells, one would never suspect that there was a piggery in the enclosed yard off North King Street. The Riley's have been raising pigs for four generations and Jimmy started off as a lad going around with his father on horse and cart collecting slop in buckets from tenement dwellers. As a teenager he herded the bellowing beasts through the streets to market. Today his piggery holds about a hundred animals and looks like scene from Connemara, with old stone sheds, wooden gates and a huge metal vat for boiling swill. Jimmy happily plods around the yard in boots amid muck, conceding that raising pigs in the city is "outdated" and the Corporation will close him down one day soon.

'I go back four generations, to me great grandfather, in pigs. I was helping me father out in the yard since I can remember ... five, six years old. We gathered pigs' swill in a horse-drawn cart from the local tenement houses. It'd be mostly scraps that they'd keep for you, mostly bread, potato peels. Just to get rid of it, never had to pay. They'd leave a barrel in the back or just bring out the bucket. In me father's time there was a lot more people around here and a lot more piggeries too. See, back in them times a family had a batch of pigs — anything from six to ten or twelve — and they'd just fatten them up and sold them. It was an extra few pounds a year. There was several big yards around North King Street, Stoneybatter, Henrietta Lane. There was a yard on North King Street known as Brannigan's and it was fierce the size of it. Couple of hundred pigs.

'Years ago me father went to fairs all the time and done a bit of dealing and brought the pigs back and you'd fatten them up and sell them. If he went to a fair in the country he used the railway and then we'd draw them off the railway with the pony and float. Now the pig market and cattle market and sheep market was up on the North Circular Road. If we had only a small amount of pigs (to sell) we'd load them on a small pony float. Eight or so pigs it would take. And if we had a lot we'd just let them out and hunt them up the street. It was quicker to let them just walk up and we'd make a couple of runs. We could let out twenty or so. I had me two brothers and one of us would walk in front and the others behind. The first couple of hundred yards would be the hardest when you'd let them out because of the sense of freedom. Then they'd settle down after a while. But they'd get stubborn and we'd use a stick to just prod them up, a gentle urge. It would be about half-six in the morning and there'd be no people. The only thing was that you'd get an odd motor car in later years and the lights of the car in the eyes of the pigs would turn them back. That used to be a problem. So you'd ask the man driving the car to switch off the lights.

'Ah, it's much the same now as in me father's time. You buy young pigs, you fatten them up and you sell them. We buy the pigs in the country, about five stone in weight, and keep them maybe four or five months, up to maybe eighteen stone. Now gathering swill, that died out about twenty-five years ago. A lot of the people moved out of the area. Nowadays my main supply is hotels and restaurants and Mountjoy Prison. They have bins in the kitchens and they dump that into our drums. Now pigs won't eat anything. And it's not advisable to give them anything with grease on it, that'd be very dangerous. I'm watching all the time and if I see grease I'll take it off. I always boil the swill down and make a stock pot, the meat and the skins and the bread and whatever. I use timber for that boiler. I can get three barrels in there and I boil it overnight. There's a bad smell sometimes ... but sometimes there's a good smell. Like when I put chicken offal in it people often remark how good that smells.

'Now pigs can be contrary. Pigs'll take to fighting. Oh, in me father's time you could be standing over them for a couple of hours watching them scrapping. See, back then he'd go to a fair in the country and got different farmers' pigs, different scents, you know. It was from *mixing* the pigs. And they'd fight for the kill.

They'd do serious damage to one another. Oh, often I've seen them in bits. They'd eat the ears and they dry up and they fall off. You'd often see them without their ears. And they'd chew at each other's ribs. Oh, they'd bite each other's tails and just keep going. Ah, we'd often have a chain hanging in the sty and we'd swing the chain and they'd bite the chain, sort of to occupy them. You'd have to give them a tip of the stick on the nose and they even used to have to stick rings in their noses to prevent them from fighting and rustling. We used to do it ourselves with special pliers. They were steel rings and if they pushed against another pig it would hurt them, keep them off.

Pig raiser Jimmy Riley in his piggery near North King Street

'Now the health inspector from the Corporation comes around. It's a known fact that the Corporation wants piggeries out of Dublin. That's been going on since me father's time. It's a slow process. If you'd come to me here fifteen years ago and asked me if I'd be here today I'd have said "no". There's not many pig raisers around now. Some people think that you shouldn't be here, that it's not suitable for the city. But if you know nothing else what can you do about it? Raising pigs now in the city is outdated, like keeping chickens and hens. But I spent me life in it. I'm just seeing an old thing out, you know?'

JOHN CLARKE — Bird Market Man, Age 54

From five years of age he accompanied his father to the Sunday bird market just around the corner in Bride Street. For the next half century it was just a weekly ritual. As a skilled catcher, he peddled his bike out into the countryside packed with gear. As a respected bird market man he mixed with all the old-timers and learned their lore. Gradually, he realised that the bird market was declining and doomed to eventually fade away. Because of the secretive nature of old bird men there was no written record of the market. His conscience dictated that he become the custodian of history and lore about the market and share it for the written record.

'The bird market originated with the Huguenots in the middle of the seventeenth century. As far back as I can remember the bird market has been part of my life. My father and my grandfather were in it. Oh, at least three generations that I know of. My grandfather used to keep larks. He often had nine, ten larks on the wall in cages. Now just to give you an idea of what they thought of birds back then, when my mother and father were married things in Dublin weren't good. But me grandfather gave them as a wedding present two larks in cages. That's all he had to give. And even that — to give away two good singing larks — that *meant* something.

'I went there with my father as a boy of five or six. It was just around the corner in Bride Street. Always on a Sunday morning from half ten till the pubs opened. People from all around the Liberties would come and people from beyond. You'd go to church and then go to the bird market. After each Mass you'd have a fresh crowd. It was a bit of a Sunday morning ritual. Then the men used to gather at Cole's Public House and it's *unbelievable* how they could talk birds. For *hours!* I remember in the forties that there was a falling-out among some of them. There was a split and they had two bird markets going for a time. One was in Hanover Lane and the other was in New Street. The one in Hanover Lane drew the biggest crowd.

'Years ago the place would be packed with birds, four or five hundred. The yard was approximately forty feet long by about ten feet wide. We used to have a stick with a nail on it and you'd hang the cages with the birds up high on the wall, about ten feet off the ground. When people came in there was a cardboard box on the ground to put money in and that was to pay for the rent of the yard. You put in a penny or a ha'penny. And children were always accepted in the market. They'd depend on children for sales. That's why they'd sell birds very cheap. Back then you'd get a redpole for three pence and a goldfinch for a shilling. We used to just put the birds in a brown paper bag. Blow the bag up and put the bird in and tear a little piece out of it to let air in. Now some (writers) say that they (bird dealers) used to squeeze them in their hand (so the bird would die and customers would return to buy another) — that's *fallacy!*

Sunday morning scene at the old bird market near Bride Street

'On a Sunday morning this man, Barney Finnegan, used to go around with a little box car with two wheels and he'd sell sods of grass for a ha'penny a sod. The sods were about seven inches by seven inches. The idea was that it would have life to it, and insects. They used to say about him that they wouldn't let him into the Phoenix Park or Stephen's Green ... that he had a tract cut all the way to Mullingar! Another man, Jemmy Oates, used to sell drinkers (made from tins) and he used to keep five or six redpoles under his cap. Each one he'd take out (to sell) he'd say that was the last one. He just did that with kids. And there was men that made cages of timber and scrap wire and sold them in the market. Now my grandfather, he'd make drinkers out of anything, like mustard tins and liver salts tins, and he'd make feeders and cages himself all decorated with fancy brass.

'There was never a woman (who) sold in the market. And in my young time you'd never even see women come into the market, even to look. Or very, very rarely. It was only in the sixties that they started coming in. But in the 1950's this woman used to come into the market on a Sunday morning, a woman in her fifties I'd say. No one ever knew who she was. And she'd buy whatever birds would be left at the end of the day and she'd let the *whole lot of them free!* Ah, she'd buy forty birds, pay cash for them, and just open the cages right in the market. She wouldn't hold a conversation with anyone. I suppose she was a bit eccentric. I was a bit curious about her, all right. I wondered *why?* I suppose she thought it was cruel, that was the reason she let them out. I remember her over a period of about three years. Then she just disappeared.

'In my time, the forties, men specialised in certain types of birds — larks, goldfinches, linnets, the redpole., Basically, birds was bought for their song. People just liked to hear the bird singing. And in the tenements a bird, psychologically, would boost your morale, you know? They'd hang it outside on the window and take it in at night. And a good looking bird appeals to people. You hear them bragging about their bird. At that time most of the barber shops in the Liberties would have a bird. It was an attraction for the kids. Plus, they liked to hear birds singing themselves. There was a barber on Stephen's Street named Willie Pigeon — that was his name — and he'd have three or four birds. Another barber, Tommy White, trained his bird to pull a little toy truck on a fine chain with his beak.

'Bird catching was seasonal. You'd start catching about the second week of September till February. You would never catch after February when birds would start breeding in the wild. Ah, we'd bicycle out. You'd go off about eight in the morning and bring the makings for a cup of tea and sandwiches. Make a fire and tea in a can. Years ago you never had to go very far cause Dublin wasn't built up the way it is now. I used to go to Ringsend, to Tallaght and Ballyfermot. It was just fields and no one ever bothered you. On some farms you would ask permission and with others you wouldn't bother. Catchers all kind of had their own areas. Oh, you'd often pass them when you'd be going on the road. Or you'd see them setting their nets in the field. There was an unwritten law that you didn't encroach on another man's territory.

'So we'd bicycle out and the nets were rolled up in your box. You had two nets and they were about sixteen feet long and three feet wide. And there was poles that were three feet long and they'd tie on the crossbar. And then your hop cages and your store cage would go on the carrier on the back. Hop cages, they were about eight inches cube, wire on top and all around the sides and you'd put a call bird in that. Now we used to catch linnets and goldfinches. So if you were going for goldfinches you'd have a couple of goldfinch call birds. See, when you'd catch birds you'd hear a bird *calling* and you'd put him aside and keep him as a call bird. Oh, no one would ever part with a good call bird. Then you had a hen bird that you put on a thing called a "flirt stick". That was a piece of timber and the bird had a little harness on it and a ring and when you'd see a bird going over you'd pull a string and it would make the hen rise up about eighteen inches and that would attract the attention of the bird flying over. You'd have to be hidden behind a bush or somewhere so they wouldn't see you. You usually had someone with you. Oh, you *could* catch on your own but it was more for the company. You often got four or five dozen birds. But then near the end of the catching days when the (housing) schemes started building up you could go out and mightn't get a bird at all. You see, the land was overtaken by houses and you had to go further afield. I'd often go out and didn't get *anything*.

'Men had their own feed recipes and basically you worked out of five different types of seeds. There was hemp, Niger seed, flax seed, red and black rape seed and maw seed. Thistle was another seed. The Ravendale Mills sold seeds for all the birds. Some men used to grind the seed in an old coffee grinder with the old handle on it. And in the summer season you'd give them as much wild foods, natural foods, as you can — dandelion seeds, chickweed — that you'd get in the fields. Years ago that was no worry, you could get them up along the canal bank. Men still go out and gather wild dandelions and chickweed and groundsel and sow thistle but it's hard to get them now because of insecticides, it's been sprayed.

'Fifteen years ago this market would be *packed.* In 1976 the Wild life Act come out and it's completely illegal to catch birds now. They're all aviary bred birds now. See, it was *always* illegal to catch wild birds but the police never bothered you. They *knew* it was illegal but they kind of kept it quiet. That's why they (bird men) never gave information to anyone or interviews. Even to the present day they're like that. Some of the old lads were very secretive. They've always been secretive. I realised when I was about twenty-five that the bird market is going to die out eventually. And the old fellas are dying. And there was *nothing* written about it. I realised that I'd have to get whatever little bit of information I could. So I talked to the old fellas. Some of them were very secretive about it. Some of them just don't realise that when it's gone, it's *gone.* It's the end of it. Now with you I know that it's going to be recorded somewhere so that someone will know something about it. I want to let someone *know about it* so that if I'm gone tomorrow at least *somebody* knows about it.'

TONY KIELY — Pigeon Fancier, Age 74

An ardent northsider, he proudly professes that the area has long been a hotbed for pigeon men ... "it was their religion". In 1936 at eighteen years of age he started raising and racing pigeons and became recognised as one of the best. What most sets him apart from other good pigeon men is his keen sense of history about the activity and the important role it has played in the life of poor working men in the inner-city.

'Ah, pigeon racing has been a great part of the history of Dublin. You'd hear them talking about pigeons in tenement houses and in pubs. That was their life. They could talk about nothing else. See, pigeon racing was actually known as the poor man's race horse. At that time men hadn't got the money. In the poor tenement areas the pigeon fancier, that was his sole hobby ... that was his *religion!* And he would deny himself his pint or his cigarettes to go and save up and buy something for his pigeon loft. Dream and talk of pigeons ... a kind of religion.

'Belgium, of course, is the home of pigeons. Pigeons came in here from England and Belfast. The oldest pigeon club in Ireland started in 1900 as the Workman's Club — it was all working men — and changed its name to the Dublin and District. It was a pigeon racing club. Working men in various walks of life all congregated for the sole reason of pigeon racing. A terrible lot of dockers were famous pigeon men. This area of north Dublin around Ballybough and the North Strand was a hotbed of pigeon men. Now years ago the tenements had no back garden so they'd have an allotment where they'd have their pigeon lofts. An allotment would be common ground. A vacant site. There were patches of open field around the North Wall and Ballybough back then and you could have four or five lots in the one field. Some of them were very high off the ground. It was just a tradition here.

'During the 1914 War pigeons played a very big part here. They were carrying messages between Belfast and Dublin and throughout all Ireland. The famous Colonel Osmond, a famous pigeon man himself, came over from England and took control of all the pigeons in Dublin because they were needed. And anyone that had pigeons had to be registered during the war. Then during the Troubles of 1916 it was illegal to keep pigeons. But pigeon fanciers brought pigeons under their coats and their shirts to a show behind closed doors and the British didn't know about it. Actually, one of the venues where it was held was the Catholic Commercial Club on O'Connell Street facing the Gresham Hotel. They smuggled their pigeons in. That'll tell you how *keen* they were on pigeons, to take the risk. Oh, at a pigeon show they'd come in and kill them. There were an awful lot of the pigeons found and they'd be killed immediately.

'I've had pigeons since I was seven years old. Since 1936 I belonged to the Dublin Homing Club and raced them. There'd be terrible rivalry and you had some colossal flyers in Dublin. Old Charlie Ingle, he was one of the greatest fanciers, and Peter Melhorn and the Dixons. In Dublin here they named pigeons after their own names because they built up their own strain of pigeons like the old pedigree, same as a horse. It would take twenty or thirty years to have a strain of pigeons named after yourself. And fathers pass this knowledge down to their sons. But they'd only hand it down to their sons! And pigeon fanciers used to meet regular in McDaid's Pub in the old days and talk about pigeons. Of course, the more drink they'd get, the more lies that'd be told.

'There was great secrecy in feeding pigeons. People were secretive and *still are*. You just *wouldn't tell*. The basic food was maple peas and tick beans from Australia and then wheat and corn. But fellas used to make up their own mixture of seeds and this was all high secrecy. Trial and error and when he'd get the proper formula, that was *his*. A fella'd be winning a lot of races and, of course, other men would try to find out. You know, a few jars in the pub. Oh, they'd often get it from the wives! There were various ways. Like a man would make sure that the fancier would be out and he'd say to the wife, "oh, I'm running out of pigeon food, could you give me a few handfuls?". And he'd see the mixture then. It was friendly but, God, very serious competition.

'It's in the pigeon's orientation that he has the homing instinct. He'll fly to his own loft. So you just build up endurance like an ordinary athlete. The pigeon is like a racehorse or a marathon athlete, you'd just build them up. Going back forty or fifty years men didn't have motor cars so we'd send them by rail or go on bikes with them. Put their basket on their bike and cycle ten miles out and let out the pigeons. Then pigeons were put onto trains. Women often used to take the pigeons (for husbands) to the trains in baskets on prams. It would be addressed to the station-master and we'd put "please liberate at such a time". You could send them for training as far as Dundalk, Wexford and Arklow and Wicklow.

'The racing season starts in April and goes until the end of September. They start off with maybe a 100-mile race and it increases every week. Every pigeon fancier has his own clock and when the pigeon comes back his rubber ring with his number on it goes into a thimble container and the clock stamps the time. Then the clocks are brought down to the club that night and opened. Now before clocks come into being when the pigeon would come back from a race they'd bring it to the G.P.O. in a box — or any way at all — and the pigeon was verified there and the times taken. Some of them would come with the pigeon under their coat. Some of them had bikes. At that time your mode of transport was mostly trams and if you *missed a tram*, well, you'd lose. So there was the man's performance in getting to the G.P.O. ... and the element of luck. And if the husband was working it was the women that'd catch the pigeons and put them in boxes and they'd be running. And they'd try to hold each other back. Oh, women used to pull one another back. The rivalry used to be something *terrible*. Oh, there are some great tales told about that. Sometimes in the excitement the pigeons escaped in the G.P.O. when they'd be taking them out of the box or from under their coat. And, of course, it wasn't verified and that was it! And, ah, there was some famous fiddlers — they fiddled the clocks. Back then when pigeons were sent by rail they'd be all marked and in baskets ready to go off to the race point and maybe the train wouldn't leave till one in the morning. Well, your man would go there about half twelve and sneak out his pigeon and take it home. Sometimes they wouldn't get the pigeon at all, they'd just get the rubber ring off him. Oh, he'd be disqualified for life. There's no second chance if you're caught fiddling.

'There are races where you go across the water into England and France. The homing instinct is very, very strong and they've come through terrible ordeals, like in bad weather. You can imagine now a pigeon let go from France to fly 600 miles and all that pigeon is flying to is his nest with two little eggs or maybe young ones. Could be a hen or a cock. It's *courage* and a *big heart* in the channel races. You'll lose some. Some fly only a foot over the water and the waves will come up and gets them in the feathers and they go in. And *fog* is a killer ... they're lost. And birds of prey know the tired pigeons coming in and they're easily caught and killed. Now if there's bad weather — fog or mist — and the pigeon couldn't cross the channel they'd get a night's rest on a safe building and then they're up at dawn and away. But if they come down on walls they're easy prey for cats. There's a good story about the pigeons in channel races that land for the night. One pigeon lands on a Catholic Church and the other fella lands on the Protestant Church. Well, the pigeon that lands on the Catholic Church has a big advantage because the church bell goes at six the next morning and frightens him! Oh, you've got these tales when you get pigeon men together. A pigeon is about fourteen or fifteen ounces and when he comes home from a hard race he's only about half his weight. If you lose half your weight you'd die! But with good husbandry you'll have him back up again. Ah, after a race the pigeon is treated as one of the family.

'Oh, God, there's big money in it now, a lot of betting. Last year a pigeon won three races and it sold for £1,000. In the 1930's it would have gone for about five shillings. And now they fly the "widowhood system". It's *unnatural.* You mate up two pigeons, a hen and a cock, and then you put the cock away where he can't see the hen, and vice versa. Then before the race they'd put him in with the hen for maybe ten minutes, but they'd watch that nothing would happen. Then they'd take him away and he'd be *mad* to get back to the hen. He'd go through the *wall* to get back to the hen. Then he'd be taken to the race point. Oh, he's in a state of frenzy. The widowhood system is cruel in this respect.

'When the war came things were very restricted and you couldn't race outside your own country. In Dublin here then we'd go down as far as Cork and Skibbereen. Interest declined because even food and grain was restricted from other countries. They can give it up for "x" many years, but then they'll go back to it eventually. Once a pigeon fancier, *always* a pigeon fancier.'

HARRY DIXON — Pigeon Fancier, Age 75

The name "Dixon" is one of the most famous in Dublin pigeon circles. Harry is quick to let you know that a 1911 photograph of his grandfather's famous racing pigeon hangs prominently on the wall of the Fluther Good's Pub in Ballybough, a sort of shrine for pigeon men. He and his brother Jimmy live together in Whitehall and have 240 pigeons in their rear yard lofts. Raising pigeons has been the core of their life and there isn't anything they don't know about "the game". As Harry divulges, "me and Jimmy never got married ... there's no time for it with pigeons."

'I was reared with pigeons. Me grandfather was a great pigeon man. He could tell you about young birds, whether the pigeon was going to be a duffer or not, and what pigeons would win channel races. From the time I was five I'd go down to him after school and clean out the pigeons for him. And when he'd be training young ones we'd go on the tram up to the Phoenix Park. He'd put them in the basket and bring them up to the park and let them out and then they'd fly back to the loft. Me father, he was a good flyer too. He had a pigeon and we had a wireless and he (pigeon) loved Irish music. He'd come up on me father's shoulder and fan his tail and you'd think he was dancing! And out in the garden he'd fly onto his head and walk on his shoulders all day. All pigeon racing goes back in families. It went from grandfathers to sons and from fathers to sons. It's just bred into you. Fathers handed down papers on pigeons just like you got papers on race horses. In me father's time they were real gentlemen and their sons the same. And if you won a race there was a hooley in the house. Ah, banjo players and fiddle players. And you got medals and silver watches. Oh, there used to be plenty of medals in our house.

Devoted pigeon raisers Harry and Jimmy Dixon

'Me grandfather was the first man ever to give me pigeons. I was about ten. Then me father bought me some. When I was starting out I rode a bike to the Curragh, thirty miles, with a basket of pigeons. Then release them and let them come home. Then you'd bring them to the station and put them on a train and you could send them to Wexford or Cork and that station-master used to let them out. That's all part of the training. So I bred pigeons and trained them hard and then I said, "it's time to get into a club". Now our club (Dublin Homing Club) goes back to 1924 but when I went into pigeons there was only about three clubs. And we had no club rooms at that time, it was just a field. Just an old field and there'd be big drays for horses in it and all the clocks used to be put on the drays and be set. And there was a pub (in Ballybough) and he (publican) had two white-washed cottages alongside of it and we used to rent them for meetings before we built our club. And he had a sliding door so he could hand in the drink till all hours of the morning. Ah, there was murder with their wives cause some of the fellas wouldn't go home till maybe five in the morning.

'Dublin was always one of the best cities for pigeons, men very well dedicated to it. Oh, you had some great birds winning channel races. People are very dedicated to their birds. You *have* to be. Can't be half-hearted. You have to go the whole way or it's no good. They really love their birds. Oh, there's very few pigeon men gets married. Very few. It has to be that way. But there were some rogues in the game in those days and they used to be able to fiddle the clocks. But you had to be caught before you could be proved a fiddler. Oh, I seen arguments between fellas. Nearly came to blows. A few of them was caught. They were suspended for life and they never raced pigeons again. Oh, you couldn't join another club — suspended for life.

"It's a funny thing, you could train pigeons and they'd be no good, they'd be dead last. You'd want to have good pigeons, like a good racehorse. Then it's the way you train them and everyone had their own ideas on pigeons. Pigeons are very intelligent. When you think that a pigeon can fly out of France into Dublin ... if I was brought to France and they said, "well, make your way to Dublin" you wouldn't know where to go! No way. You'd be lost. In the war the Germans and the British and even your crowd, the Americans, had pigeons trained to fly to the army trucks and that's how they were getting all their information out. A lot of them were shot down but a lot of them got through with very important messages. They saved a lot of lives. For years the Germans wrote books and they'd say pigeons fly by the eyes, that they have a kind of built-in radar in their eyes. Now, the experts say they do it by smells. They're only surmising. It's a mystery.

'A fella like me that was always used to pigeons, if you didn't have them you'd miss them. You definitely would go queer. It's bred into you. My father used to clean out the pigeons up till a few months before he died. And he died at ninety-six. They were his life. Pigeons kept him going — it's as simple as that. Pigeons is a better cure than doctors. Why, there's little wild birds, like sparrows, that comes up here at six in the morning and they come on me hands and all. Come and pick out of me hand. Keep calling for grub. A priest in our club, when he sees the birds coming along he thinks I'm St. Francis of Assissi!'

Chapter 7

Entertainers and Performers

PADDY "BONES" SWEENEY — Busker, Age 70

I first spotted him on a wet, drizzly evening on Grafton Street playing his harmonica and old bohdran drum. He was the genuine article — no doubt about it. "I'm the last of the old buskers, all right", he certified. At sixteen years of age he packed his gear and hit the road travelling the thirty-two counties on foot, bicycle and horse-drawn caravan. He played in country pubs, at fairs and slept in graveyards. He always saw himself as a "wandering minstrel". As age slowed him down he left the rural roads for the streets of Dublin where he is respectfully regarded by the younger musicians as the grandaddy of the buskers.

'My father was a lock keeper on the canal and we lived outside Dublin. I learned a lot of the traditional music at home. Me father, me mother, me grandmother, aunts and uncles, were all traditional musicians. There was a whole mix of accordion, concertina, banjo, fiddle, tin whistle. Just played for the family. At that time neighbours would come in and have a set-to or a hooley. And the old buskers that would come into Dublin, they would *amaze* me. I would always say, "I'm going to be one of them some day". That was me dream ... and so me dream come true.

'When I become sixteen I decided to hit the road meself. So I packed up me gear one day and I was off. I went travelling around Ireland on a bicycle. I had a wattle tent. You cut the hazel sticks and make ribs and pull your canvas over it. I learned it from the Travelling people. I always had a change of socks and underwear and a towel. I was like a wandering minstrel. You'd cycle about six, eight, ten miles and you'd come to a village. On a good day I could do about twenty miles on me bike. I had a banjo and a harmonica and a pair of bones in me pocket. And I got the name "bones" on account of playing the bones. They were cattle ribs. It was a clicking sound, same as playing spoons. I'd sleep mostly on the side of the road. Sometimes I slept in graveyards. It was safer. Local farmers would ask you into their house to play and in villages they'd bring me into the pub and put me sitting up on the counter. And they'd say, "will you play a few tunes?". They'd give me a bottle of orange and a packet of biscuits and pass around a hat for me and I'd make a few bob. When I was young I could play for five or six hours in one go. At that time me parents were fairly objecting to it … "why is he so much of the gypsy?". I was away for a good while and then I come back. They saw that I come back more harder, more tough in meself. And the father, he says, "you know, Rose, he's a *real man* now, isn't he? He's really made it".

Busker Paddy "Bones" Sweeney performing along Grafton Street

'Years ago there were hundreds of buskers all around the country. And there were all different showmen at fairs, like jugglers, mimers, fellas doing tricks. It was more colourful then. And the old buskers, we all knew each other. We'd come into a bar and do a few tunes and always got a few beers and a few bob. We had good crack. And nicknames ... there were three brothers called the "Three Blind Mice" and "Mick the Whistle" and "Banjo Harry" and they called me "Paddy Bones". All good accordion players, flute, banjo, fiddle, whistle players. And we all played by ear. I don't know of any buskers who could read music. And we used to have what was called "swapping tunes". They'd say, "I like that tune you're playing" and they'd a good ear and they'd pick it up. Then they'd give you one. I have hundreds of tunes now up in me mind. Some jigs and reels I just made up, like "Saddle the Pony", "A Penny Swing", "The Bag of Spuds", "Kid on the Mountain". But there's hundreds and hundreds of tunes I've still to learn yet.

'Most buskers weren't married. They were all wanderers. They could never settle down to that type of life. Now some buskers would marry a woman busker and they'd travel together, team up and travel through Ireland. There was Margaret Barry who used to go around to all the football matches and race courses in the 1930's and 1940's. She walked and used to wear a big black shawl and a banjo would be tied on her back. Another woman used to play the banjo up at the Dublin Cattle Market and she'd only one leg and a wooden crutch. She used to stand outside Hanlon's Pub on the North Circular Road when all the big farmers and cattle dealers come in and that's how she made her living. They were very good to her. And they'd bring her out little glasses of whiskey and brandy. She used to sing "Mick McGilligan's Daughter, Mary Ann".

'I was always moreless a loner but I was married when I was about twenty-four. I met her in Tipperary on a fair day. We'd be living here in Dublin and I'd go out for two or three months. I had a horse and caravan at the time. It was hard, that's why we split up. She was getting contrary over it ... "don't go away". I'd say, "I *must* get away. I want to travel. I can't bring you with me, the road is too hard for you". See, I used to go to the thirty-two counties, the whole of Ireland. Always met up with other musicians and learned a lot from them. And on the road you met up with philosophers, historians, writers and they'd be interested in you. And there were old story tellers and great old step dancers. They'd travel on the crossroads. Step dancing there'd be eight people, four men and four women, and it would be crossroad dancing. Musicians would come down and all the neighbourhood would be down for the crossroad dancing. You might be lucky and be the only busker in the area.

'Busking at fairs was the most beautiful part of me life. They used to hold the fairs on the street at that time selling cattle and sheep and horses and pigs. All the drovers around and there'd be dealings and clapping hands and splitting the difference. All that tradition was beautiful. Farmers that might only come once a month to fair day would be *delighted* to see you. If you got about six bob you could eat well and keep going. Now during bad weather and snow you couldn't travel so much. I'd go into a town. A lot of old buskers, they'd come in and base themselves in Dublin for the winter. They'd keep out of the mountainy country. On the road in the mountains would be very hard. I got stuck in Donegal some years ago with the two horses in a heavy drift of snow and couldn't move. My worry was that the horses would die of hunger. But the local people got to find out and they come down and helped me out, brought me down hay and straw and turf for me fire. And the women sent me down homemade bread and tea

Old-time Dublin street busker Paddy "Bones" Sweeney

and sugar and milk. They were really good. That's real hospitality, the *real* thing.

'So I travelled throughout the country with the horse-drawn caravan but traffic was beginning to get heavy on the road (early 1950's) and it became unsafe. So I played around Dublin on the street. I play there now on Liffey Street by Arnott's and up on Grafton Street most Sundays. They all know me name now in Dublin. Some say, "that's really beautiful. You're the best in Dublin streets that we've ever heard". When people stop and gather around it's a form of appreciation. I love to speak to the people. And kids will be dancing in front of me. Ah, I've had forty or fifty people around me. I make enough money on the street to have a flat, buy me food. When I get twenty-five pounds I'm quite content. But this is the only town in the whole of Ireland where cops say you have to move on. You have to move on ... but then we come back. Some of the buskers here had a battle with the law a few years ago. I got six months probation in 1983 for busking and a two pound fine. Most towns, none of them bother you!

'Ah, it's changed today. Too much bowsers (boozers). Guys get drunk and try to steal your instruments, especially the bohdran drum. Four years ago I got knifed in my back and they kicked me neck in. I lost me speech for a while. It's not safe now. But now I like to encourage the younger buskers. Ah, but the buskers today wouldn't stand a hope in hell — a snowball's chance in hell — against the old buskers. I seen the best of them. I say to the young buskers today, "if you want to be a *real* busker you've got to hit the road. You've got to face a lot of hardships and you have to cope with it". You've got to have in in *here* (tapping heart) and up here (tapping head). But some of the younger ones, they're not buskers. They've no *character,* no talent. To me, to be a busker you've got to have character ... you're a *showman,* an entertainer.

'There's only a few of us old-timers left. I'm the oldest busker here in Dublin. God, it's been a hard life! But I'd do it all again. Going along the road from place to place, whistling to yourself. Meeting lovely people and other musicians. It's a beautiful way of life as far as I'm concerned. It never leaves you. You eat it, you sleep it, you drink it and you play it. It's me life. I don't know anything else. Buskers are rich in that they love what they're doing. And money can't buy that. No money can buy my lifestyle, not the whole world's money put together. Just to be left alone and do what I'm doing. A life that I loved ... independent ... adventurous ... you know? I've been *free!'*

JOHN MAHER — Busker, Age 63

Born in a caravan to Travelling parents, he began as a child singing barefooted beside his father on the streets of country towns. Dirty and raggedly-clad, he looked like some Dickensian urchin. But he drew a crowd and that was the objective. He ran away from home at twelve

*years of age and took to the roads as a nomadic busker. He lived by his
wits, songs and tin whistle. In his later years he "wintered in" in Dublin
and found that he could earn a fair living from the city streets.
Wearing a huge Mexican sombrero for show he prefers busking along
Henry Street where on Saturdays he draws massive crowds of curious
onlookers. "They think I'm from another century", he muses.*

'I was born.in a caravan when we were travelling. Cities were completely taboo
for Travelling people back then. Now if you were doing the music it was O.K.
but if you were begging you got hassled. In those days me father often went
singing in the streets and he used to sell ballad sheets as well. And I'd be going
around selling them when I was small, seven or eight, and a fella would say to
me, "if you sing that song I'll buy it". So, straight away, I'd start singing the song.
Just the voice. Then I'd start playing it with a whistle. Oh, I wasn't a bit shy. It
just came natural.

'My father used to play what they called the "box", the accordion, and he'd sing
with it. Very often he used to pawn it. When he hadn't got the box, well, he'd
sing in the streets and get the price of it back again.We used to do all the weekly
fairs in different towns and you'd walk up and down the street singing. Now on
me mother's side they'd be doing the "hoopla", the roulette wheel, at different
fairs. We called them spielers. In those days a lot of the buskers, even me father,
would go on a bicycle rather than the horse and cart from town to town. Up to
ten or eleven me father used to carry me in the carrier on the back of the bicycle.
In rainy weather we used to have the old soldier's cape. He'd wear that and I'd
be under the back of it. And the box, you had to keep that dry. And you'd carry
maybe a sleeping bag or a few blankets. We often slept out under the tree with
plastic or the cape over us. It was completely safe back then.

'Now I ran away when I was twelve. The father was drinking and kind of giving
me a hard time. Very difficult in those days. Trying to sing or play in the street
and sometimes you'd get soaked to the skin. I started off with a penny whistle
and I often did a jig, but it wouldn't be proper dancing. But I had a crowd
around me and I'd play up to them, you see, that was the idea. And I was
raggedy completely. I had no shoes, me hair would be unkempt and you
wouldn't have proper clothes. Trousers was always too big or too small for me.
Something like out of Dickens in a way ... it looked Oliver Twistish or Artful
Dodger, like that. But people were kind. People'd throw you money in the
streets, ha'pennies and even farthings. Everything counted. I've often had me two
trouser pockets full of copper. If you made a pound in a week it was doing
good. But you'd get days with no fairs or bad weather and then you were
finished.

'There was a load of travelling musicians at that time. And in the old days I used
to bicycle and I played the tin whistle and the box and the mouth organ. And
back then there was no traffic, no sound (in towns). Like if you'd walk into a

206

town like Clondalkin and Jim the Barber, one of the street singers years ago, if he was singing in the middle of it you could hear him several streets away cause there was no traffic, no sound, and the voice carried. Now for years I had a beard real long and hair real long and big rough boots and an old coat, like a tramp, and I called meself "Rambling John". People used to stop and look. No matter where you'd go you'd get the kind welcome. The things people did for me was *unbelievable*. People on the street in little towns ... "have you a place to sleep tonight? You can come to my house and sleep there". And I was playing away outside and it was heavy frost and people'd bring me mittens and out comes a lady with a big pot of tea and bread and sandwiches and a man brings

John Maher, one of the last of the traveling buskers, performing along Henry Street

me a glass of hot whiskey. Next thing, the butcher comes out and says, "call into me and I'll give you a few chops" and another fella says, "here you are" and he threw me a chicken. *Honestly.*

'Now one day me and Paddy O'Brien — and the two of us half drunk — was going along the road and I said, "well, that's a big crowd, there must be an awful match on here ... we'll set up". So we get the instruments and sit down and start

A busking harpist along Grafton Street

playing by the gate. Now this is as true as I'm here! And the crowd's coming out and we're getting a few bob and a nun comes over to us and says, "hello, that music is lovely … he *would have loved it!*" And I says, *"who* would have loved it?". "Ah, me father". He was after being buried! We were playing outside a graveyard. At a funeral. We never seen it. It looked like a football field. There was a huge crowd in it.

'Now about ten years ago I was travelling around and when you're busking you have to think of the weather. You see, in the winter time if the weather is bad you can't travel with the ice and snow so you have to try and get a place for the winter. So I said, "the hell with it, I'll settle down in Dublin for the winter and wait for the spring again and get off the road". Now the only place in the whole of Ireland there was trouble with the guards is here in Dublin. For the last years I was getting a lot of hassle and I was arrested at least five times. And you'd be moved on. Like I'd go into Henry Street and the police'd say, "move on … go on over to Grafton Street". And I'd say, "I don't like Grafton Street". And he'd say, "why not?" and I said, "there's all Barclay cards and Diner's cards and no change in the pocket". But on Henry Street it's a real shopping area for people from the country and the average, normal person. But Grafton Street is kind of the Yuppies. I did Grafton Street once but it didn't have the same atmosphere for me at all as Henry Street. Now last Saturday on Henry Street I picked up eighty quid!

'Now when I appear here in Dublin I get great crowds. One time I had a crowd of 400 to 500 people. I'm playing all tunes of the forties, the ballads, all Irish songs. It hits them. Oh, people get emotional. I've observed that. They'll come along and say, "Oh, that's lovely. It's been years since I heard that". Like one day I played "Danny Boy" and when I stopped for a smoke this old man comes over, an old age pensioner, and he gave me a pound and he says, "could you play that again?". So I did. And the next minute he was busting up crying and there was a crowd around. "I never heard it as nice as that", he says.

'I still make all the festivals. Last year I travelled 4,000 miles in Ireland. See, I busk the trains and the buses down and back. Country buses. I go to the back seat and start playing and just put the box down and collect. And I busk the train down to Galway. I stay in one carriage and play there and then pack up and go to the next one. See, anywhere there's a crowd, you can busk. It's like me father used to say to me, "where you meet two bicycles at the crossroad you'll get the price of a pint". I was all around the country last year and the people in Mayo and Galway said, "we haven't seen the likes of you here in thirty or forty years". See, there are none like me now that go from town to town in winter. They think I'm from outer space or from another century.

'There are none like me now … well, there's Johnny "Melodion" Hogan, Paddy "Bones" Sweeney, Michael Dunne, John Wilson and then there's "Blind Joe" Ganor, he's in Galway. It has to be *in you.* You have to be able to rough it and you'd have to like it. I'd rather be out in the fresh air and earning a few bob.

Please, God, when it's time for me to go I'll go to the Gateway waiting for the crowd to come in ... I'll busk outside first.'

FRANK QUINLAN — Busker, Age 60

His favourite haunts are along Grafton and Henry Streets where his booming voice is certain to attract attention. His wind-swept grey hair and moustache create a striking appearance perfectly fitting a street balladeer. People stop to look and listen. He's good — good enough, in fact, that he can play at such pubs as the Wolfe Tone and The Chinaman in the evenings when he wishes. But he clearly sees the streets as his stage and prefers the intimate rapport with people gathered close around. And he's savvy enough to break into a sentimental rendition of "Danny Boy" when he sees a contingent of Americans approaching.

'The first time I saw buskers was in Limerick. I was about nine or ten. They were brothers, both of them blind, and both played the fiddle. They were quite good. I accepted it naturally as part of the scene. The busker, I'd say, was originally the story teller or versifier. What I know of busking, originally they were news bearers, people who travelled from town to town bearing news of what happened in the last town. Eventually the minstrels and the ballads all came into it.

'I left home at sixteen and travelled around England doing this job and that. I came back to Ireland and had some taxi jobs. At night time in the rank waiting for somebody to come along I'd sit in the back seat and play the guitar. Just teach yourself sort of thing. Two years later I was in Amsterdam and buskers were part of the street life. I got into a scene where some of us were playing in youth clubs, but never busked. But in Amsterdam I developed the flair for entertaining.

'My first experience at busking was here in Dublin up on Grafton Street. There were no jobs and I started off broke. I walked up Grafton Street and took out my guitar and started playing. My knees were like jelly ... shaking. And I put it back in the box and walked up the street. Then I said to myself, "I *have* to do it". It was desperation. I just said, "you *have* to do it!". So I walked back down again and three or four months later I was an old busker. There were maybe a dozen real buskers around then and we'd meet on the street. Buskers, they have this nomadic sort of thing in them and they don't want to be tied down to times and places. It's a kind of a fraternity.

'Dublin is a good city for busking, especially the northside. Amongst the working people you have a much better rapport. I used to do six to eight hours a day some time back. In winter it's no fun. Your hands are freezing, your back is cold and the wind is blowing — but you've still got to make money. People might be passing you by and not stopping. Or maybe just throwing the odd copper in. If it was summer the whole year around it would be infinitely preferable to busk. But money warms you as well and Christmas time you get very good money. I once got a drop of fifteen pounds ... a couple of Americans. Or you'll get offered a drink or flowers from young girls. Or from children sometimes apples, half-eaten bags of sweets and things like that.

Well-known Dublin street busker Frank Quinlan (right) chatting with some appreciative listeners

'Busking is the same as getting up on a stage. As a busker you'd do more on the street than you would do in a pub. On the street when you're giving out, doing a pitch, when your crowd comes around they're all facing you and you're looking at them and the closer the contact you have with them the better. You're not only singing and playing but you talk to the audience, crack a joke or two. So you'll have more of a rapport on the streets than you will in a pub. You get more of a kick out of it. And I'm a watcher, I learn a lot about human nature on the street. You see all the lunacies and down-and-outs and dingbats. And you can sense the mood of the crowds. You can *feel* it on the street. There's an eyeball-to-eyeball contact. You'll look at your audience and try to gauge what's nice for them. I always stick with a certain number of Irish songs. You can see the smiles and the memories … and tears.

Busker Frank Quinlan and mate being "cheerfully" interrupted by police

'Nice experiences. Like the old professor of music who comes down Grafton Street and sits down listening for a while and then he comes up and tells you that you're not playing this one properly. But then at the same time says to you, "sing me a song that'll make me cry and I'll give you a pound". He was telling me that he was sort of getting on (in age) and found it hard to relate to women. So I sang him a song that had something to do with that. It didn't make him quite cry and he put fifty "P" in the box. So I think it was nearly successful.

'Another nice experience now, and this was in the heart of winter, a very cold night, raining, hardly anybody on Grafton Street and I'm standing in a doorway. Down the opposite side come a Traveller (Itinerant), a male, and on this side a female Traveller begging. And I said, "sorry, there's nothing at all". So she says, "will you sing 'The Fields of Athenry?'. So I started to sing and she put fifty "P" in the box. And she sat down on the ground. Next thing, I hear him shout, "get up off your ass, woman, and go and do some work". So he comes over to join her and sits down and they ask me to play something else. And I sing a song called "Bo Jangles". They finished up putting about four pounds in the box and it was the only four pounds there that evening. This was years ago and I still meet them on the streets and they still call me "Mr. Bo Jangles".

'Years ago it was much simpler, much easier. They (guards) can move you on now if you're causing an obstruction. Sometimes you're threatened with arrest. My partner now, he's been prosecuted under the 1840's Vagrancy Act. I've avoided that by talking my way out of it. The shopowners on Grafton Street and Henry Street, for all intent and purposes, *own* the street. So about three years ago we got together a union of buskers to try and make peace with the shopkeepers, not the police. We collected 8,000 signatures (of public support) and had meetings and it came to a kind of agreement that they, the shopkeepers, would calm down a little bit on their side and we would too.

'With busking you can guarantee *nothing* ... with the weather and police, the people, the frozen hands. But I wake up with it and I go to bed with it and I live it during the day. I'd hate to lose this street level.'

BRIAN HUDSON — Pavement Artist, Age 35

He is one of the most gifted "chalkies" on Dublin's streets. At nineteen years of age in Vienna he began learning his artform from fellow pavement artists. Today the skin on his fingertips is worn away from blending chalk colours on rough pavement surfaces. Dark-haired, introspective and deadly earnest about his work, he is the stereotypical "struggling artist". He earns enough to survive from day to day, but little more. But most important, he is free to express himself. To him, that is the very essence of life. A few summers ago he won first prize in the Westport competition for pavement artists.

'In Dublin we're called pavement artists, or "chalkies". I reckon that pavement art goes back millions of years, like what the cavemen used to do on the walls with burnt wood or whatever they used. I reckon they expressed themselves in the sand as well. Now on the streets it must go way back. Back in the fourteenth century chalk was the most dominant thing and tubes of paint came after chalk. Leonardo DeVinci, he used chalk ... or charcoal. Same principle in using it, same effect. Doing it on the ground you don't have paints and brushes. The colours are just mixed with your fingers. The lovely thing is that there isn't a brush between you and your picture. It's your *fingers*. I put colour and an image on just a grey ground and that's a contribution. I think Dubliners appreciate it.

'I'm from Churchtown, kind of a working-class area. In school I had some art and was told that I was quite good. I never went into secondary school cause I mitched a lot. After unsuccessfully starting a few trades I travelled to Hamburg, France, Spain and eventually found myself in Vienna. I saw a lot of people

213

drawing in the street and thought, "I like drawing, I know the fundamentals of it". So I started off in Vienna and on the very first pitch got myself a quiet place. I was very uneasy about it, you know. I just did it with school chalk. I had my Irish passport and the old ones had a gold harp. So I thought that was simple to draw, with just lines and curves. It was kind of patriotic actually. It was really bad that first day and nobody left me anything. I was there for only about a half an hour and then I just ran away from it. After that first day I thought about it a bit more cause I was just getting by by begging. And I'd been doing some drawing at home. So about a week later I went out again and mixed with other pavement artists in Vienna. I did a scene from the bible and it turned out very well. And I found that when I did get down on the pavement to draw it wasn't only a means of getting money but it was also a means of *expression*. From Vienna I went to Munich and continued street drawing.

'I got back to Dublin in 1979. I had a lot of experience I got in Munich, Vienna, Stutgart, Hamburg. Henry Street arcade was the first place I did a drawing. I did a Mother and Child picture. I can get it so it looks like there's motion in the picture with shadows and when the light shines on it it looks like the hair is blowing. That day I made nearly fifty pounds! That encouraged me. The best picture I ever done here in Dublin was the Children of Lir, an old Irish legend of three children who were turned into swans and it was in dark blues and light blues. Irish take pride in their history and mythology but they also respond to religious pictures.

'I'd be out for about six hours and I might take out 200 different pieces of chalk. Just carry them in a box. And it's either a good surface or a bad surface. A pavement stone is better if it's about a hundred years old or more. These new ones are kind of "biscuity" and your chalk is wasted because of the little pores and lumps. It just eats your chalk away. And blending the chalk with my finger I'm rubbing the skin away. On the pavement it's your knee joints that hurt the most. And in the winter it's cold but when you're absorbed in something you forget about the cold. It's that motivation to get something on the ground, to create something ... a way of expression. That's as important as the money. With drawing nobody can dictate to your mind. *Nobody!*

'Dubliners appreciate it. A lot of people come up and hit me on the back and say, "keep up the good work, you're a very talented artist". Ah, it's good for the old ego. Sometimes a guy who admires what I'm doing will bring me a pint out of the pub. Just puts the pint down beside me. Maybe pat me on the back and walk on. It's beautiful, actually, when people do that. I find that the old people stop and really, really admire it. A good day would be about fifty pounds. I made £120 one day. It was at Christmas and everyone was very givish. But there's always a percentage of what you take home that's sympathy money. I know this because I'll often finish a picture and watch an old lady, not looking at the picture but watching *me*. She hasn't even looked to appreciate the picture. It's just the fact that I'm sitting on the ground.

Talented Dublin pavement artist Brian Hudson

'I'd say that there's only about eight serious pavement artists in Dublin now who are constantly at it. When you're drawing maybe a thousand people might see it and then it's *gone*. In a day. It bothers me in a way. Some I'm glad to walk away from but others, especially the ones that come out of me head, I would like to have. It's as if, "here I am after doing this and all I have now is this money". The picture's not with me anymore. Funny thing, after I go home I feel kind of empty.'

COLLETTE MEEHAN — Pavement Artist, Age 30

She honed her artistic skills on street pavements in Germany, Spain and Italy. Her favourite pitch in Dublin is on College Green where she creates colourful works by the French Impressionists. As people admiringly engage her in conversation she flashes a warm smile and pauses in her painting. Then there are the "odd crazy" individuals she has to suffer on the street. But pavement art provides her with "bread and butter" money and a sense of creative expression in the midst of an immediately appreciative audience.

'I used to come into town every Saturday when I was a child and just go to see the buskers and the street artists. Ah, I wanted to do it. Teachers at school taught me art and when I was eighteen I left school and went to art school in Dun Laoghaire for one year. My first pavement drawing experience was when I was nineteen. It was on Grafton Street. It took courage to do it. I was a bunch of nerves. But the sun was shining and it was fun to be out. At that time I wasn't very good at choosing work to catch people's eye. But I'd say I made about a fiver the first day.

'I wanted to make drawing my way to make money and so I went travelling to Germany and France with one busker and another girl who was drawing in the street also. The standards really varied a lot in France, religious paintings to Impressionistic. When I started I didn't know that there was a tradition behind it. It was only later in Italy I heard that the tradition began with artists who needed to advertise their work and they'd come out on the street. And famous people — maybe Michelangelo — came out and did this to attract work. I guess they were quite supreme then. It must have been amazing. And the tradition was to do it on the pavement. It gave it respectability. I spent two months in Rome and this is where I got my experience, a very good place to draw because the city is totally surrounded and filled with art.

Passers–by intrigued by pavement art

'I came back to Dublin and the police moved us off a lot … complaints about obstruction. You can't just go where you want. It may be an unwritten law. You generally keep away from shops. Shopowners have a say because you can block people. On College Green it's safe because there's not many shops there and part of O'Connell and Henry and Grafton Streets are O.K. College Green pavement is good because it's smooth and this is important. You tend to burn your fingers on the pavement. See, you can have a good patch to draw on and then suddenly one slab won't be smooth and it won't take the chalk. I've drawn on stuff that was so rough that my fingers were cut. And I find that my back is getting very bad. Generally I need about eight hours and I sit cross-legged or crouched down. By the end of the week you can feel it.

'Being out on the street you meet a lot of different kinds of people. There can be so many people passing your drawing and somebody will say, "Oh, that's not the way a Holy Family should be presented" ... criticising your interpretation of it. But somebody else will come up and say, "Oh, that's beautiful". So sometimes it's good criticism. Basically, it's all communication and that's what we're there for. People have given me money, flowers, ice cream, pizza, everything. And a whole cake — probably from some woman who suddenly decided to go on a diet. But I don't like it when people stand for an hour watching and maybe want to chat you up. And drunks are sometimes a problem. You just hope they go away. And sometimes you get the odd crazy. Like the woman here in Dublin in black who carries the cross. Well, one time she criticised my drawing, it was a religious picture. And I'm very touchy about people with dogs. They can walk around the picture but the dog will take a shortcut.

'Pavement drawing gives you enough to live on. I'm on the street making my bread and butter money. In Italy there was a book made of street artists. There's a lot of respect for it. Oh, yes, I can say I contribute to beautiful things on the street. There's even a pavement artist in "Mary Poppins"!'

URSULA MEEHAN — Pavement Artist, Age 28

Like her sister, Collette, she does mostly French Impressionistic work but also likes classical Italian and Dutch Renaissance paintings. On a sultry August afternoon she hunches over her pavement art, hands and face smeared with chalk but seemingly contented in her work. Describing herself as a "free spirit", she takes pride in contributing a colourful scene upon a dead grey pavement.

'When I was ten or eleven I used to draw in school all the time, from my head. Oh, I did great monsters. When I left school I did graphic art for two years. I was seventeen when I started to street draw in Dublin during the holidays to make money. My first day I did a Reubens up at St. Stephen's Green. I only made six pounds but it was "Oh, great!", you know?

'So I did one summer drawing and then the next summer I went to Germany. It was that sense of freedom to leave. I went off with a friend and we worked as chamber maids in a hotel in Munich. On my day off I'd go out drawing. Then we went down to Italy and stayed in Rome for the winter and that's when I really got into street drawing. I was travelling with a rucksack on the back and in Rome I used to live outside all the time … very rough. We used to live in a monument in a park during the winter. There were a lot of street drawers around in Rome and ten or twelve of us from different countries would all live together. It was really very close. A lot of really interesting people. You get all kinds of street artists, really good ones and really terrible ones, but we were all learning. I did a lot of drawing in Italy. They've bigger pavements and you've more sunshine. And in Rome it's a very high standard of street drawing. In north Italy there's a street drawing competition every year. They have a lot of history of it.

Dublin pavement artist Ursula Meehan

'Street drawing in Dublin has always been good. Now I did a lot of Italian art in Italy and Europe but in Ireland you try to do "Irishy" work — Oscar Wilde, Bernard Shaw, Beckett, Joyce, Yeats. I did some pictures of some Irish writers and I used to write a poem underneath and they were very popular in Dublin. A lot of people draw religious things but I find them very annoying. If I draw a religious picture it's only because it's a masterpiece work of art, not for the religious end of it. But if you're drawing a religious picture the gypsy Tinkers will never steal from you because they're very religious. My work mostly uses classical pieces and Renaissance. Irish people say, "Oh, great, something a bit different … not Madonna's everywhere".

'In Dublin people *do* appreciate it. It can be very good for your ego … people coming up and saying how brilliant you are. You're mixing with people in a way that I like, whereas if you're just in a studio and painting you're *alone*. You'll be surprised at the young, tough guys who'll come along and they'll really appreciate it! I do a lot at Christmas time and I put candles around the picture at night cause it gets dark very early. It's lovely at night. Fifty pounds would be a

218

good day. I once got thirty-five pounds from a man in Dublin, an artist, a landscape painter. But one time I was arrested outside Trinity. I was up for begging and obstruction. And I just said, "I don't think it's begging at all. It's a form of art and in other countries it's respected and it has its own place". In the end it was kind of laughed out of court.

'You have to be a free spirit. I've met people who have drawn for ten and twenty years. You might just end up doing street drawing for the rest of your life ... and that kind of bothers me. But I've always felt that it was worth people giving money for street drawing because you've made something beautiful. I love seeing the colour that you're doing on the street. That attracts people and for the moment people enjoy it ... the colour that you add to the street and the way that people react to it.'

THOM McGINTY — Street Mime and Clown, Age 40

"Dublin's most famous street walker", he likes to acclaim him-self. There's no disputing that. To Dubliners he's best known as the "Diceman" on Grafton Street. Of course, he's also been a teapot, tennis ball, Easter Egg, Dracula and countless other oddly shaped and coloured objects and personages. As Dublin's premier street jester, he has been featured on R.T.E. shows and in magazine articles. Despite his commercial success in doing costumed promotions for business firms, there is no doubting that Thom's great love is the street itself and the grand crowds on a sunny Saturday afternoon. Although he has been abused and accosted many times, he fully intends to continue providing Dubliners with high amusement. After all, he admits, "I'm a street character ... part of the history of street life in Dublin".

'I was born in Scotland — on April Fool's Day! The father's father was from Donegal and from six weeks old I started coming over here every summer. So when I was twenty-four I moved over to Dublin sort of bag and baggage. I had something ridiculous like forty pounds at the time. I sold stuff to keep going, odds and ends like teapots and candle sticks and stamp collections I'd collected over the years. I wasn't aware that I could claim dole here and so I reckoned I'd have to go out on the street for handouts. And I thought, "God, I can't do that, can't just stand with my hand out". So I thought, "well, maybe I can *give* them something for their money. I can't play an instrument and I can't sing but I can make-up in gear and give them something to look at". I'd seen the Dandelion Market and it looked O.K., it wasn't exposed on the street. It had the kind of atmosphere that might take it. So I took bits and pieces and a jacket and looked sort of bizarre like a clown and a little mat and actually sat there with a little note on a brown paper bag saying, "In love with country but unable to gain employment — please give generously, thank you".

'I was in the main mall and I just sat there — motionless. I think the immobility was fear! I approached it as a bizarre way of begging, rather than performing, as you can see from the note. I was very, very scared, very nervous, and I thought, "well, if I get two pounds off it ...". But I think I made *sixteen* pounds that day. What happened was, people seemed to be *fascinated* by this beggar and I'd thank them.with a wink and thumbs-up. Now after a couple of weeks the note went because it was no longer valid. Also, I started to *stand*. I think it was a psychological thing — from sitting to standing — that I was no longer timid. And I was a model in art school (previously) and I'd be in one pose in front of people

Thom McGinty, Dublin's premier street mime along Grafton Street

for six hours and so I got this idea of making (standing) pictures in front of people. I enjoyed it enormously, enjoyed it as a way of performing. And I found that it provided me with an income. Then the Dandelion closed down in 1979.

'Now there was this shop called the Diceman on Grafton Street which sold games and the owner was interested in a bit of crack in the street to promote his shop. So I thought I'd give it a go for a couple of weeks to see if it'd work out. His logo was a man in black and a broad-brimmed hat and his hand out with dice on it. Now we didn't have that gear, so I did it dressed in a black and gold "magiciany" turban thing with the hand out and the dice, but not moving. Now there was never any intention of collecting, but people put money into the hand with the dice. Completely unexpected. Try and tell the police that! And because the owner was into fantasy games there was as whole realm of visuals I could get into and relate with the shop. So I'd change the colour and shapes. But I tended to keep the face that worked. Now a lot of people, they'd watch at a distance. Wouldn't come *near* me! No. They wouldn't. But I could take in sixteen to twenty pounds on a day. And there were days when I'd take in fifty.

Famed street mime Thom McGinty along Grafton Street

'He was happy with the attention I was getting and the business I was bringing in but other traders in the arcade were concerned that my presence was keeping people from coming into their shops because the entrance would be blocked. So these traders had me forcibly removed from there by the police. So I couldn't just stand outside there and then I tried standing in the middle of the road. But again I was moved … couldn't stand. So, the only way to do it was to *move*, that's what the gardai wanted. So I practised out in the street to move and still get those qualities of stillness — but to be on the move so he (guard) can't get me for obstruction. I just started trying it. To me it was a Godsend because the problem of obstruction with a crowd gathering was very real. But when you're moving — a sort of ethereal gliding effect — the act was even more effective. It was just very mobile and I could deal with lots of situations.

A bit of lively street theatre along Grafton Street

'I was being called "The Diceman" then by the public. I was creating phenomenal media attention for the shop. But I was so strongly associated with the Diceman that there was no way you could work for other people on Grafton Street. There was a lot of frustration because I wanted to create. Once the shop went (closed) I was in big demand. This triggered all sorts of weird ideas. I took a job with Brown-Thomas advertising their late night openings as a sort of Edwardian newspaper seller. And I did a fair bit of work for Bewley's advertising as Dracula for their bracks, and as an Easter egg. But I discovered that whoever you worked for, the identity of the Diceman was with you as a character. And when I started moving people still put money in my hand. There's only so much you can hold in your hand and so I'd sort of mechanically put it away with moves. At this time I saw myself as a *walking picture*, a performing walking picture. It was a form of visual documentation. Like, rather than having a picture up on a wall or a statue in a gallery, I was there walking down the street in front of them. I saw myself definitely as a creative performing artist.

'Oh, Dubliners are appreciative. There's supposed to be 53,000 people who go down there on Grafton Street each day. But people on Henry Street are much more alive and immediate with their reactions. All sorts of looks and reactions. Shapes really attract people. Like I was a tennis ball and a teapot. And I do thousands of winks in a day. The strongest response is definitely from the young and the old. Oh, you can get some "looks" on their faces. And there's moods in crowds. You can feel the waves of the people's moods as they change during the day.

'And people do things to you sometimes out of anger. That's another kind of story. If you're in the street you have to deal with hecklers. In the past years I've been set fire to by a cigarette, people stuff a cigarette in your neck or on the back of your heel, people spat in my face, poured hot cups of coffee over me. Sometimes they'll just give you a punch to try and move you cause you're so straight. And office girls, they'll give you clouts in the back of the head. A crowd of young guys set fire to my costume. On Grafton Street. It just melted. People helped to put it out. Setting fire … that's cheating. You set yourself up with a public exhibition, right? But not to be abused. In the street sometimes they'll come up and stick you with a safety pin. I've done a lot of stuff in bare feet and people will throw thumb tacks on the ground in front of you. You're not sacrosanct out there.

'Some of my friends say to me now, "oh, that's great — you've *made it* at last and you don't have to do those streets anymore". And I say, "what are you *talking about?*". I couldn't just go to commercial work. I still go out on my own and don't collect — as a matter of *principal.* You give people a special delight, a visual delight. You're giving them a moment or a second of making them laugh, amusing them. The ability to create visuals is endless. I've certainly got the imagination for that. Lots of stuff I'd like to do on the street. Dublin has a strong history of street characters and street presences. I think I'm a street character, a street presence. People do see me as part of the history of street life in Dublin.'

EOIN RABBITT — Street Mime and Clown, Age 32

As a dancing clown attired in black clothing with stark white-painted face, bright red nose and red heart on his cheek, he is quite a novelty on Dublin streets. People halt, stand motionless, get perplexed expressions on their faces. Then they smile and enjoy the show. He calls himself a "performing artist" whose stage is the city's streets. He is highly sensitive and there is an apparent vulnerability about him. His moods swing from joyful to sad and he has openly cried on the street before his audience. Charlie Chaplinesque in appearance, he is a fluid dancer with expressive face and hand gestures. Some people seem mesmerised by his motions.

'Through history, since the beginning, every country had clowns. I didn't really plan to be a street performer ... this image on the street was just created. It's a totality of myself. I'm a social clown, meaning I socialise with people when I'm on the street. People say, "Bravo" and "thank you" and give me flowers. On Henry Street sometimes I've drawn a hundred, maybe two hundred people. People get drawn to me. I find the real, real Dublin people in the centre of Dublin. They're beautiful people. I'm less inhibited when I put on my clown clothes and take on the characters of other people. People can fall in love with a clown.

'I was born in Galway and when I was a child I saw a lot of people playing music, fiddles or violins, but I saw no street mimes. But I'd make believe. I had a good fantasy. When I was six I spent a year in the hospital for T.B. and when I came back I always had a little bit extra observation. And I began classical ballet when I was seven. I was very thin and small and the only boy in it. When I was twelve we did a lot of Irish dance in our school and I started dancing on my own and I'd imagine expressions in my mind. And I'd see Charlie Chaplin and Laurel and Hardy and I was intrigued. I'd often spend hours just dancing in the back room of the house with music.

'When I was sixteen I left school and came to Dublin and joined a religious group called "The Jesus People". I believe that somebody put L.S.D. in something I ate because I had a "trip" and seen great big flowers and everything. I only stayed a few days because they were way out of their minds. Then I worked here in Dublin as a social worker at a hostel for men, I was interested in *people*. At twenty-one I joined the Trappist Monastery in Waterford. But I left it a year later, and a day. While I was there I did a lot of yoga, became a vegetarian and I also danced there, practised movement on my own. My music was inside of me. And I heard there about one monk 300 or 400 years ago who was a clown in a circus once and then he became a monk and did mime and dance.

'I began performing back on the streets in Galway. I just sort of put this thing around my head, a kind of scarf, and moved slowly to the sounds of this blind man (busker) playing there with an accordion. And other people were playing music and I moved to their music. And also the cars passing ... their sound was my music. *Street sounds* were my music. No make-up, no music, just movement. People would just stand around (watching). And I liked to dance in the street to the people playing music. I danced a lot in my barefeet. Now the first day I put down a hat, but no money in it. See, if you put money in the hat and people see it, it attracts other money. But to me it was important not to start that way, to see if people would give me any.

'I really started as a performance artist in Dublin in 1982 on the street. I just *felt* it. There was an inner voice. I always had this kind of artistic energy. And I was influenced by Thom McGinty (see preceding pages). I bought some colours and painted my face. I had this white face — not black or red — always a white face.

Street mime and clown Eoin Rabbitt

A very dramatic white face. And a little heart on my face and the red nose and the black lips I do for my black-haired curly clown I do. And red or black clothing. And I always start by standing as a statue. If you do the statue it holds people's attention and then you can perform in front of a lot of people. I improvise. I think of Gene Kelly and "Singing in the Rain" ... you know, that set-up — theatre on the street — and I improvise with a lamp-post or waste paper box. And I like a background or pitch with shop windows with mannequins and colour. I love to dance, dance, dance. But performing on the street is difficult because you don't know what's going to happen. Practical problems. Like the problems of young people and delinquency. Like today a boy threw something at me. Or they'll try and steal my radio. And the police are a problem. Here in Dublin they allow more music than theatre on the street.

Grafton Street puppeteer and street mime Eoin Rabbitt clapping in approval

'I'm aware of what's happening on the street and the people that are watching me. Dublin people, they're beautiful people. Oh, beautiful things have happened. People will say, "Bravo, Bravo!", give me flowers, write me notes. One woman came over today and danced with me. It's nice to see people feeling happy. And you can feel the *energy*. People share the good energy through the dance and music and sharing. Like there was this one woman standing there in her fur coat and a gypsy woman standing beside her watching me. I don't really notice what individuals put in but it's mostly ten or twenty pence. Sometimes they'll put in a pound.

'Some people can fall in love with a clown but they don't really want to know *you*. So sometimes I'm feeling O.K. physically but something isn't right (emotionally). But I use that sadness in a very dramatic way. I mean, there have been times when I've cried in the street ... because of some negative energy that happened from the people. But it's my life and I'd like to continue street performing. I've seen people of eighty and ninety in Vienna doing it.'

PAT TIERNEY — Bardic Street Poet, Age 35

Surely there is no more curious, anachronistic sight on Dublin's streets than bardic-style poet Pat Tierney. Seemingly out of time and place, he recites poetry along Grafton Street with a sincerity that can move listeners to tears. Like many poets before him, he experienced a lonely and tortured childhood turning him toward in introspective life. After years of living as a "wandering minstrel" and bardic poet in the wilds of Newfoundland, he returned to Dublin's streets to bring poetry to the city folk. There is an almost mystical aura about him and his lofty poetic quest. He has formed the Irish Bardic Society and after his recitations and a warm applause he softly reminds people, "please don't forget the poet's pot" as they drop in a few coins for his supper.

'My earliest memories were in St. Anne's School run by the Sisters of Mercy. When I was about four or five I remember having to line up and get slapped every day for wetting the bed. And in the classroom one teacher was particularly fond of using the stick. You were afraid of the nuns. When I was seven I went to the Christian Brothers' School and they were very strict and you got beaten up and there was a lot of fear. All the Brothers carried leather straps and they used these on you very often. Beating you by slapping your hands with fifteen or twenty of those or slapping you across the face with the palm of their hands and you'd be there begging them, "please, Brother, don't hit me again!". But they keep slapping you. Constant abuse. The only emotion you have is fear and survival. I think that the normal emotions that people have who are raised in families don't really develop in people raised in institutions.

'I don't ever recall having enough food. That may account for the fact that I'm kind of small stature. I remember very distinctly learning this trick where I could swallow my food and bring it down as far as there in my chest and bring it back up again. It was almost like a cow chewing the cud. Another thing I recall about being hungry, one of the teachers used to bring in an apple for himself every day and he'd peel the apple and throw the skin in the bin along with cigarette ashes and everything else. And he was always coughing and spitting this green phlegm into this bucket. Now whenever he left the classroom for any reason there was always a big dash up to the bin to get the skins of the apple out of there. So that'll give you an idea of the situation there as far as people being hungry.

'When I was ten years old I was taken out of the orphanage and brought out to a family in Castlegar. They had a farm and wanted a child they could bring up. It was quite a bad situation. She'd slap me and belittle me. But I went to the local

Castlegar National School and the first connection I had with poetry was there. The Headmaster was from Mayo and he was very nationalistic and you could see tears swelling in his eyes when he would talk about the men who died in 1916 and about poetry. He would talk about a poet named Anthony Raftery who died about 1834. I was in awe of the idea of this blind poet travelling the roads. One day in class we were asked to write a little verse or poem and I remember writing the line, "the roofs of the houses all shiny with rain". The teacher read it and asked me if I had really written this myself and I said "yes". That was significant for me that he had said that.

'When I was fifteen years old I wrote my first poem. It was about the 1916 Rebellion. The second poem I wrote around this time was called "A Parable" and I wrote it from actual experience. When I was in Castlegar we used to go to Mass on Sundays and at certain times of the year the priest would read off the altar how much each household had paid into the Church and that inspired me to write the poem. It goes:

> *The Canon stood at the altar side*
> *a large book spread before his eyes,*
> *The congregation was quiet and still*
> *Then from holy lips began to spill,*
> *The names of each one in the village,*
> *Those who worked in town and tillage.*
> *And as each name was called aloud*
> *Their monthly offering was unshroud.*

'When I was writing the poems it almost seemed like somebody else was writing them rather than myself. There must have been this thing inside me ... this need to express. I think when people are raised in bondage there is this need to express. That's possibly why the Irish nation has produced such great writers, because of this historical bondage. For me, I believe it was the *need to express.*

'When I was seventeen I went to Dublin. Places like the Garden of Remembrance, the G.P.O., Kilmainham Gaol had a strong effect on me. I liked Dublin. I knocked around and wrote various little poems. When I was eighteen I joined Sinn Fein and became a recruiting officer. Then I was arrested for various political activities. Like I burned a Union Jack in front of the St. Patrick's Day reviewing stand. Then we got into selling books on the street at the G.P.O. And I remember this one man mentioning Yeats and sometimes he'd quote a line here or there. The people who I met in the Republican circles were the ones who really made me literate and gave me the sense that I could achieve things myself. Then I decided I wanted to go to America. I saved money and went over on holiday but, of course, remained illegally. I went to Detroit and worked as a janitor, then went to Arizona and met some Irish people there and started to organise poetry readings. Then I went to Massachusetts to work on fishing boats and went to Wyoming and worked in an oil field and on a ranch during branding season. I was accumulating a larger wealth of experience to draw from ... I knew I wanted to get to poetry.

Street poet Pat Tierney earnestly sharing poetry with passers–by on Grafton Street

'Then I decided that I was going to Newfoundland, Canada. I had the idea that there was something rural about it and I still had the great interest in the lifestyle of this Raftery fellow. I feel it's a kind of a *destiny*. I got the ferry to Newfoundland and arrived at six in the morning in the foggy damp. I'd absolutely no money, nothing. There was a Mass going and I went outside and played a few tunes on the mouth organ, so that I could get some money to get some breakfast. I put a cap down and made a few dollars. And someone told me

229

that if I went over to this lounge that afternoon there'd be traditional music. It was a terrible afternoon and the rain coming down and so I decided to go inside and have a pint and listen to the music. I sat down there on my backpack and wrote out a small poem about the band that was playing. "There's a little poem I wrote for you", I said to one of the band members, thinking no more about it. This fella read out the poem on the stage and I got a big round of applause. This stunned me a bit. Next thing I knew there was about seven pints of beer in front of me and five dollar bills being pushed into my hands and people gathering around me. This actually was the first time this bardic tradition — this idea of writing poetry and getting paid for it — came upon me. It was almost like I was destined to go to that particular place on that particular day and write that particular poem.

'When it was time to go home they asked me where I was staying. I said that I saw a shed out back there and I'd probably stay there. One man says, "you're welcome to come and stay with me". And I says, "well, I wouldn't want to stay with you unless you had some work for me to do so I could repay you". So I helped for three or four days putting in the potatoes. Then I wrote a poem for the family I stayed with — and that was the start of it. From then on I was *stuck*. I *had to write poetry* ... fate ... had to write poetry as an expression. I had the *sense* now that I was at the right place at the right time to see if it was possible to live in this bardic style. And the people seemed to be interested in the poems. It was very romantic, very free spirited ... the idea of rambling the roads in the sunshine and being your own man and singing to yourself. Something romantic and peaceful and pleasant and fulfilling about that. I'd carry a backpack and a sleeping bag and a change of clothes and a few books of poetry and I'd find a sheltered spot in a shed or under a stairwell. Of course, there were times when I'd be hitch-hiking on the road to the next village and the rain would be pissing down on top of me. I was always hitch-hiking and footing and if I went to somebody's house I wrote them a little poem. When I'd walk into a village the first thing I'd say, "where does the local school teacher live?". I found the best contacts were school teachers and musicians. And I was writing little poems and selling them to the local people.

'Now I had been nearly nine years travelling around and I was thinking it was time for me to go back to Ireland. I arrived back in Dublin with less money than when I had left but so happy because I'd always wanted to come back. It's almost like Ireland had become my mother ... I could not forget Ireland, not for a minute. I decided to thank this God that brought me back to Ireland safely and so I walked from the Garden of Remembrance to Croagh Patrick. It took me seven days with a backpack to walk there, a kind of pilgrimage in thanks. Along the way I would stop at people's houses and recite poetry for them and do a bit of work. Got to Croagh Patrick, climbed the mountain and then came back to Dublin.

'I decided that I wanted to bring poetry to the *streets* — of Dublin. To see if it was possible to revive the bardic tradition, this idea of the travelling poet. Now in the city you're not really a travelling poet as such, you're a stationary poet living in the city. But I think that poetry can be brought back to the people and it's as important to do it in the big city as it is in the country areas. Street life in Dublin is diverse and varied. We have an awful lot of musicians that play on the streets here but bringing literature to the common people going up and down the streets, that's my contribution. I want to affect the people who do not go to poetry readings. That's the secret of doing it on the street ... bringing poetry *to* the people. That's my goal.

'The problem on the streets is you can't be reading this highfaluting stuff that nobody understands. I read poetry by Yeats but simple poems that everybody can understand. Some people are amazed that I would have the neck and the nerve to stand out on the street and read poetry. People have walked by me and said, *"poetry?* You must be joking!". And I've said, "come here, just let me read you one ... let me recite you just one poem and just see what you think". I recite them a poem or two and they say, "that's *fantastic!"*. Bringing poetry, my poetry and the works of great Irish poets, *to the people* ... I *love* it. I am moved myself sometimes by things I read because I can *feel* so much of what I'm saying. I can feel the words and the words become part of me. I express that and I think the people actually feel that. I can actually see people on the street trying to choke back a tear.

'I'm going to spend the rest of my life involved in writing poetry — with the help of God — and bringing poetry to the people. I *must* bring poetry *to* the people. The lifestyle and idea of travelling and writing poetry is the closest I can come to the bardic tradition. I read poetry now morning, noon and night. I can't get away from it. Poetry gives me dignity and self-esteem that I never had before. I find poetry to be spiritual. I get great comfort from it. I find that I'm close to God when I read a poem.'

Notes

INTRODUCTION

1   Rev. Canon F.F. Carmichael, *Dublin — A Lecture*, (Dublin: Hodges, Figgis & Co. Ltd., 1907), p. 13.

2   *Dublin Explorations and Reflections*, Anonymous Author, (Dublin: Maunsel & Co. Ltd., 1917), p. 29.

3   Sidney Davies, *Dublin Types*, (Dublin: The Talbot Press Ltd., 1918), p. x.

4   Christine Longford, *a Biography of Dublin*, (London: Methuen & Co. Ltd., 1936), p. 6.

5   John J. Dunne, "Cabaret of the Streets of Dublin", *Evening Press*, Jan. 15, 1981

6   Jane Jacobs, *The Death and Life of Great American Cities*, (New York: Random House, 1961), p. 30.

7   An Taisce, *Amenity Study of Dublin and Dun Loaghaire*, (Dublin: An Taisce, 1967), p. 36.

8   Robert Gahan, "Some Old Street Characters of Dublin", *Dublin Historical Record*, Vol. II, 1939, p. 105.

9   Paddy Crosbie, *Your Dinner's Poured Out!*, (Dublin: The O'Brien Press, 1981), p. 95.

10 Eamonn MacThomais, *Janey Mack Me Shirt is Black*, (Dublin: The O'Brien Press, 1982) Frontispiece.

11 Richard Dorson, "The Oral Historian and the Folklorist", in Willa K. Baum and David K. Dunaway (editors), *Oral History: An Interdisciplinary Anthology*, (Nashville, Tennessee: American Association for State and Local History, 1984), p. 295.

12 Paul Thompson, "History and the Community", in Willa K. Baum and David K. Dunaway (editors), *Oral History: An Interdisciplinary Anthology*, (Nashville, Tennessee: American Association for State and Local History, 1984), p. 38.

13 Charles T. Morrisey, "Introduction", in Willa K. Baum and David K. Dunaway (editors), *Oral History: An Interdisciplinary Anthology*, (Nashville, Tennessee: American Association for State and Local History, 1984), p. xxi.

14 Mary Maloney, "Dublin — Before All is Lost", *Evening Press*, May 17, 1980, p. 91.

DUBLIN STREET LIFE AND ORAL URBANLORE

1   Seamus de Burca, "Growing Up in Dublin", *Dublin Historical Record*, Vol. XXIX, No. 3, 1976, p. 96.

2   John J. Webb, *The Guilds of Dublin*, (London: Kennikat Press, 1970), pp. 53-55. Originally published in 1929.

3   A. O'Neill, "Dublin's Eighteenth Century Trade Processions", *Ireland's Own*, Vol. 64, October 20, 1934, p. 487.

4   Sidney Davies, *Dublin Types*, (Dublin: The Talbot Press Ltd., 1918), p. x.

5   Bill Kelly, *Me Darlin' Dublin's Dead & Gone*, (Dublin: Ward River Press, 1983), pp. 3-4.

6   Rev. Canon F.F. Carmichael, *Dublin — A Lecture*, (Dublin: Hodges, Figgis & Co.,

1907), pp. 26-27.

7   John J. Dunne, "Cabaret of the Streets of Dublin", *Evening Press*, January 15, 1981.

8   P.J. McCall, "Zozimus", *Dublin Historical Record*, Vol. VII, No. 4, 1945, pp. 134-149.

9   *Ibid.*, p. 135.

10 Davies, *op. cit.*, p. xxvi.

11 Eamonn McThomais, *Me Jewel and Darlin' Dublin*, (Dublin: The O'Brien Press, 1974), p. 35.

12 Jane Jacobs, *The Death and Life of Great American Cities*, (New York: Random House, 1961), p. 35.

13 *Moore Street: A Report*, (Dublin: School of Architecture, University College, Dublin, 1974), p. 10.

14 Constantia Maxwell, *Dublin Under the Georges, 1714-1830*, (Dublin: Gill & Macmillan, 1979), p. 240.

15 F.J. Little, "A Glimpse at Victorian Dublin", *Dublin Historical Record*, Vol. VI, 1943, p. 19.

16 Charles T. Morrissey, "Introduction", in Wilma K. Baum and David K. Dunaway (editors), *Oral History: An Interdisciplinary Anthology*, (Nashville, Tennessee: American Association for State and Local History, 1984), p. xxi.

17 Louis Starr, "Oral History", in Willa K. Baum and David K. Dunaway (editors), *Oral History: An Interdisciplinary Anthology*, (Nashville, Tennessee: American Association for State and Local History, 1984), p. 4.

18 Eilis Brady, *All In! All In!*, (Dublin: Comhairle Bhealoideas Eireann, University College, Belfield, 1984), Frontispiece.

19 Mary Maloney, "Dublin — Before All is Lost", *Evening Press*, May 17, 1980, p. 91.

HISTORICAL PERSPECTIVES ON DUBLIN STREET TYPES

1   Lar Redmond, *Show Us the Moon*, (Dingle: Brandon Books, 1988), p. 95.

2   Joseph V. O'Brien, *Dear, Dirty Dublin*, (Berkeley: University of California Press, 1982), p. 67.

3   J. Nolan, *Changing Faces*, (Dublin: Elo Press, 1982), p. 101.

4   Tom MacDonagh, *My Green Age*, (Dublin: Poolbeg Press, 1986), p. 125.

5   John J. Dunne, *Streets Broad and Narrow*, (Dublin: Helicon Ltd, 1982), p. 18.

6   Pete St. John, *Jasus Wept!*, (Dublin: Temple Bar Studios, 1988), pp. 39-40.

7   Kenneth Hudson, *Pawnbroking: An Aspect of British Social History*, (London: The Bodley Head Press, 1982), p. 13.

8   Maura O'Kiely, "Pawnbrokers Lament the End of an Era in Hock", *The Sunday Tribune*, January 26, 1986, p. 5.

9   Edward MacLysaght, *Irish Life in the Seventeenth Century*, (Dublin: Irish Academic Press, 1979), p. 195.

10 *Ibid.*, p. 196.

11 Mary E. Daly, *Dublin — The Deposed Capital*, (Cork: Cork University Press, 1984), p. 78.

12 *Ibid.*, p. 78.

13　O'Brien, *op. cit.*, p. 176, footnote 2.

14　*Moore Street: A Report*, (Dublin: School of Architecture, University College, Dublin, 1974), p. 8.

15　Deirdre Henchy, "Dublin 80 Years Ago", *Dublin Historical Record*, Volume XXVI, No. 1, 1972, p. 23.

16　Rev. Canon F.F. Carmichael, *Dublin — A Lecture*, (Dublin: Hodges, Figgis & Co. Ltd., 1907), p. 26.

17　John Edward Walsh, *Rakes and Ruffians*, (Dublin: Four Courts Press, 1979), p. 62. Reprint of original 1840 publication.

18　Robert Gahan, "Some Old Street Characters of Dublin", *Dublin Historical Record*, Vol. II, 1939, p. 99.

19　Henchy, *op. cit.*, p. 23, footnote 15.

20　Bernard Neary, *North of the Liffey*, (Dublin: Lenhar Publications, 1984), p. 21.

21　Bill Kelly, *Me Darlin' Dublin's Dead and Gone*, (Dublin: Ward River Press, 1983), p. 3.

22　Paddy Crosbie, *Your Dinner's Poured Out!*, (Dublin: The O'Brien Press, 1981), p. 69.

23　P.J. Flanagan and C.B. Mac an tSaoir, *Dublin's Buses*, (Dublin: Transport Research Associates, 1968), p. 8.

24　Barra Boydell, "Impressions of Dublin — 1934", *Dublin Historical Record*, Vol. XXXVII, No. 3, 1984, p. 92.

25　Eamonn MacThomais, *Janey Mack Me Shirt is Black*, (Dublin: The O'Brien Press, 1982), p. 122.

26　Moira Lysaght, "My Dublin", *Dublin Historical Record*, Vol. XXX, No. 4, 1977, p. 126.

27　Crosbie, *op. cit.*, p. 95, footnote 22.

28　Peter Somerville-Large, *Dublin*, (London: Hamish-Hamilton, 1979), p. 243.

29　O'Brien, *op. cit.*, p. 64, footnote 2.

30　*Dublin — 1913*, (Dublin: The O'Brien Press — Curriculum Development Unit, no authors cited, 1982), p. 24.

31　Dunne, *op. cit.*, p. 91, footnote 5.

32　Refer to: Jim Kilroy, *Howth and Her Trams*, (Dublin: Fingal Book Publishers, 1986).

33　Kevin Murray, "Transport", in Tom Kennedy (editor), *Victorian Dublin*, (Dublin: Albertine Kennedy Publishers, 1980), p. 93.

34　Flanagan and Mac an tSaoir, *op. cit.*, p. 8, footnote 23.

35　*Ibid.*, p. 8.

36　*Ibid.*, p. 8.

37　O'Brien, *op. cit.*, p. 64, footnote 2.

38　*Ibid.*, p. 65.

39　*Irish Times*, January 11, 1934.

40　O'Brien, *op. cit.*, p. 65, footnote 2.

41　*Ibid.*, p. 66.

42　Kevin C. Kearns, *Stoneybatter: Dublin's Inner-Urban Village*, (Dublin: The Glendale

Press Ltd., 1989), p. 36.

43 MacThomais, *op. cit.*, p. 120, footnote 25.

44 Constantia Maxwell, *Dublin Under the Georges, 1714-1830*, (Dublin: Gill and Macmillan Ltd., 1979), p. 242.

45 Micheline McCormack, "Bid to Ban Bird Market in Bride Street", *Irish Press*, March 24, 1969, p. 28.

46 Elgy Gillespie, "Pigeon Fanciers in Dublin Unite", *Irish Times*, September 1, 1973, p. 6.

47 Mairin Johnston, *Around the Banks of Pimlico*, (Dublin: Attic Press, 1985), p. 108.

48 Peter Thompson, "When It's Busk or Broke", *Irish Press*, March 8, 1988.

49 Gideon Sjoberg, *The Preindustrial City*, (New York: The Free Press, 1960), p. 136.

50 MacLysaght, *op. cit.*, p. 196, footnote 9.

51 Brian MacGoilla Phadraig, "Dublin One Hundred Years Ago", *Dublin Historical Record*, Vol. XXIII, 1969, p. 60.

52 Sidney Davies, *Dublin Types*, (Dublin: The Talbot Press, 1918), p. 36.

53 *Ibid.*, p. 36.

54 P.J. McCall, "Zozimus", *Dublin Historical Record*, Vol. VII, No. 4, 1945, p. 135.

55 P.J. McCall, *In the Shadow of St. Patrick's*, A paper read before The Irish National Library Society, April 27, 1983, (Dublin: Carraig Books, 1976 reprint), p. 31.

56 *Ibid.*, p. 34.

57 The following articles discuss the legal and practical plight of buskers in Dublin's streets: "Buskers Set Up Guild", *Irish Times*, June 18, 1986; Kathryn Holmquist, "Why Buskers May Blossom in Dublin's Streets", *Irish Times*, January 27, 1987; "Free Buskers", *Irish Independent*, August 10, 1988, p. 7.

58 Susan L. Mitchell, "Out of the Dust", *The Lady of the House*, December, 1917, p. 11.

59 Paddy Kehoe, "Thom McGinty", *In Dublin Magazine*, August 4, 1988, p. 12.

60 Nolan, *op. cit.*, p. 222, footnote 3.

61 Corina Thomas, "Pat Tierney" A Modern Day Minstrel", *The Newfoundland Herald*, October 19, 1987, p. 18.

Bibliography

An Taisce, *Amenity Study of Dublin and Dun Laoghaire*, (Dublin: An Taisce, 1967).

Baum, Willa K. and Dunaway, David K. (editors), *Oral History: An Interdisciplinary Anthology*, (Nashville, Tennessee: American Association for State and Local History, 1984).

Bloxham, Peter, "The Little Sweeps' Scandal", *Evening Herald*, August 28, 1970, p. 6.

Bolger, Dermot (editor), *Invisible Cities: The New Dubliners*, (Dublin: Raven Arts Press, 1988).

Boydell, Barra, "Impressions of Dublin — 1934", *Dublin Historical Record*, Vol. XXXVII, No. 3, 1984, pp. 88-103.

Brady, Eilis. *All In! All In!*, (Dublin: Comhairle Bhealoideas Eireann, University College, Belfield, 1984).

Brewer, John D., *The Royal Irish Constabulary: An Oral History*, (Belfast: Institute of Irish Studies, Queen's University, 1990).

"Buskers Set Up Guild", *Irish Times*, June 18, 1986.

Cahill, Gerry, *Back to the Streets*, (Dublin: Housing Research Unit, University College, Dublin, 1980).

Carmichael, Rev. Canon F.F.,*Dublin — A Lecture*, (Dublin: Hodges, Figgis and Co., 1907).

Cashell, Ronan, "A Dublin Character", *Dublin Historical Record*, XLI, No. 1, 1987, pp. 28-30.

Chesney, Kellow, *The Victorian Underworld*, (London: Temple, Smith, Ltd., 1970).

Clarke, Desmond, *Dublin*, (London: B.T. Batsford, 1977).

Cole, Herbert, "The History of Signwriting", in W.G. Sutherland (editor), *The Modern Signwriter*, (Southport, Lancashire: The Sutherland Publishing Company, 1954).

Collins, James, *Life in Old Dublin*, (Cork: Tower Books, 1978). A reprint of original 1913 edition.

Corkery, Tom, *Tom Corkery's Dublin*, (Dublin: Anvil Press Ltd., 1980).

Cosgrave, Augustine D., "North Dublin City", *Dublin Historical Record*, Vol. XXIII, 1969, pp. 3-22.

Cosgrave, Dillon, *North Dublin: City and Environs*, (Dublin: M.H. Gill & Sons, Ltd., 1909).

Cosgrove, Art, *Dublin Through the Ages*, (Dublin: The College Press, 1986).

Coulter, Carol, "Old Market May Get New Life", *Irish Times*, July 30, 1986.

Crosbie, Paddy, *Your Dinner's Poured Out!*, (Dublin: The O'Brien Press, 1981).

Dalton, Martin, "Monday is Pawnday", *The Bell*, Vol. XIV, No. 5, 1947, pp. 46-51.

Daly, Mary E., *Dublin — The Deposed Capital*, (Cork: Cork University Press, 1984).

Davies, Sidney, *Dublin Types*, (Dublin: The Talbot Press, Ltd., 1918).

de Burca, Seamus, "Growing-Up in Dublin", *Dublin Historical Record*, Vol. XXIX, No. 3, 1976, pp. 82-99.

Dickens, Charles, *Sketches by Boz*, (London: Oxford University Press, 1957).

Dickinson, Page L., *The Dublin of Yesterday*, (London: Methuen & Co. Ltd., 1929).

Dickinson, David (editor), *The Gorgeous Mask: Dublin 1700-1850*, (Dublin: Trinity College Workshop, 1987).

Dublin — 1913, (Dublin: The O'Brien Press — Curriculum Development Unit, no authors cited, 1982).

Dublin Explorations and Reflections, written by an anonymous Englishman, (Dublin: Maunsel & Co. Ltd., 1917).

Dunne, Derek, "Grafton Street Lives", *Irish Times*, August 16, 1988.

Dunne, John J., "Cabaret of the Streets of Dublin", *Evening Press*, January 15, 1981.

Dunne, John J., *Streets Broad and Narrow*, (Dublin: Helicon Ltd., 1982).

Fagan, Patrick, *The Second City*, (Dublin: Branar Press, 1986).

Flanagan, P.J., and Mac an tSaoir, C.B., *Dublin's Buses*, (Dublin: Transport Research Associates, 1968).

"Free Buskers", *Irish Independent*, August 10, 1988, p. 7.

Gahan, Robert, "Some Old Street Characters of Dublin", *Dublin Historical Record*, Vol. II, 1939, pp. 98-105.

Gilbert, John T., *A History of the City of Dublin*, (Dublin: Gill & Macmillan, 1978). Reprint of the original three volumes, 1854-59).

Gillespie, Elgy, *The Liberties of Dublin*, (Dublin: The O'Brien Press, 1973).

Gillespie, Elgy, "Pigeon Fanciers in Dublin Unite", *Irish Times*, September 1, 1973, p. 6.

Henchy, Deirdre, "Dublin 80 Years Ago", *Dublin Historical Record*, Vol. XXVI, No. 1, 1972, pp. 18-23.

Holmquist, Kathryn, "Why Buskers May Blossom in Dublin Streets", *Irish Times*, January 27, 1987.

Hudson, Kenneth, *Pawnbroking: An Aspect of British Social History*, (London: The Bodley Head Press, 1982).

Jackle, John; Brunn, Stanley and Roseman, Curtis. *Human Spatial Behavior*, (North Scituate, Massachusetts: Duxbury Press, 1976).

Jacobs, Jane, *The Death and Life of Great American Cities*, (New York: Random House, 1961).

Johnston, Mairin, *Around the Banks of Pimlico*, (Dublin: Attic Press, 1985).

Kearns, Kevin C., *Georgian Dublin: Ireland's Imperilled Architectural Heritage*, (London: David & Charles Ltd., 1983).

Kearns, Kevin C., *Dublin's Vanishing Craftsmen*, (Belfast: The Appletree Press, 1986).

Kearns, Kevin C., *Stoneybatter: Dublin's Inner-Urban Village*, (Dublin: The Glendale Press, 1989).

Keatinge, Edgar F., "Colourful, Tuneful Dublin", *Dublin Historical Record*, Vol. IX, No. 3, 1947, pp. 73-85.

Keena Colm, "Busking in Dublin Isn't Easy, But It's Thriving", *Irish Times*, June 23, 1986, p. 12.

Kehoe, Paddy, "Thom McGinty", *In Dublin Magazine*, August 4, 1988, p. 12.

Kelly, Bill, *Me Darlin' Dublin's Dead and Gone*, (Dublin: Ward River Press, 1983.)

Kennedy, Tom, *Victorian Dublin*, (Dublin: Albertine Kennedy Publishers Ltd., 1980).

Kenny, Carlos, "The Pawn Ticket Climbs Up the Social Ladder", *Evening Herald*, October 28, 1982, p. 19.

Kilroy, Jim, *Howth and Her Trams*, (Dublin: Fingal Book Publishers, 1986).

Lemass, Peter and Lavelle, Paul, *The Urban Plunge*, (Dublin: Veritas Publications, 1988).

Levine, June, "The Decline of a Famous Street", *Sunday Independent*, March 7, 1971.

Lewis, R., *Dublin Guide*, (Dublin: Lewis Correcting Co., 1787).

Little, F.J., "A Glimpse of Victorian Dublin", *Dublin Historical Record*, Vol. VI, 1943, pp. 8-24.

Longford, Christine, *A Biography of Dublin*, (London: Methuen & Co. Ltd., 1936).

Lummis, Trevor, "Structure and Validity in Oral Evidence", *International Journal of Oral History*, No. 2, June, 1984, pp. 109-120.

Lysaght, Moira, "My Dublin", *Dublin Historical Record*, Vol. XXX, No. 4, 1977, pp. 122-135.

Lysaght, Moira, "A North City Childhood in the Early Century", *Dublin Historical Record*, Vol. XXXVIII, No. 2, 1985, pp. 74-87.

MacDonagh, Tom, *My Green Age*, (Dublin: Poolbeg Press, 1986).

MacLysaght, Edward, *Irish Life in the Seventeenth Century*, (Dublin: Irish Academic Press, 1979).

MacThomais, Eamonn, *Gur Cake & Coak Blocks*, (Dublin: The O'Brien Press, 1976).

MacThomais, Eamonn, *Janey Mack Me Shirt is Black*, (Dublin: The O'Brien Press, 1982).

MacThomais, Eamonn, *Me Jewel and Darlin' Dublin*, (Dublin: The O'Brien Press, 1974).

Maloney, Mary, "Dublin — Before All is Lost", *Evening Press*, May 17, 1980, p. 91.

Maxwell, Constantia, *Dublin Under the Georges, 1714-1830*, (Dublin: Gill & Macmillan Ltd., 1979).

McCall, P.J., *In the Shadow of St. Patrick's*, (Dublin: Carraig Books, 1976). Reprint of original 1893 paper read before the Irish National Library Society.

McCall, P.J., "Zozimus", *Dublin Historical Record*, Vol. VII, No. 4, 1945, pp. 134-149.

McCarthy, Justine, "Little Left in an Old Tradition", *Irish Independent*, November 4, 1982.

McCormack, Micheline, "Bid to Ban Bird Market in Bride Street", *Irish Press*, March 24, 1969, p. 28.

McCourt, Desmond, "The Use of Oral Tradition in Irish Historical Geography", *Irish Geography*, Vol. VI, No. 4, 1972, pp. 394-410.

McDonald, Frank, "Traders Gather to Celebrate Grafton Street's New Look", *Irish Times*, August 17, 1988.

McGrath, Raymond, "Dublin Panorama", *The Bell*, Vol. 2, No. 5, 1941, pp. 35-48.

McGregor, John James, *New Picture of Dublin*, (Dublin: Sealy, Bryers & Walker, 1907).

Messenger, Betty, *Picking Up the Linen Threads*, (Belfast: Blackstaff Press, 1988).

Millman, Laurence, *Our Like Will Not Be There Again*, (Boston: Little, Brown & Company, 1977).

Mitchell, Susan L., "Out of the Dust", *The Lady of the House*, December, 1917, p. 11.

Moore Street: A Report, (Dublin: School of Architecture, University College, Dublin, 1974).

Morrissey, Charles T., "Introduction", in Willa K. Baum and David K. Dunaway (editors), *Oral History: An Interdisciplinary Anthology*, (Nashville, Tennessee: American Association for State and Local History, 1984), pp. XIX-XXIII.

Mumford, Lewis, *The Culture of Cities*, (New York: Harcourt, Brace & Co., 1938).

Munck, Ronnie and Rolston, Bill, *Belfast in the Thirties: An Oral History*, (Belfast: Blackstaff Press Ltd., 1987).

Murray, Kevin, "Transport", in Tom Kennedy (editor), *Victorian Dublin*, (Dublin: Albertine Kennedy Publishers, 1980), pp. 90-98.

"The Mysteries of Smithfield", *The Dublin Builder*, February 15, 1861.

Neary, Bernard, *North of the Liffey*, (Dublin: Lenhar Publications, 1984).

Nolan, J., *Changing Faces*, (Dublin: Elo Press, 1982).

"North City History", *City Views*, December, 1980, pp. 4-5.

Nowlan, Kevin B., *Travel and Transport in Ireland*, (Dublin: Gill & Macmillan, 1973).

O'Brien, Joseph V., *Dear, Dirty Dublin*, (Berkeley: University of California Press, 1982).

O'Donnell, Peadar, "People and Pawnshops", *The Bell*, Vol. 5, No. 3, 1942, pp. 206-208.

O'Donovan, John, *Life By the Liffey*, (Dublin: Gill & Macmillan Ltd., 1986).

O'Kiely, Maura, "Pawnbrokers Lament the End of an Era in Hock", *The Sunday Tribune*, January 26, 1986, p. 5.

"Only Two Birds Sold at Market", *Irish Press*, March 3, 1969.

O'Sullivan, Seuman, "The Lamplighter", *The Dublin Magazine*, September, 1923, p. 153.

"Pawnbroking in Ireland" (no author), *Dublin University Magazine*, Vol. XIV, No. LXXXIV, 1839, pp. 675-682.

Peter, A., *Dublin Fragments*, (Dublin: Hodges, Figgis & Co., 1925).

Peter, A., *Sketches of Old Dublin*, (Dublin: Sealy, Bryers & Walker, 1907).

Phadraig, Brian MacGoilla, "Dublin One Hundred Years Ago", *Dublin Historical Record*, Vol. XXXII, No. 1, 1978, pp. 15-26.

Redmond, Lar, *Show Us the Moon*, (Dingle: Brandon Books, 1988).

Robertson, Olivia, *Dublin Phoenix*, (London: The Alden Press, 1957).

Sheehan, Ronan and Walsh, Brendan, *The Heart of the City*, (Dingle: Brandon Book Publishers, 1988).

Sjoberg, Gideon, *The Preindustrial City*, (New York: The Free Press, 1960).

Sommerville-Large, Peter, *Dublin*, (London: Hamish-Hamilton Ltd., 1979).

Starr, Louis, "Oral History", in Willa K. Baum and David K. Dunaway (editors), *Oral History: An Interdisciplinary Anthology*, (Nashville, Tennessee: American Association for State and Local History, 1984), pp. 3-25.

St. John, Pete, *Jasus Wept!*, (Dublin: Temple Bar Studios, 1988).

"The Street Life of Old Dublin", *The Lady of the House*, Vol. XXIII, No. 248, 1909.

"Street Traders:", *Irish Times*, August 7, 1985.

"Street Traders Seek Support of Public", *Irish Times*, July 27, 1985.

Thomas, Corina, "Pat Tierney: A Modern Day Minstrel", *The Newfoundland Herald*, October 10, 1987, p. 18.

Thompson, Paul, "History and the Community", in Willa K. Baum and David K. Dunaway, *Oral History: An Interdisciplinary Anthology*, (Nashville, Tennessee: American Association for State and Local History, 1984), pp. 37-50.

Thompson, Peter. "When It's Busk or Broke", *Irish Press*, March 8, 1988.

Walsh, John Edward, *Rakes and Ruffians*, (Dublin: Four Courts Press, 1979). Reprint of original 1840 publication.

Webb, John J., *The Guilds of Dublin*, (London: Kennikat Press, 1970). Reprint of original 1929 publication.

Wren, Jimmy, *The Villages of Dublin*, (Dublin: Tomar Publications, 1982).

Index